FROM THE
MISSISSIPPI
DELTA *A Memoir*

Endesha Ida Mae Holland, Ph.D.

SIMON & SCHUSTER

SIMON & SCHUSTER

Rockefeller Center

1230 Avenue of the Americas

New York, NY 10020

SIMON & SCHUSTER and colophon are registered trademarks

of Simon & Schuster Inc.

Designed by Barbara M. Bachman

Manufactured in the United States of America

10   9   8   7   6   5   4   3   2   1

Library of Congress Cataloging-in-Publication Data

Holland, Endesha Ida Mae.

From the Mississippi Delta: a memoir / Endesha Ida Mae Holland.

p. cm.

1. Holland, Endesha Ida Mae.

2. Afro-American women—Mississippi—Greenwood—Biography.

3. Afro-Americans—Mississippi—Greenwood—Biography.

4. Greenwood (Miss.)—Biography.

5. Delta (Miss. : Region)—Biography.

6. Afro-Americans—Civil rights—Mississippi—History—20th century.

I. Title.

F349.G82H65   1997

976.2'46—dc21

[B]   97-22663   CIP

ISBN 0-684-81011-5

This book is dedicated to the memory of the entire

Greenwood community, both living and dead; and to the

honor of my son, Cedric, and granddaughter, Kashka.

Yet, deep down, I knew that I could never

really leave the South, for my feeling had

already been formed by the South, for there had

been slowly instilled into my personality and

consciousness, black though I was, the culture

of the South. So, in leaving, I was taking a part

of the South to transplant in alien soil, to see

if it could grow differently, if it could drink of

new and cool rains, bend in strange winds,

respond to the warmth of other suns, and,

perhaps, to bloom. . . .

—RICHARD WRIGHT, *BLACK BOY*

Prologue

IF SOUTH IS A PERSPECTIVE AS WELL AS A DIRECTION, THEN THE MISSISSIPPI DELTA MAY WELL BE the most southern place on earth.

"South." It doesn't come easy on my tongue like I thought it would. Fingers trace lines of red and black on a map. "Here, right here," you say. But it's neither here nor there. If only I could make you understand that geography can never map my heart.

It's an old story. Once upon a time, it was written in brilliant black ink, but now it's faded, nearly invisible. The tired old lies take up a lot of space, pushing the sad truths to the margins and beyond. Where does it begin?

Ol' Man River had touched all the other points of the compass: north, near the Great Lakes; east, in the fertile valleys of Ohio; west, and the Great Plains—he'd come from all these places. Now he was headed south. He rolled and rushed, ebbed and flowed in eternal migration to destination and destiny. Where he crossed Yazoo, he cut her, but soft. And where he cut, Delta was born.

It was baptism. Ol' Man pushed her down, tried to hold her beneath his rushing waters but couldn't. Delta rose, she floated. Ol' Man claimed her as kin, gave her his rightful name, Mississippi. Mississippi Delta.

She was fertile, Miss Delta, giving birth to a paradise where deer, bear, panther, wildcat, raccoon, peacock, and flamingo roamed wild and free—until the settlers came. White folks from the southern colonies—now states—came greedily and in increasing numbers to steal from the Delta, down to her very ground.

What they couldn't steal, they slaughtered, including the Choctaws, Chicasaw, and Yazoo who had mostly been relocated there by treaty in the first place.

Stealing from Delta wasn't easy. So the white man brought people he had enslaved—my ancestors—to do the hard work. With chains around our necks, we were forced to clear the land he claimed, to build his levees, to work his plantations. We were forced to plant his cotton, our hands scarred by the boll's spurs, our bodies scarred by the bossman's whip, our souls scarred by the white man's cruelty. Our men were castrated and lynched, our women forced to bear the white man's lust—and oftentimes his children.

We were Africans who knew nothing of Guinea, Senegal, Nigeria, or Ghana. We were Caribes who had never seen the sun set on Montego Bay. Yet we remembered home.

After the Civil War we were made citizens of the land we'd helped to build. Citizens—just like our former masters—and we were promised . . .

But by then it was too late for promises. Mississippi Delta had given birth to something that was neither a paradise nor its promise. Mississippi Delta remained a world apart—another country, another time, she refused to rejoin the Union that had "saved" us.

Saved? No, we had not been saved. The rules remained the same as before, only the names had changed. Now we were called "sharecroppers," cropping for shares to pay back loans at prices set by the plantation masters (only now they were called "plantation owners" or "planters"). We had swapped the chains of slavery for the bonds of debt. And what did we own at so steep a price? Nothing but miserable shacks and weedy gardens that could never bear enough fruit to fill a belly.

The Jim Crow caste laws that kept slavery alive after its so-called death did more than preserve America's "peculiar institution" well into the twentieth century. They kept our black lives medieval.

In my hometown of Greenwood, in Leflore County, Mississippi, whites had sworn since before Reconstruction that we blacks would not only know our place but stay in it forever. They celebrated as a holiday the Leflore County Massacre of 1889, in which three thousand blacks seeking political rights had been slaughtered by white posses. Here, in this paradise lost, black people could take nothing for granted—not life, not liberty, not "the pursuit of happiness."

Into this magnolia jungle, on August 29, 1944, I was dragged, kicking and screaming, from Mama's womb.

A story, a story.

Another story is coming.

Stop talking and listen.

Let it go, let it come.

—*African Griot's Preamble*

FROM THE

MISSISSIPPI

DELTA

One

Fire is eating Mama up. Her dress is burning off, up around her waist. Her titties look like charred black lanterns. Her pubic hair is scorching her thighs.

Hands reach out for her. My arms reach out, my hands beckon to her. But I don't have enough fingers. I have two fingers on my right hand; my left hand is missing a finger and thumb. Where they should be are smoldering, charred stumps. Hot blue fire licks my face. The flames turn into a swarm of bumblebees —stinging, stinging—my face, my neck, my back, my legs. I scream and scream and scream.

"Git up from here, gal—you done pissed in de bed!" Mama's voice just about woke me—snatching me from the fire but not the stinging bees. "Git yo'self up here, runnin' 'round actin' all grown —you jest a pissy-tail 'omanish pee-de-bed chile!"

Mama's angry face filled my view. She pulled the heavy quilt and sheet off the bed. "I was havin' a real bad dream, Mama!" I frantically wiggled all my fingers and held out my arms—no charred bones, just good chocolate flesh. Relieved, I sank back on the wet, lumpy mattress, then recoiled at the sharp smell of my pee.

"Lawdy, Lawd, Lawdy! Dis here old gal done laid up here and ruint my tick!" Mama exclaimed to our tar-papered ceiling.

"Ain't gonna pee de bed no mo'!" I hollered, jumping out of the bed and away from the piece of electric cord Mama used as her spanking strap. I could see the strap in her hand, poised high above my head, but I never felt it land on my backside because my pee had started stinging—a million bees at work between my legs and my shoulders. Mama always said that I peed up instead of down.

"Gal, you jest 'bout nine years old and you *still* pee-de-bed!" Mama twirled the cord 'round and 'round her head like Lash LaRue, the white cowboy dressed all in black we saw up at the Walthall picture show.

I jumped up out of my bed and threw my skinny arms around her neck before that strong brown arm could strike. "You ain't burnt up, Mama!" I was so glad to see her whole, glowering down at me in her big flowered smock.

"Doncha be huggin' on me, ol' pishy gal!" Mama said. She swatted at me halfheartedly, but her voice had softened.

"Can't help it, Mama!" I hollered as I dodged her blows, jumping to keep from stepping on all the roaches that danced at my feet.

Our roaches weren't afraid of anything. They didn't even run when Mama lit the kerosene lamp—they just went on about their business. There were at least three generations: nut-brown old folks, beige teenagers, and tan babies, some with long hulls hanging beneath their bellies. Black folks who lived on the other side of town called our side—Gee Pee—"the roachy heaben o' de Delta." Black folks hunted roaches and sold what they caught, a penny apiece, to the local bait store, where white fishermen came to buy lures for their hooks.

We be some kinda proud of our roaches, since it was our roaches that helped hook the bass and catfish that ended up, battered and fried, on white supper tables. We weren't proud of *having* roaches, but they were one of the few ways that black folks and white folks could be part of the same thing, without violence or anger or hate. It was a funny kind of line that connected the roaches to the fish, the blacks to the whites, and Gee Pee to the rest of the world.

Gee Pee is where we lived—Mama, my older brothers, Simon

Jr. and Bud, my sister, Jean, me, and all the roaches. Gee Pee was the "respectable" black neighborhood uptown, closer to Main Street and the white folks. Its dusty streets were lined with shotgun houses—long, narrow structures that shot back from small porches through the front door, out the back, and across a barren yard to hit the bull's-eye, the outhouse.

In summer, the hot air shimmered over our dusty sidewalks and the few lazy wires serving electricity to Gee Pee dropped down lower. The patched streets crumbled at the edges and the potholes overflowed after each summer shower. Few of the houses ever looked finished; some were just less decayed than others.

Inside Gee Pee stores, dented, rust-rimmed cans were stacked in pyramids on the floor and on beat-up shelves, and packages of meat rotted in leaky coolers. Ads for Coca-Cola, Royal Crown cola, Double Cola, Falstaff beer, Camels and Lucky Strikes, and Garrett and Tube Rose snuffs were painted on buildings. Faded ads also lined the cardboard and tin we used to cover our windows.

Dogs were tied to woodsheds or to sticks in the ground in people's yards, or they roamed the streets and alleys, foraging for food and greeting passersby. Teenage girls in pedal pushers and upswept hair scuttled by in groups, giggling at boys who walked with a slow, jerky, "mannish" leg drag. Between the tumbledown buildings, in vacant lots and alleys, the younger kids would play, pulling ticks and cockleburs from their legs and arms before going home. If you didn't believe what your mama said about ringworm, you didn't mind the lack of shoes, which I never wore regularly until I started school.

I was born into the double shotgun house 114 East Gibb Street. Mama rented both sides of the clapboard house, which stood on raised posts. A confused patch of petunias hugged the ground at the end of the front porch. Inside, the crudely painted walls were peeling and patched with newspaper. The ceiling was so low that I could read "Little Lulu" on the funny pages pasted there. Wide floorboards, some of them covered with linoleum, lay close together but never touched. In between you could see the earth beneath the house. The heavily patched roof over our heads kept neither daylight nor raindrops from finding their way indoors.

Black folks in Gee Pee who had some money—schoolteachers, undertakers, and preachers—lived in dark, mustard-colored houses with gas, electric lights, indoor toilets, and pretty knickknacks. We were one of the poorest families in Gee Pee, and our house was a dirty gray. But Mama never failed to remind us, " 'Member now, you livin' in Gee Pee, not Baptist Town nor Gritney!"

Baptist Town and Gritney were on the "wrong" side of the railroad tracks that ran through the town, northeast to southwest. Baptist Town was the run-down part of town where the poorest black people lived, boxed in by the tracks. In places the tracks were almost hidden by the smelly black mud that oozed from the "bayou," an open cesspool that held the waste from outhouses. Gritney, with its juke joints, was for the "disrespectable" black folks—"sin jest a-waitin' to happen," Mama always said. There, on the low end of McLauren Street, drunkards and rabble-rousers lived and danced and died. In Gee Pee, people dreamed of riding the night train or hoboing up the Illinois Central line to Chicago. In Gritney, people dreamed of moving across the tracks to Gee Pee. In Baptist Town, people dreamed of escaping the maze of railroad tracks, to anywhere.

Since I was the baby in the family, most days it was just me and Mama in the house alone, while my brothers and sister were in school—when they weren't playing hooky, "tryin' to act all mannish or 'omanish, smellin' dey pee," as Mama said.

Even now, I remember Mama creaking back and forth in her green-planked rocker in our front room, wearing a white flour-sack smock, holding a big dip of snuff in her mouth. She would lean forward and aim a shot of brown liquid at her coffee can, titties hanging against her thighs. She could spit so straight that the juice hardly ever ran down the side of the can.

She was a mountain of a woman, big-boned, with lots of flesh on her frame. She had smooth, snuff-colored cheeks, a little hint of a mustache, and a Sphinx-like gaze that stared out from behind the wire-rimmed glasses she removed only to go to sleep. If you've seen pictures of those little clay statues, those Great Mother goddesses dug up in North Africa, or a West African fertility fetish— all fat and sassy and gazing off into time—that was my Mama.

When she wasn't rocking, she was ironing a big stack of starched laundry that never seemed to get smaller, no matter how fast or long she worked—that was how popular she was with her white ladies. Sometimes she got so tired she'd put the ironing board on the floor and iron lying down, but she never quit. "Mr. Glazer needs dem closes to be right, wit'out no cat-faces. Dey is gwine to Jackson to see de lawyer," Mama said from the floor, as she lay next to the ironing board. "All dem 'portant white folkses be axin' Mr. Glazer, 'Who do yore pressin'?' He say to dem, 'I gots de best in de Delta, but you needs a 'pointment!' " She would stretch out full-length on the floor and laugh and laugh until her eyes welled up and she started coughing.

For a long time, I had to content myself with what Mama told us about the enticing and forbidden white sections of Greenwood that began where Gee Pee ended, several blocks north of Walthall Street. I never tired of Mama's description of "de white folkses' part o' town." She talked about streets and boulevards overshadowed by hickory, walnut, magnolia, china, and hackberry trees, and about big plantation-style houses set back from the tree-lined street, with many big rooms and bright, soft rugs on the floors. In the front of each house lay a beautiful green carpet of grass, cut short and edged, with pretty flowers set in borders along the walkway. Unlike our bumpy Gee Pee and Gritney roads, the streets were paved and no open window was without its screen. Every house seemed freshly painted—mostly white and trimmed with all the colors of the rainbow. Dirt never seemed to stick to them, and Mama said that inside, they got "thangs so purty dat dey hurt de eyeballs."

Although I didn't know it then, the houses in Greenwood gave me my first lesson in race. I learned that color and money went together. I learned that houses had skins, just like people, and just like people, they were segregated by color and money. It took me a long time to learn that houses and people wore their skins only on the outside. And then I wondered why nobody ever bothered to look underneath.

In the white neighborhoods, there was no traffic except for the shiny, late-model Chevys and Plymouths and DeSotos cruising along the quiet, shady boulevards, resplendent with chrome. Young white boys on bicycles dodged the cars as they tossed Greenwood's daily newspaper, the *Commonwealth,* onto the neatly trimmed lawns. Mama's white ladies used to give her old copies to paper our walls and ceiling. Mama couldn't read, so she favored the comic pages. But I noticed that the paper hardly ever featured a black person on its front page—or anywhere else, for that matter, unless it was for a knife fight in Gritney or, more rarely, the burglary of a white home.

Black folks went into the white section of town cautiously, and only during daylight. It was a long time before I set foot inside a white person's house, and no white folks ever went inside mine. I wondered about the white folks and how they lived. I wondered whether they wondered about me.

Nearer our house on East Gibb, the shade got sparser and the flies got thicker. Kids were everywhere, playing Post Office and

Kick the Can, jumping rope, and chanting their ABC's. Women gossiped and fanned themselves and sipped RC on one another's porches. They spoke pig Latin so that we children couldn't understand them when they talked about sex or white people. At noon, when the sawmill whistle blew, the women would go inside to put the men's dinner on the table. The few kids who were lucky enough to have fathers in the house would stop playing and run to meet their daddies.

I was luckier than most kids because, though I never had a daddy to meet, I had three daddies come to visit, depending on the time of year. My Christmas daddy was Mr. Ethan, who lived in Ohio and came to Greenwood when the winter cotton harvest was over. He'd take me and Mama out shopping on Main Street, but he never stayed long, because he had another family someplace else. My Easter daddy was Mr. Warren, who lived in Chicago with his wife. Jean said he was my real papa. He took us shopping, too, on Easter week, to buy me new clothes. My birthday daddy, Mr. Goosch, came every year in August, and gave me five dollars. Although he lived in Baptist Town, I didn't see him but once a year. Mama said that was " 'cause his footses be real bad." Maybe it was just as well I didn't see any of them more often, because when Mama talked about them, she usually called them "low down an' dirty scoun'ers."

When she finished ironing for the day, Mama would sit in her favorite chair, rocking, remembering, and talking, her nappy shoulder-length hair almost hidden under the headrag that my Christmas daddy gave her before I was born. She never got tired of telling me why she left home. Since she was the oldest child, she felt it was right that she be the first to go out on her own. "I tell you dis here, Ida Mae, so dat when you has chilluns—you won't have no mean old man—no stepdaddy—over dem."

Mama rocked faster and faster as she spoke, as if by pushing up and back with all the weight of her body she could pump the story out of her. "My stepdaddy, Cal, was a real mean man. I 'spect Suaar had to marry up wit' him, 'cause her be big wit' me. I weren't none of his—I'm glad a dat—'cause his own dear chilluns say he be a mean old man."

I knew by now that whenever she talked the "stepdaddy talk" it was my job to hurry to the back room and get her slopjar, quick. It was always the same, this story that she seemed to choke on. The only time she threw up was when she talked about her stepdaddy. She'd rock even faster, sweating and breathing harder and harder until it came rushing up, the stinking green bile so thick and slimy that it choked her as she tried to spit it out.

It was a frightening thing for me to watch, but I got used to it. I understood, somehow, that it was brought on by a deep hurt and anger she felt toward her stepdaddy, Cal; a hurt she usually held on to—deep inside, way down in her gut—a hurt that sometimes she just couldn't hold any longer, so she worked it out with her story. If a baby gets ahold of something she shouldn't and swallows it, if you're quick enough and stick a finger down her throat you can make her gag and throw it up. Mama's story was like that finger, only it reached down a whole lot farther than a finger—and what it pulled up had been swallowed a long time ago. And what she had swallowed was more bitter and raw than anything any baby could ever get at.

Mama was born on a plantation in Belzoni to a family of tenant farmers. Her mother, Suaar, had thirteen children but only seven lived to be adults. Mama's given name was Ida Mae, which she passed on to me. But everybody called her Aint Baby, meaning that she wasn't the baby anymore. My Delta nickname was another matter.

When I was a toddler, Suaar would bounce me on her knee singing:

Jump rat,
Jump cat,
Jump all night long!

I would giggle and egg her on so she'd bounce me higher and get me hysterical. Some people said that little game is why everyone started calling me Cat. Another story was that I had been scratched over one eye by a stray cat while Mama was out on the town. My brothers said it was because I had skinny little legs, like an alley cat, which was why they always called me "Little Leg Cat," though nobody else did.

"My real daddy's name is Pierce Garner," Mama would continue. "He live in Prairie Point. I'm gwine take you dere, Ida Mae, so dat he kin see you." She had a faraway look in her eyes. "I wish dat Suaar had marry my daddy, but I 'spect she couldn't—bence he had a wife already. I went down yon'er to see my daddy 'bout nine years ago—when I was big wit' you. He be so glad to see me. His wife, Pecola, and dey chilluns, my little sister and brother, Josephine and Willie James, act like I be de Queen o' Sheba. Dey was some kinda good to me. De first thang us'n talk 'bout was old man Cal Conner."

At the sound of that evil name, I stopped pouring dishwater down the neck of Sister Girl, my doll, and fetched Mama's homemade fly swatter. She would swat flies as if she could swat away the memory of her mean old stepdaddy and her life in the hills, with him and her mother and her half-brothers and sisters.

While Mama swatted flies and rocked, agitated, I went back to my doll. Sister Girl's hair was long and blond, like Shirley Temple's, and she had blue eyes. She could actually pee on the floor when you pulled off her head and poured water down her neck. I'd spend hours water-waving that long hair, slicking it down with lard or tallow and making snake curls with a pencil, then covering it with one of Mama's headrags.

Mama's voice interrupted my hairdressing. "Us chilluns be real hongry. My brother, Bruh, his belly use ta git twisted up 'cause he be so hongry. He say he couldn't stand for it no mo', he had a git somethang to fill his belly. And we ain't got no somethang. So Bruh, he jest go and et de post dat prop our house up. He be chewin' de wood like it be meat, till he ain't hongry no mo'. Dat's how hongry us be. And half de time, meat be in de house, but his own dear daddy won't gi'e him none—'cause he say he be savin' it for de dog. After us be done work de field all day, makin' a crop for de white folkses an' ain't got nothin' in us belly! Now dat be some mess."

Mama smashed a fly. "Suaar'd be some kinda tired but she had to go git Cal some grits or he'd whup her wit' de bullwhip till her closes be soaked down wit' blood. An' dere be nothin' dat us chilluns could do 'bout it neither."

Mama was the master of the silent cry, so I had to take my eyes off Sister Girl to see when she was weeping. "Dose boys, Bruh and Son, act like dey don't see it, but us girls jumped on Cal Conner's back to pull him off'n Suaar. Den Cal turn on us—he thowed me 'gainst de wall, hit Annie wit' a wood plank, an' he like to beat Sweet to death! 'Course now, he never got de nerve to beat Mag —'cause he be 'fraid o' her daddy. Eversomebody on our plan'a-tion knowed dat de white man be Mag's daddy—she favors him a lot. De onliest girl dat Cal took to is Doll. Suaar said it's 'cause Doll be his only child that favors his mother." Mama took another dip of snuff and rolled it inside her bottom lip. She continued to swat flies and mash any bold roaches that crawled across her floor.

"Set up, Ida Mae, and lissen to dis." She took a halfhearted swing at me with her snuff rag or fly swatter to get my attention. "Cal, he ruther spit on me den say a civil 'howdy do.' He treat me bad but he treat his other chilluns worst—like de dirt on dis here flo'. Many a time us chilluns drunk water jest to git our own belly full. I never let him see how hongry I be, bence I seed Bruh eat de wood off'n de house." Mama spit more brown snuff juice precisely into the slop jar. "I 'members de day I run off. I jest up and say to my own dear self, Ida Mae, you gots t' git 'way from here—'fore yore stepdaddy kills you!"

I listened more intently now, because I knew from experience that play-like was about to happen. I tucked Sister Girl into her shoebox and gave Mama my undivided attention.

Mama got out of her chair, shuffled to the door, and looked up and down Gibb Street, as if to reassure herself that her stepdaddy was not marching down the street. All of a sudden, she wheeled around and went into a crouch. She was reliving her escape from the plantation and Cal Conner. I leaned back and watched her, wondering for all the world why she never joined the Silas Green or Rabbit Foot shows—she was better then half the actresses I'd seen, including those at the Walthall picture show.

Her voice had dropped to a whisper. "It be in de summertime, right after Bruh et de wood. I be layin' on my pallet—dead hongry —dat I 'cided t' git up an' go to de Delta. I crept up outta my kivvers an' went t' de outhouse, where I hide my grip, an' set out into de dark o' night—wit' onlies de moon t' keep me comp'ny. I set out walkin' t' dis here town. A great big truck pull up 'longside me, it brakes squallin', an' de white man axed me, 'Wherebouts you gwine to, gal?' I tol' him dat I be gwine t' de Delta t' work on de plan'ation. He gi'e me a ride t' de cutoff out yon'er by Valley Hill."

Mama would play like she was climbing down from a big truck

seat. She'd look around like she was expecting a car to come driving through our front room. "Den I cotched a ride wit' dis old, old white man an' 'oman. She read de Bible all de way here. She didn't even look at me. De white folkses got a sayin', ' 'F'n a white 'oman look at a colored 'oman 'fore seven, it gwine rain 'fore 'leven.' I 'spect she didn't want de colored folkses t' leave de cotton field on 'count o' rain."

Mama sank back into her rocking chair. Silent tears ran in rivulets from her eyes and gathered beneath her chin, but she was smiling. I slid across the floor, careful not to touch the mashed roaches, and laid my head in Mama's lap. I felt my own tears sting my eyes. Whenever Mama acted out her escape from her stepdaddy's shack, I went through the whole journey with her. Although I was glad that I was still the baby, I vowed to cry just like Mama when I grew up.

Two

IN ADDITION TO TAKING IN IRONING, MAMA
RENTED ROOMS BY THE HOUR OUT OF BOTH SIDES OF
our house. We had our own alley, Dixie Lane, which allowed men
to come in by the front door and leave unseen out the rear. Business
was so good that Mama started renting out the woodshed that sat
directly behind our house. It was so small there was barely room
for a single cot and wash basin, but the renters found the setup
sufficient, as long as it came with the clean sheets that Mama's
roominghouse was known for. We were taught never to greet the
men who waited until dark to come to our house, and we were
forbidden to go into the backyard after dusk. Mama never made us
children wash any of the sheets "soiled in sin," either. She washed
them herself with her own homemade soap, boiled them in bluing
water, then rubbed and rubbed them on a washboard in the big
tin tub.

Whenever a neighbor tried to chastise her about the men who
beat a steady path to our house to have sex with any number of
women, she would say, "I be jest tryin' to make a livin' for me and
my chilluns." The neighbors would turn their heads and snicker, or
rant and rave about how Gee Pee was a place to bring up a family,
not to carry on that sort of business. After a while our house got a
bad reputation, and so did we. Some women would cross to the
other side of Gibb Street so they wouldn't have to walk past our
house.

Still, despite the nasty things they may have said behind Mama's
back, to her face the adults in our little community were very

respectful. The town needed Mama, and they knew it. Back then, women in love and trouble had no one to turn to for advice about sex or pregnancy or even love—no counselors or social agencies or therapists. Instead, they came to Mama—perhaps because they knew about the rooms she rented and trusted her not to judge them or gossip about their business. Much of Gee Pee confided in Mama—which is how I came to know everything that was going on. I was always listening.

MAMA ALSO had permanent roomers, like Dossie Ree, a pretty young woman with two children, a failed marriage, and a brutally jealous boyfriend. She took her children with her everywhere. The boy, who was older, walked at her side, while the girl rode on Dossie's hip. Dossie could sing the old-time spirituals so that the people in them came to life. When she sang about Jesus it was like he was in our house. Mama always said, "Dossie, her be a good girl dats run into a bad-luck man." Many years later, Dossie would distinguish herself as a spy for the best-known civil rights organization of the day.

Late one afternoon, way past the time her boyfriend usually ate his dinner of hot-water cornbread, cabbage, and rabbit, Dossie still hadn't come home to cook for him. Young as I was, I could see right off how mad he was. He slipped around the side of our house, peeping in the window and "cussin' to beat de band," as Mama said later. "I knowed dere was a dead cat on de line!"

By the time Dossie Ree finally came home, her boyfriend was sitting on our back steps, calmly shuffling and cutting a deck of cards—he gambled for a living. As she approached him, smiling like she didn't have a care in the world, he could see that his meal was the furthest thing from her mind. He picked up a hammer that lay just underneath the steps and with all his strength, he brought it down on Dossie Ree's head. Blood flew everywhere. It covered the boy and girl. It ran down Dossie Ree's neck to her arms and feet and the grass of our backyard. Her children were hollering and crying and so were we. Folks came running from every direction to stop the fight and patch Dossie Ree up before she bled to death. I remember her blood dripping into the washtub as she held her head sideways. She never cried out, never said a word—she just started singing "Amazing Grace" as Mama and the other women wrung the blood out of her hair.

That was the first and I believe the last time that I saw a woman being beaten by a man. Over the years, I saw many fights between men and women in Greenwood, but it was always the man who got beaten.

Mama also let a room by the week to Easter Mae, another pretty young woman who had a superb head for business. She always had a new money-making scheme going. She'd talk the clerks at the big department stores into letting her have clothes on credit. When our food got low, she went up to the chain grocery stores, Piggly Wiggly or Liberty Cash, and got food on credit. The men she dated paid dearly—up to three dollars a trick—and she made them bring a bottle of Garrett snuff and an RC cola for Mama, and candy for us kids. She always had something smart to say to the black men, and she talked sassy to the white men, too—behind their backs. Her claim to fame was that not a drop of white blood coursed through her veins. "Ain't like y'all," she'd brag. "I is plumb-dee black. I is real sweet, too!"

One time Preacher, the jackleg minister, said, "I'm gwine upside o' dat ole black-ass 'oman's head! 'Cause her be a fool 'f'n she thinks I'm gonna pay for some poon-tang!"

When Easter Mae heard what Preacher was saying, she went to his house, called him out—in front of his wife, Flower Bell—and dared him to repeat what he had said. "I done got too old for you t' be runnin' 'round here broadcastin' a slander 'gainst my name —'cause I ain't never gon' gi'e myself to you, or to nosomebody!" Easter Mae said, with all the dignity she could muster.

"Ain't tryin' to court you, gal, doncha be actin' like I done wrong by de church or my sweet lovin' wife, Flower Bell!" Preacher protested.

"You's a lie, Preacher!" Easter Mae said with a scornful voice. "You wants to git underneath my closes, but I ain't let you 'cause you ain't got 'nough money. And," she added, "you be stanking so bad I *hopes* you ain't got de money—I don't know how Flower Bell puts up wit' you." Easter Mae stood in front of their house, her hands on her hips, her hair lying flat against her head, her chin and bosom stuck high.

"You git from in front o' my house, you drunken 'oman!" Preacher hollered. "You git on 'way from here, 'sturbin' my sweet Flower Bell!"

"Is I 'sturbin' you, Flower Bell?" Easter Mae asked.

"Naw, you ain't—de truth never hurt nosomebody," Flower Bell said softly. "I'm gonna see to it dat Preacher bathes, 'cause he do have a bad odor. And I wants you to look after his man-for-ness. Come over here ever week and I will give you de money."

That's how Easter Mae got to be famous in Gee Pee. Women who were pregnant or sickly or dying with cancer, the way Flower Bell was, started hiring her to have sex with their husbands. Maybe she was the reason folks let us stay in Gee Pee—Mama had Easter Mae, who provided a community service.

If you cut catty-corner across Gibb Street, you ran right smack dab into Miss Laurel Stokes's Cafe. Mama and her friends said that Miss Laurel propped sick old Mr. Stokes up in bed, then sent for Brother Pastor and married him, just to get his cafe. Even so, she always looked out for us and let us eat for half price. She made the best fried chicken we ever ate.

Another line of shotgun houses ran from her cafe down Walthall Street. Mama Lena's house was a ways up the street, near the Walthall picture show. Mama said that when I was real little, Miss Lizzie Bell and Mama Lena had a prayer war at the Turner Chapel African Methodist Episcopal Church across the street.

Mama Lena had taken to walking around her yard shouting out to "de Lawd," barely pausing for an answer back. Miss Lizzie Bell, who tried to best Mama Lena in all things holy, did not take this lying down. She waited until the next Sunday, when all of Gee Pee was in the church, then launched her own attack.

"Ida Mae chile, you oughta seen dem." Mama's face lit up, and I could tell she was about to do her play-like. "Lena was doing some kinda prayin'. Her be walkin' and talkin' and callin' out to de Lawd —voice like a great big trumpet." Mama picked up her imaginary cane and hobbled like Miss Lizzie Bell. She stopped suddenly and turned back—I swear, she even looked like Miss Lizzie Bell. She stood on her tiptoes, raised her arms over her head, threw her head back, and started laughing. "Ya don't say . . . well, well, well now . . . Yassir . . . yassir, Lawd! Ya don't say . . . Do Jesus! . . . I shore will, Lawd . . . yassir, yassir . . . I knows it—I knows dat we be kinfolkses!"

By this time, Mama had laughed and cried her way down the imaginary church steps. I saw she was at the end of her play-like, so I rushed to our icebox and got her a cold bottle of RC cola. If you didn't have money for the Walthall picture show, you could always spend the day watching Mama.

A lot of fine, God-fearing people lived in Gee Pee—and a lot of famous folks, too. Right next to Miss Lizzie Bell's house was Mr. Samuel Smith's house. One night Mr. Samuel had been sleeping with his outside woman, Miss Daffodil, who was known as Miss Daffy. He got up in the dark and put his clothes on and went home to his wife, Miss Loddie. But just as he was about to get into bed, Miss Loddie started screaming and hollering until she woke the whole neighborhood. She told Mr. Samuel to go back where he came from, give the woman her bloomers, and get his undershorts back. After that, everybody in Gee Pee, Gritney, and Baptist Town knew Mr. Samuel.

For me, Mr. Samuel's house was already a landmark because it was right next door to the Walthall picture show. The crumbly old theater was just for us colored people, though white people came sometimes when big-time gospel groups performed there. They always sat up front, with a buffer of several rows behind them. I remember sitting in those stiff-backed wooden seats, watching Hopalong Cassidy, Lash LaRue, Gene Autry, and Roy Rogers, King of the Cowboys, mow down hundreds of Hollywood Indians to make the Old West safe for decent folk. I thought for a long time that "decent folk" meant me, too, so I rooted for the cowboys to beat the Indians. I could hear Bud and Simon Jr. and the rest of their noisy friends screaming with pleasure at every move Old Hoppy made—flashing and twirling that silver gun. They cheered even louder when they saw the whites of Mantan Moreland's eyes —just before he ran from "the haints." But Tarzan was by far Gee Pee's favorite action hero. He could do anything and knew every-thing about surviving in the jungle—with the help of the African tribesmen who threatened and then befriended him.

We missed the big movies that showed in white theaters—with the exception of *The Ten Commandments*. When it came to the Walthall all the schools and churches let out early so we could stand in the lines that stretched around the block. For a story that took place in Africa, it didn't have many black faces, but few of our movies did.

When Jean was young, she and I adored Shirley Temple, who charmed all the men with her singing, dancing, and snake curls. I could sit in that stiff-backed seat all day and watch her bouncy curls, wishing they were mine. But Mama made Jean go with us to the picture show even when Jean would rather be down on McLauren Street in the juke joints than looking after us children in the pee-smelling picture show.

On the far side of our house, away from the alley, was Mr. Put's garage, where most of the black people in Gee Pee took their cars to be serviced. Mr. Put was white, and Mr. Put wasn't his real name—people said that whenever he wasn't sure where a part went, he just "put" it anywhere.

Mr. Put had two other traits that didn't endear him to the residents of Gee Pee. He was fond of black women and had the habit of fondling them and making sexual remarks about them even in the presence of their men. And he was one of the Leflore County good ol' boys—a group that would become formally known as the White Citizens Council by the 1960s.

All the black folks were afraid of Mr. Put. Black men didn't like the way he treated their women or their cars, but nobody dared to challenge what he did to either. The men would mutter, "Ain't gonna take my car to de garage for fixin' no mo'!" But the next week, most of them were lined up, waiting for Mr. Put to work on their cars. It was just the way things were done.

Straight down East Gibb, with a front door that opened nice and proper on Main Street, was the store owned by Mr. Pete and his barren wife, Miss Ellen. They were white folks, too. Miss Ellen came from somewhere in the North, and she never quite fit in with the other white women. Mama said, "Dat Miz Ellen, her be a good 'oman, when ole Mr. Pete ain't 'round." Mama would wait until she saw Mr. Pete leave the store in his white pickup truck. Then she'd go to the store to get snuff, salt meat, and other "grocies," which Miss Ellen would give her on credit. They had an unspoken agreement not to tell Mr. Pete about Mama's account.

Mr. Pete liked to tease Gee Pee's women as much as Mr. Put did, but he restrained himself when their men were present. And although he called grown black men "boy" and didn't allow black men in the store with Miss Ellen when he was out, he wasn't a good ol' boy. But he liked being with Mr. Put. They'd sit for hours in front of the garage, drinking Falstaff beer from paper bags—out of Miss Ellen's sight—commenting on Gee Pee women's behinds and laughing loudly.

Down on the low end of Gibb, across Walthall, right next to the railroad tracks, was the Century Funeral Home. Mr. Simon, a black man, was an embalmer extraordinaire. He did his best work when he was drunk. He was on duty that hot, still afternoon in 1955 when they brought in Emmett Till's body. Emmett Till was a black teenager on a visit from Chicago who didn't know his "place" in Mississippi. He dared to call a white woman "baby" and got killed for it.

A group of us were playing Post Office behind Turner Chapel AME Church when they brought his mutilated corpse in for Mr. Simon to work whatever magic he could. We sneaked a peek at his body while Mr. Simon was rummaging through his cupboards in search of an extra-stiff drink. We were horrified at the swollen, lumpy face with the eyes gouged out. Alix Sanders pointed to something stuck between the lips. "Dat's his thang," I said. We stood for the longest time staring down at the body, which seemed to have served as food for the fish. Finally, some white men shooed us away with the warning, "Y'all see what kin happen when you sass-out white women."

After Emmett Till's death, I began to see, even if I did not understand it all, that we black folks had to be careful around whites, and mind never to get out of our "place" around them. Shortly thereafter, a man named Mr. Matthews, who lived in Baptist Town, stood up to a white man who wanted to lie with Mr. Matthews's wife. Later that day, I watched as a mob of white men beat him down and poured acid over his body. It melted his skin right off and burned three holes clean through him, but it took him a whole day to die, hollering pitifully all the while.

When Mama heard the news, she shook her head and took a big dip of snuff. "He ain't de onliest one, neither." She hawked and spat. "De thangs I done seed. Our mens done paid de price—our brothers, our daddies, and dey daddies 'fore dem, be sont to dey grave wit'out dey fingers, eyes, ears, and privates."

"Yas'm," I'd nod, and get Mama her slop jar.

Lately, Mama talked to me more and more often about staying in my place around white folks: "Us 'omans was not kilt like de mens, but alotta us hopes dat death be quick, when de straw boss be whippin' us; or when us had a let de white mens have dey way underneath our closes." Mama would tremble a little and miss her aim, spraying the side of the coffee can.

My sister, Jean, had discovered Gritney and liquor and beer—sploe and homebrew—at the age of ten. My brother Bud (who is really my cousin, but that's a story for another day) had discovered hooky and used his time away from school to win marbles from the Gritney kids, who were expected to drop out. Simon Jr. had just discovered the power of his fist; he'd beaten up six men without getting a scratch on himself.

"Dese here ol' chilluns ain't got bat sense, but dey knows 'nough not to sass out de white folkses!" Mama used to say, shaking her head. "My boys ain't like dat Till boy. My boys knows not to look no white 'oman in de face, 'cause 'f'n dey do, de white 'oman kin say dat dey wolf-whistle at her—den dey gon' git us all kilt!"

For us, being safe meant staying close to home. We knew all the folks on Gibb Street, and they'd look out for us—even when they were busy looking out for themselves.

But in the fall, I saw a lot of the Delta countryside, from the back of a flatbed truck. It was important to get the cotton harvest in before the winter rains began, and anybody who wanted a job —even townfolk and children—could sign on as day labor. In fact, Leflore County's black schools usually opened a couple of months after the white schools to ensure that enough hands were available in the fields. I remember the headlights of those flatbed trucks sticking out like a bullfrog's eyes, perched on bent fenders above dirty grilles that protruded like buck teeth, ready to chomp anything in their path—rabbit or skunk, or the occasional dog carcass we passed with its guts strewn over the road.

Although most of our rains came in late winter or spring, an autumn storm could leave the rutted dirt roads impassable. "Muddy road call de milepost a liar!" Mama would say when our usual twenty- or thirty-minute ride turned into an hour or two. When we finally got off the truck, the sticky Delta mud would suck our shoes off and grab our bare feet like quicksand.

Once in the fields, we'd make a long line. The grown folk wore straw hats and trailed long sacks shroudlike over one shoulder. We'd fill one bag with damp white cotton, then another, stopping only for our midday meal—sardines, moon pies, and RC's. After eating, the adults would take a big dip of snuff or a chew of tobacco and bend again, under the unrelenting sun. We pulled the cotton out of the bolls until it got so dark we couldn't see.

After the day's work, we'd stumble tired and dusty back to the trucks for the endless ride home. Mama would point out the tarpaper shacks where the poor colored folks who lived on the plantation were housed. "I praise de Lawd dat I gots me a house in town —in Gee Pee," Mama would say, shaking her head sadly and skeeting snuff juice into her empty sardine can. She was bigger and stronger and did more work than us kids, and the long day hit her hard. Sighing softly, she would rest her head on my shoulder and nap all the way to Gibb Street. Behind us, the road stretched out into the darkness, straddled by lights from the scattered shacks that melded into the quilt of stars.

Three

All the black people in town have gathered in one place. There are no white faces anywhere, which is odd, because wherever blacks are gathered in large numbers there are always whites present—to make our gathering official and to make certain that we stay in our place.

No one moves, but there is a restlessness in the air. The people want to move but they can't. They wait and wait until they vibrate in their stillness. Only their eyes move, following me as I pass. Why is it that I can move and they can't? They seem afraid but I feel no fear at all. I look into their eyes and their eyes seem to be talking, offering me encouragement. I am still confused, but I keep moving.

I stop and face the crowd, and suddenly giant waves roll slowly over and around them until they are engulfed. Then the waters calm, and legs, bodies, and heads emerge. I am so glad to see them whole and not drowned that I smile, and my smile seems to mobilize them. They begin to wiggle toes and snap ankles back and forth as if they're testing them out for the first time. Still they do not move from their places. They're waiting again. No one breathes. Somehow I understand that they're waiting for me, for a signal from me.

I turn away from the huge crowd. I throw my shoulders back and straighten my spine so that my head pushes up high toward the sky. I realize that there is a baton in my hand. It's the one that Bud made for me, nothing fancy, just an old broomstick whittled down, with tape wound thick on each end. I raise my hand and point the baton toward Heaven. The people behind me start to breathe again, with one big breath. Everyone is breathing together in the same rhythm, to the same beat, a pulse that grows stronger and stronger until it almost seems to race.

I lower the hand holding the baton halfway, and then, quick as a flash, I throw my hand up and the baton flies out of my grasp and soars straight up. All heads are tilted back, watching its flight. Now it zooms back to earth, and somehow it has turned from wood to shining silver, a bolting arrow aimed at me. The crowd holds its breath as I spin and catch it, easy and without looking, in the hand behind my back.

People holler and shout and whistle and cheer. Somebody brags, "It be like Cat th'owed up thunder, an' cotch lightnin'!"

I raise my baton again, take a breath and step out, first forward and then wide-legged to the side, like I'm clearing a path down Gibb Street, pushing everything out of my way. Magically, the street grows wider and the curbs seem to jump back. Even the clouds in the heavens draw back like curtains to reveal a bright yellow ball of sun shining down on me and all the people of Gee Pee, who have gathered behind me in one endless line.

This is a parade for sure. Everyone is following me, imitating my grand, high steps. We are marching joyously, prancing to the sounds of the Greenwood Colored Marching Band, but the beating and thumping of our hearts drowns out the music.

WHENEVER ANYTHING important happened in our town there was a parade to mark the occasion. If a visiting preacher came to town, or when Silas Green and the Rabbit Foot Minstrels came to perform, a parade announced their arrival. Holidays like the Fourth of July or Labor Day called for a parade, too.

It would begin small, with the Greenwood Colored Marching Band and their family and friends. Then, as the parade passed along the streets, everyone would drop whatever they were doing and come to see what all the fuss was about. The parade would swell larger and larger as people joined in, trying to see what everyone else was doing and where everyone else was going. All of Baptist Town, Gritney, and Gee Pee, and a few white kids would follow the parade to the fairgrounds where the performance or festivities would take place.

This was what I dreamed of every day, a parade—with me leading it. My dream wasn't an unusual one for a little black girl back then. Majorettes were beautiful, glamorous—or what passed for glamorous in my little town. Men and boys talked to them nicely and treated them with respect. Majorettes were like movie stars to the black people of Greenwood. They were beloved, even idolized. And they were always the center of attention.

I kept dreaming my dream, and every day after school, I practiced my majorette step. I marched up and down Gibb Street near Dixie Lane, stepping high and twirling my baton. I paraded until I was wet with sweat, refining my wide-legged step and throwing my baton up in the air and catching it behind my back. Just like in my dream, I could twirl better than any other girl in Gee Pee.

"Don'cha be marchin' out yon'er in de road, Ida Mae," Mama shouted from inside the house, where she was ironing on the floor. I ignored her. I had to practice.

It was early evening, and although the sun had begun to dip to the horizon, the heat of the day still hung heavy in the air and on the skin. It had driven everyone outside to the edge of their front porches, where they sat in rickety old chairs or on the steps to catch whatever breeze could be caught. And when there was no breeze to catch they took up their fans, either the special ones, saved and brought from church, or the ones they made from old newspaper or the cardboard they'd used as a dustpan earlier in the day. They talked in whispers between long, loud gulps of cold RC cola and dips of snuff that made them sneeze. From time to time, they'd glance my way. I could feel their eyes on me, like in my dream, so I marched real sassy and flipped over backward and caught my baton.

Somewhere amid my bump-and-grind strut and the brassy sound of that imaginary band I heard the squeal of real brakes. An enormous expanse of chrome and green paint flashed in the corner of my eye, and the next thing I knew I was in the airless dark, with gravel that smelled like burnt oil plugging my nose, covering my face. I couldn't breathe. *This must be the way it feels to be dead,* I thought. My nine short years of life passed quickly through my mind.

I heard people hollering, then the sound of flip-flop shoes flapping against the gravel. Suddenly I realized I wasn't dead. It was dark because I was underneath the car. I couldn't breathe or cry out because my nose and mouth were filled with gravel. I coughed and spat and heard someone screaming but it wasn't me. Then I felt big strong hands grab my puny wrist and pull me out into the daylight.

"Ida Mae—Ida Mae!" Mama shouted over and over as she picked the gravel from my nose and mouth. "Lawdy, Lawdy, please don' take my little chile from me!" she prayed as her hands searched my body for broken bones. I followed her eyes down to my right leg. It looked worse than Jean's, the night she'd been cut up with a razor in a Gritney juke house.

The crowd around me parted and I saw a nicely dressed but paler than usual white woman, Miss Lussie Bee's white lady, crying and shaking in the big green Packard that sat crossways in the alley.

"A kinder 'oman ain't been born," I remember Miss Lussie Bee saying. "Dat dere white lady done gi'e me her dresses an' other closes; she even gi'e me de bloomers off'n her backside!" Miss Lussie Bee bragged to all of Gee Pee. Now, with her arms around her weeping employer, Miss Lussie Bee escorted her white lady to the corner store, away from the staring, blaming eyes.

Mr. Simon, the embalmer, and Son Boy Brown, the town drunk, carried me to just inside our back door, lowering me onto a quilt covered with newspaper to sop the blood. I smelled the whiskey on Son Boy's breath and the dead folk on Mr. Simon. Mama sponged my gritty face and bloody leg. Son Boy Brown, having lots of experience with police protocol, staggered back into the street and directed traffic away from Dixie Lane.

I recognized many of my schoolmates among the crowd around the back door. They looked scared and sad and excited. There was one jet-black, skinny girl with thick, waist-length hair whom I hadn't seen before. I didn't know it then, but that girl was Everlena, and she was to become my best friend. The crowd parted again and I saw Miss Lussie Bee's white lady, leaning on Miss Lussie Bee and Miss Ellen. Behind them, Mr. Pete moved the shiny green car from the mouth of the alley and parked it on Gibb Street.

It was the sight of Miss Lussie Bee's distraught white lady that really brought my leg back to life. I began to twist and moan. The white lady opened her purse and took out a dainty handkerchief. Gently she began to wipe away the blood and dirt from my leg. Mama didn't say anything, but kept working alongside her.

I wiped my snotty nose with a bloody hand and clutched my leg like it was on fire.

"Mama—Mama! It hurt!" My own tears made the white lady cry even harder. I felt mighty important each time she sobbed aloud. I could see the envious stares of my schoolmates, and I knew they wished the white lady's car had run over them. I didn't think I was hurt bad—I didn't feel any worse than I had the time I fell playing Post Office and scraped my knees all bloody. But I knew how to take the stage, how to play-like, and just then I was playing-like I was in a lot of pain, to make all of Gee Pee—and especially Miss Lussie Bee's weeping white lady—sad to see me hurtin' so.

Miss Ellen and Mr. Pete took Mama aside and whispered in her ear. Mama's head bobbed up and down as she listened to them, but she never took her eyes off me. Miss Ellen patted Mama on the shoulder and Miss Lussie Bee's white lady gave her a hug. People started making 'mirations over Miss Lussie Bee's white lady, and I knew that this day would be included forever in Miss Lussie Bee's Saturday night stories. I could see right away that the Gee Pee folks were play-liking, though. It was a reflex for black people to act that way around white people. As Mama and her friends said, "De white folkses be kind t' us coloreds, 'f'n us kick up a fuss over dem."

Mr. Pete squared his shoulders and said to Mama, loud enough so the crowd could hear, "This here gal, little Ida, she got mo' life in her then a cat! She ain't hurt bad. Y'all come on up to the store, Big Ida, and git some RC's. And git this gal a box of them moon-pies." Mr. Pete looked pleased. It was the longest speech he had ever made to a group of black people. The crowd started moving away. "All y'all got to do is rub some tallow and sage on her leg," Mr. Pete continued with authority. Another knot of people left.

Miss Lussie Bee steadily worked the remaining onlookers, re-minding them of the good works her white lady did for us black people. "You gwine git a great big sack of apples and oranges an' p'cans—an' a new baby-doll!—dat dis here good 'oman gwine brang you," Lussie Bee announced to me. The white lady patted my face and gave me her bloody handkerchief as a souvenir. She hugged Lussie Bee, who stood proudly in her embrace.

"Big Ida," Mr. Pete said, "y'all kin git groceries on credit till Little Ida gits well in the next week or two."

"Lawd, I show nuff 'preciate dat, Mr. Pete," Mama said, looking around to be sure that the remaining neighbors had heard. It wasn't enough to be well thought of by white people—everybody else had to know it, too.

I searched the thinning crowd for sympathy. Mr. Simon—who, except for a colored dentist, was the nearest we had to a doctor—gave me his attention. My eyes fluttered as he bent to examine my leg with an air of great importance.

"Say dere, Mr. Embalmer, she ain't dead yet," a bystander shouted. Mr. Simon suppressed a smile and kept examining my leg. Everybody waited with bated breath to hear his diagnosis.

"Dis chile's leg be in pretty bad shape," Mr. Simon said, looking Miss Lussie Bee's white lady in the eye. "Run over yon'er an' git my bag," he said to one of my schoolmates.

The boy left for the funeral home, running to beat the band. This was Mama's signal to start crying. Great big silent tears rolled down her cheeks and gathered around her neck. Miss Lussie Bee and her white lady took each other's arms. The mood of hope and congratulation evaporated. I just lay there and played dead and waited for the examination to end. A couple of my schoolmates, bored with the show, left to play tag while two men carefully moved me to our front room and laid me on Mama's bed.

Suddenly, a hot tong gripped my leg, and I couldn't straighten it out. The pain surprised me, and it dawned on me that I'd never been hurt this bad. I was scared I wouldn't be able to walk again. I cried out, and Mama knelt at the side of the bed and hugged me tight.

The boy returned with Mr. Simon's bag. After he examined my swollen leg, I was commanded to lie where I was for two weeks, on pain of mortal affliction. Miss Lussie Bee and her white lady left solemnly, along with the rest of the crowd. I never saw a real doctor, so I never knew how close I really came to losing my scrawny leg.

Sure enough, though, Miss Lussie Bee's white lady drove up in front of our house every Sunday morning. Mama listened for the honk, then went out to the big green Packard to get two big bags filled with apples, oranges, pecans, and other groceries, and secondhand clothing from the white lady's closet—but no doll. I tried not to look too disappointed from my makeshift hospital bed by the door. Sometimes the white lady would get out of her car and stand, arms crossed, next to the shiny bumper. Mama said she always asked about me, but never accepted her invitation to come in and see for herself.

"Hmph," Mama grunted, watching the car lurch from the curb. "Dat 'oman oughta be branging me some money for de way she done tore up yore leg. She ain't gots no business drivin' up and down dese streets like dat—she ain't gots no business to be drivin' dat car!"

She continued to low-rate the white lady, especially when she took something out of the bags that we didn't want. " 'F'n I was Lussie Bee, I never would git in de car wit' dat 'oman. Dey tell me when she went to git her permit to drive, de man wouldn't git in de car wit' her, 'cause eversomebody knows dat 'oman can't drive." Mama took a box of waffles out of the bag. "Wafers?" she barked. "Dat 'oman mus' not like dese thangs. But de Lawd knows I's thankful she didn't hurt yore leg real bad. Leastways you kin still march in de parade and turn yore stick. Lussie Bee say dat 'oman's husband tol' her not to be drivin' 'round up town, jest down here to Gee Pee to pick up Lussie Bee. Now ain't dat somethang? He don't care how many us colored folkses she hit wit' dat car. Dat's how come yore leg gotta take a long time to git well." Mama laughed. "Us'n gotta collect her due for de neighbors, too!"

We had a real good time, eating and talking, making jokes about white folks we'd never dare say to their faces. My whole class came to visit and sang me a song, and there was talk that the school was going to make me an honorary majorette. The African Methodist Episcopal Church sent me a brand-new Bible, and Mama's white ladies gave me fifty cents. Many of the people who lived in Gee Pee would stop on their way home from work to inquire about my health.

"Hey dere, Aint Baby," a woman yelled from the sidewalk, "how's Cat feelin' deday?"

"Dis here gal o' mine's doin' tol'able well deday," Mama hollered back. "She gwine be up an' 'round in no time."

Then people felt called upon to make 'mirations over Miss Lussie Bee's white lady. "Let me say one thang: dat 'oman dat Lussie Bee work for, she is show nuff gwine to see de face o' God!"

"Amen!" Mama declared. "Lussie Bee be some kinda blessed to have such a good white lady."

Miss Lussie Bee's white lady was as famous as I was. The white firemen took turns trying to teach her to drive better. The white women's sewing circle invited her to make a speech. And the white picture show showed a picture in her honor. Undoubtedly, we were the most famous pair in Greenwood, and I understood that each of us needed the other to maintain our status.

"It's a good thang dat no colored somebody's car hit you, 'cause dey show nuff couldn't a brung me dis here!" Mama held up a jar of Garrett snuff. "Dat dere 'oman gots more sense den I gi'e her credit for," she said, grinning.

When I wasn't entertaining visitors, I spent my convalesence coloring, reading comics, and playing with my doll. And I had long talks—or rather, "listen to's"—with Mama while she ironed. We talked and acted out important things, doing our play-like to the sounds of apples bitten to the core, pecan and peanut hulls falling on newspaper, or my hard, blue-eyed, yellow-haired doll nursing at the tiny water bottle I held to her lips. We spent so much time together that sometimes it felt as if we were the same person. When Jean and the boys would return for supper or bed the house seemed crowded to me. I couldn't share things with them the way I did with Mama.

Children who spend most of their time around grown-ups grow old and wise faster than do children who seldom see grown-ups except at meals or when some teacher is talking at them. Children left to other children are only children, but children like me— with Mama always talking and telling me about life, hers and other people's—are at once child and adult. Except when Mama was scolding me, she always treated me as if I were another adult, some neighbor woman come to sit a spell and jaw away.

One of her favorite topics was how proud I'd be of her once she got her permit to practice granny midwifery, a goal that always seemed near but somehow out of reach.

"You see, chile," she said, throwing her shoulders back as she moved between the ironing board and the overflowing clothes basket with an almost imperial grandeur, "you gots ta have a dream, 'f'n you gwine be somebody. When I gits my permit, all de folkses gwine say, 'Dere she goes, dat's Big Ida Mae, Little Ida Mae's mama. Ain't she a real fine 'oman? She done got her own dear self a permit to practice!'"

In Mama's dream, she was dressed in a clean white starched dress and cap and shoes like nurses wore, and she was toting a bulging black bag like doctors carried. On a string around her neck she wore her nature sack, full of herbs. She'd rush to the side of some woman's bed to offer her comfort and skill. Gently but firmly, she'd tell the woman what to do. Her hands would roam over the woman's stomach and read the signs as she reached inside to feel the baby and see how it was "setting." Her hands would tell her everything she needed to know.

This part was not a dream. Mama had magic hands, everyone always said. She had helped women birth before. But the hospital wouldn't treat colored women, so Mama would help until Dr. Feinberg and Mama Cindy, the granny midwife, got there. Once, when they arrived much later than the baby who'd arrived with Mama's help, Dr. Feinberg took Mama's hands in his and turned them over. He looked at the baby and then at Mama and said, "Aint Baby, you sure got the hands for it. You ought to become a granny catcher your own self."

"Dat's what I done tol' her," Mama Cindy said as she checked out the baby. "Dis here navel cord is cut jest right."

That's when it started, Mama's dream of catching babies. Now some folks might have thought it was an uppity kind of dream. But then to lots of folks any dream of bettering yourself seemed uppity. It wasn't the making something of yourself they stuck up their noses at. It was the trying—the wanting, the dreaming, the play-liking and pretension. Too many of them had dreamed of a better life, even worked at it, without success. And rather than be tortured by dreams, many decided not to dream at all.

So Mama was brave, in dreaming, in dreaming aloud to others, in wanting something despite the odds. And the odds were long. For one thing, a licensed granny midwife had to be able to read and write in order to sign certificates of birth.

Mama didn't know her ABC's, let alone how to read or write, but I did. She decided that when she got her permit to practice, I would be her assistant to handle the paperwork for her. Still, she had to take classes at the county health department, where I couldn't accompany her. But Miss Elnora Maddox, the grand midwife of Greenwood who'd begun to call on Mama to accompany her whenever she had a case, took Mama to class and wrote down the rules for her.

Such was Mama's determination to realize her dream and to join the ranks of "sainted women," as granny midwives were called. This was Mama's grand dream, the dream from which I learned how to dream—big and unafraid, no matter what obstacles or bitterness are put in your way. "Don'cha never gi'e your own dear dream up," Mama said, standing over the ironing board. "You gotta start somewheres, an' a dream is jest as good a place as any!"

Mama had another dream—that I would go to college. She was proud of the fact that I could read and write; what came naturally to me seemed like a miracle to her. She understood the importance of education and the potential it offered. Although it was too late for schooling for her, it wasn't for me. She had already selected Campbell AME College in Jackson for me. I would stay in a dormitory.

I often found school boring and useless. I took reading and writing for granted, not appreciating that my mother's generation and the ones before hers—even many in my own generation—had been denied the chance for any kind of education at all. But when I first heard that word, "dormitory"—not from Mama but from Velma Lee, a girl who went to Campbell—I thought it was the most magical word I had ever heard. Dormitory! I couldn't begin to imagine it, even though Velma Lee explained it to me again and again. The idea seemed impossible to me. I also knew that I could never live away from home, in a dormitory or anywhere else, because I still peed in the bed.

Mama put the smoothing iron down on the back of the wood-burning stove and took a bottle of cola from the icebox. "I owe dis RC to my own dear self," she said between long swallows, and grinned at me.

"Yas'm, Mama," I replied. "I gots me a dream, too."

"What for!" Mama grunted. "Drempt 'bout pee-de-bed?"

Tears pooled in my eyes. Every time I tried to tell Mama about my dream, she made fun of me. "Ain't talkin' 'bout dat," I said quietly. I didn't want to get backhanded for being too womanish, but I had to speak or I would burst. I pushed my doll off my lap and propped my leg on top of the pillows. "No, Mama. I's talkin' 'bout a dream like yours."

That stopped Mama's ironing cold—and nothing made her stop ironing, except when I got hit by the car. "I beg yore pardon, chile —what do you mean?" she said.

"I mean I wants to be a majorette, a drum majorette," I said in a tiny voice. "I wants to be out front o' all de other girls!"

"Well, now, you don't say." She laughed, but it wasn't to mock me. "Well, you jest oughta do dat, Ida Mae—'cause you kin step higher den anysomebody. Ain't *nobody* kin turn a stick like you do! You jest make sho' you keep outta de streets—'way from dat alley, now, you hear me, gal?"

I thought about mentioning my other dream—the one that caused me to pee in the bed—but decided against tempting fate. Besides, Mama was tired, and now she wobbled toward her rocking chair. Lately, she'd started stumbling and falling down— play-like, she said, to keep me laughing—but even at my age, I could see there was nothing play-like about it. She couldn't keep herself from falling.

"Ida Mae, gal, you is nine years old—but you got mo' sense

den a lotta folkses ten times ol'er den you is. Yet, dere be thangs in dis world you don't know nothing 'bout."

"Thangs like what, Mama?" I hopped over on one foot and laid my head in her lap.

"Thangs dat mama hens gots to do to feed her chicks." Mama reached into her bosom to get her snuff, to take a dip, before she continued. "I knows dat you is 'shame o' me."

"No'm," I lied, "ain't 'shame o' you none." I kept my face hidden in her lap so she couldn't see my face.

I never told Mama about how my schoolmates low-rated our family. During recess, they played "the wood house game," a cross between Post Office and tag, with the child playing Mama being "it." Their insults and my curses quickly escalated into the dozens, the ritual exchange of insults we referred to as "signifying." They'd sing special songs they made up to tease me as well:

> Mr. So-and-So
> came a-knockin' on Aint Baby's door,
> and when his wife finds out,
> man, will she be sore!

They'd accompany the song with nasty gestures to illustrate what went on in the other side of our row house and out back in the wood house.

Mama looked at me long and sad, like she knew about the taunting and teasing I had to undergo. "I'm gwine git me my dream, Ida Mae," she said. "You gwine see. I be marchin' down yon'er to git my permit to practice!"

"You gonna be Somebody!" I told her. I knew what to say. This was another kind of ritual exchange, one that built us up.

"I sho' nuff will! I be walkin' like dis." Mama rose slowly to her feet. Her shoulders moved back and her head seemed to stretch off her neck. She staggered around the front room, the closest she could come to strutting. She made me feel so proud of her and she looked so pretty and so smart—I was glad she was my mama, even if all my playmates mocked her and what she had to do to feed her chicks.

I joined Mama's march and we both stumbled and hopped around the room. I stepped out like a majorette, marching to a band that only we could hear. Finally, Mama gave out and flopped back into her rocking chair.

"We is somethang, ain't we, Ida Mae!"

"Yas'm, dis is de way I be marchin'—leadin' de parade!"

"You be a good gal, Ida Mae, an' de folkses gwine make 'mirations over you."

"I is, Mama. I ain't never gone make you shame o' me," I promised, crossing my heart and meaning it. I couldn't think of anything that I could possibly do that would shame my mama. How little did I know of life!

Mama took her time spitting her snuff juice into her coffee can. "Don'cha worry none 'bout what de chilluns say 'bout dis here family; we be good as anysomebody in dis world—don't matter none how I makes our livin'."

"Yas'm," I agreed.

My good feelings lasted a few more weeks because our neighbors kept poking their heads in the door to make 'mirations over my injury and fortitude. Then the weather turned hot and sticky. Our neighbors sat out on their porches, drinking Royal Crown cola, dipping snuff, and gossiping. Every now and then someone would take a swipe at a fly. In the middle of the street, despite the heat, a gang of my friends were playing my favorite games. I couldn't stand being cooped up all day inside our house, and my leg wasn't even sore anymore, but Mama forbid me to go outside.

"A heap sees but a few knows," she said, as she changed my bandage, a piece of flour sack soaked in turpentine that she washed and boiled whenever it got soiled. "De next thang you know, dese here folkses be done run down yon'er an' tol' Lussie Bee's white lady dat you be out gal'vantin' 'round." I knew that Mama was looking forward to our weekly treats and she didn't want them to stop.

So I went from the bed to the front door and back to the bed. No matter how hot the weather got, Mama always covered my legs with a quilt that she and Miss Sister Brown and Miss Susie had sewn before I was born. I studied that quilt until the colors ran together, naming the patches and looking for a match or some kind of pattern in them.

A YEAR came and went, and things changed—little things and big things. Miss Lussie Bee's white lady passed on. I didn't see it, but a couple of Mama's women friends did. "Dead!" they said. "Seen it happen my own dear self. Awful—jest awful. Her car jest turned an' flipped, den it roll down yon'er 'neath de underpass an' fell upside down." The women pointed off in the direction of the accident, staring as if they could still see Miss Lussie Bee's white lady hanging in the windshield. "Dead," they muttered. Soon after, Miss Lussie Bee moved across the railroad tracks, to a house near Booker's Cafe, over in Gritney.

NOW THERE were no more Sunday groceries. Still, Mama and me got by and play-liked, and for a long time Mama

would say, "Dat dere white 'oman oughta be restin' in peace—
'cause she sho' nuff couldn't drive. But Lawd, she brung de bestest
apples an' oranges an' snuff anysomebody ever put in dey mouth!"

I stopped practicing. I no longer wanted to be at the head of any
parades marching through Greenwood. My homemade baton
leaned against the back of the house, waiting to be picked up and
thrown high into the air.

Four

ONE SATURDAY, WHILE MAMA WAS IRONING
AND I SAT AT HER FEET PLAYING WITH MY DOLL, I SAW
the skinny, jet-black girl with the long hair again—the one I had
seen the day I got hit by the car. She was standing on the curb
watching the other girls jump rope. I could see that she wanted to
play, but they were ignoring her. She looked as sad as the day the
car hit me.

"Y'all let her jump!" I shouted out the front door—startling
Mama and surprising myself. But none of the girls would jump
with her. So before Mama could stop me, I ran out of the house
and teamed up with her to jump double-dutch.

Her name, it turned out, was Everlena Hoskins, and from the
day we met, we were inseparable. She lived in a shotgun house in
an alley in Gritney, with five brothers, a sister, her mother, and her
father. Mr. Earl, her daddy, owned a barber shop on Johnson Street
in Gee Pee. On Saturdays, Everlena and I would hang around the
front door of his shop and watch the country people from the
plantations outside of Greenwood who came to get their hair cut.
We laughed at the women and girls who smeared their legs and
arms with tallow and lard so they wouldn't be ashy when they
came to town.

The barber shop didn't make much money, and Everlena's family
was very poor. Like most of the other mothers, her mother, Miss
Boot, worked as a maid, leaving home well before daylight to fix
coffee for "her white folks" and returning home well past dark.
Every Saturday, Miss Boot got drunk, so Everlena learned to care

for her baby sister and brothers. She was a younger version of her
mama, real pretty.

By now all those days I'd spent at home nursing my injury had
developed into a taste for hooky. Back in school now I itched to be
free again. It was a terrible itch and I scratched it, spending most
of my days at Everlena's house while her mama and daddy were at
work. We'd smoke three-for-a-nickel cigarettes, talk grown-up,
and tell stories.

Our little haven enticed several other girls to join us. Everlena
took charge of our money, bought our cigarettes, and rationed
them back to us not by the cigarette but by the puff. I didn't mind
her bossiness too much, because with her, I was accepted. My
schoolmates and fellow truants stopped teasing me about Mama
running a whorehouse or my sister Jean being a drunk. So day after
day, I sat on Everlena's lumpy couch and silently deferred to her
opinions and her will.

"Cat, girl, dey ain't gonna let you be in no parade—when is
you seen anybody dat's not bright in the band?" Everlena asked as
she blew smoke rings in the air. "Bright" meant light-skinned.

"Can't none o' dem girls beat me marchin'!" I shouted, taking
my allotted puff.

"You better wake up, girl! Yore family, dey ain't good 'nough,"
Everlena shot back. She said what we already knew, that to the
people who mattered most in our little town, our families weren't
"good 'nough."

But Everlena and I—and tiny, black Alice and fat, short-haired,
brown Gwen, and all the rest—had banded together. "So what?"
we said. So we were outcasts. "So what," we said again and now,
together, accepted it without bitterness. We had each other and
didn't need the "saditty folks" who marked the difference between
themselves and other black folks by skin color.

We were a group—no, a "gang"—now. We were our own

society, almost like a ladies' club—except we seldom acted like "ladies," and instead of sipping lemonade, wine, and gin, we drank Kool-Aid, sweetened water, and beer to quench the thirst that accompanied the sardine sandwiches that were our late-afternoon meal. It always amazes me that boys would still stop by to visit us despite our smoky sardine breath, but we had the allure of womanhood—or so we liked to think. We thought we were grown now, because we had put away our dolls, ribbons, and barrettes.

One day, after weeks of glorious truancy, we decided to go to school. Everybody, especially our teachers, was surprised to see us sitting at our desks, looking pious and ready to learn. During "rest period," we put our heads down on our desks for twenty minutes. My head was down and my eyes were closed, but my mind was roaming across the highway to the 82 Bar and Grill. I was dreaming about dancing and taking a secret sip of beer when a few of the teacher's words penetrated that happy dream: "Principal Coleman sent to the Capitol and got everybody's birth certificate, using city funds."

Heads lifted from desks and the teacher read the birth names of each student. Half the time, she had to point out which of us she was referring to; many of us were hearing our real names for the first time. Stone Street School was filled with Apple Jacks, Baby Boys, Sugar Pies, L.Q.'s, and Bright Eyes who turned out to be just plain Aaron, George, Betty Mae, Quentin, and Tommy. Everlena was astonished to discover that her real name was Evelyn—an assertion that would have drawn a bloody nose from anyone else. Again and again she asked, "How come Boot didn't tell me de truth?"

Another morning, we were smoking our last cigarette in Everlena's living room when we heard Miss Boot outside the door. It was my turn to take a drag, and in a panic I threw the cigarette under the pillow and fanned away the smoke. Miss Boot was surprised to see us sitting on her couch but she didn't say anything—she had to hurry back to work. Within seconds, though, the cigarette had burned through the cotton-filled pillows.

Miss Boot sniffed the air. "Everlena, I smell smoke!"

"Naw, Boot, dat ain't nothing but de salt meat I burnt for breakfast," Everlena lied. She jumped on the couch and tried to smother the smoking cigarette.

"Us don't have no school 'til after twelve," I added, embellishing my lie to be safe. "We is plaitin' de May Pole deday."

"Well, y'all go on to de schoolhouse when you 'spose to," Miss Boot said as she hurried out the door. "And 'fore y'all leave, be sho' to put out de fire on dat cigarette!"

No sooner had the door closed behind her then we jumped up to put out the smoldering pillows. Then we started blaming one another about just whose fault it was. We were still arguing when there was a loud knock at the door. Neither of us was brave enough to answer. Then the door squeaked open and we all hid our faces. When we peeked, there was Leroy Harper, a handsome upperclassman—laughing at us. He had seen Miss Boot return home, and knowing we were playing hooky—and smoking cigarettes—he got a big kick out of our getting caught, and wanted to rub it in.

That was the day I first heard Leroy recite Ernest Lawrence Thayer's poem "Casey at the Bat." We pooled our coins to buy a nickel's worth of cigarettes—two for us to share and one whole cigarette to seduce Leroy into reciting.

"The outlook wasn't brilliant for the Mudville Nine that day," he said, standing like a king. He took a deep drag from his cigarette while we girls sat in front of him, cross-legged, passing our butt back and forth. "The score stood four to two . . ." Leroy ran through the poem, which lasted for the duration of his cigarette.

He kept going to the window, peeking nervously from behind the plastic curtain. Unlike us, he was not a veteran truant, and he wanted to go back to school—at least in time to answer the afternoon roll call. He'd also probably begun to figure he was wasting his time with us wayward girls. We showed no interest in playing Post Office, a game he insinuated he excelled at. Still, he was a natural orator who inspired in me from the first a great affinity for the legendary ballplayer.

I had only memorized the first two stanzas when Leroy decided to leave. I begged him to stay, at least to correct me while I repeated what I could—in other words, to be my teacher. That seemed to do the trick. I got up and he sat down, taking a couple of drags from our last cigarette as compensation for overtime.

I launched into my performance like a thing possessed. They say black Africans discover the supernatural in themselves by acting out their stories in songs and dances. Gee Pee had no professional theater, and the only stars we ever saw—besides those in the sky—were the performers who toured with the minstrel shows. Still, we had our entertainment.

Saturday evenings had long been set aside for amusement in the black community. At first it had been a group of men singing with a jug band, or dancing fancy steps in the dust, or telling jokes and clowning, trying to make everybody laugh, feel good, and forget about the long week working in the fields. Later there were movies, but many people couldn't afford them. So they'd gather on each other's porches as those who had been to the Walthall picture show brought Tarzan and Shirley Temple to life, play-acting their favorite scenes. It was more fun than seeing the originals.

Even better was the chance to see someone imitating some eccentric relative or play out something that had happened earlier in the week—especially if it involved white folk, like when Mama play-liked Miss Lussie Bee's white lady. Al Jolson in blackface was never as entertaining as black folk playing like whites. It was both funny and cruel.

I never missed these sessions, and took every opportunity to perform. It was there that I began to learn what worked for an audience and what didn't. When I stood up to recite "Casey," I summoned up all the tricks and nuances I had observed on Saturday nights.

I stopped when I ran out of story. Leroy, Everlena, and the other girls just sat there, slack-jawed.

Then Everlena broke the silence. "Cat, girl, you found your callin'—you is a nat'ral-born play-liker!" Even Leroy agreed.

That afternoon, I went to school to look in my reader for the complete text. But the poem wasn't in the sixth-grade textbook, and Leroy showed no inclination to share his copy, the source of all his power, which he guarded like Samson did his hair. It was clear to me that I was going to have to learn the poem the old-fashioned way: through the oral tradition. Everlena and I decided to get Leroy to recite the poem enough times for me to learn it by heart.

But the next day Leroy returned to Everlena's house and slipped a treasure into my hands: a beat-up copy of his book with the text of "Casey." In gratitude, I let him have my last drag off our cigarette.

For the rest of the term, I pored over the poem. I memorized every word and mined them all for every nuance, every pregnant pause. I rehearsed every chance I got, trying to get every line perfect and to make the meaning clear. I recited the text out loud on my way to the store and silently while I sat on our porch. I tried new variations before going to sleep at night, or outside Miss Robertson's arithmetic class, and on Sunday morning before church. I made our flop-eared old dog, Frisgo, an audience of one as he chewed on my abandoned baton.

I finally had the courage to try the whole thing out on Mama. The poem flew out in one piece: not like a truckload of furniture, a stick at a time, but as a beautiful suite of antiques, a shining rarity. When I had finished, Mama clapped and cheered and crushed me to her big old titties and said, "You done it, Ida Mae, you kin sho' 'nough play-like!"

From then on, she would call me to recite "Casey" for her friends and anybody else who had time to listen. Whenever our neighbors passed by—Miss Nellie, who had a very nice house near the funeral home; Miss Tut, who was married to a man who owned a shoe-repair store and liked to put on airs; or Miss Susie, who lived across the street with her five "good chilluns"—she would call me to perform, shouting, "Ida Mae, chile, c'mon out chere and do dat baseball thang!" Everybody who heard me recite said that I had talent and would go far—all except Jean, who got tired of hearing the poem. She retreated farther and farther into the house to escape it, sometimes singing at the top of her voice to drown out my applause.

The entire membership of Turner Chapel AME Church knew that my recitation skills were highly advanced. Our Sunday school teacher gave me the longest Easter speech, and I amazed the church folk with my dramatic rendition of Christ rising from the tomb. Mr. Buckhanon, Easter Mae's sugar daddy, applauded and gave me a shiny quarter. With the money clutched tightly in my sweaty palm, I realized that being in front of people—talking and getting paid for it—was what really appealed to me.

EVERLENA'S MAMA didn't go to work one Friday morning, so we all, including Everlena, had to go to school. When I got there, the place was buzzing with talk that some white people from uptown were coming to the school the following Monday. The rumor gained credence when classes were suspended and all able-bodied students were recruited to clean up the more neglected parts of our building: the dirty windows, moldy bathrooms, scuffed-up hallways, and trash-strewn, overgrown lawns. Normally, Everlena and I were the first to volunteer for duties outside the classroom, but this crash beautification program seemed just one bag shy of picking cotton. Still, our curiosity about what was afoot got the better of our judgment, and we stayed around to help.

After a morning of hard labor, Principal Coleman held a pep rally during the hour normally reserved for school assembly. When we sweaty laborers were in our places, he asked us to stand and pledge allegiance to the federal flag, sing "God Bless America," and recite the Lord's Prayer. With Abraham Lincoln, Kate Smith, and Jesus Christ now suitably paid homage to, Mr. Coleman began his oration.

"Teachers, students—a *great* honor is being bestowed on us here at Stone Street School. Our superintendent called me early this morning to say that many great educators will be coming to evaluate our school—to see how we're doing. I said to him"—he stepped out from behind the beat-up podium and raised his arms dramatically—" 'We're ready! Yes, sir—we're *ready!* Come ahead with your visit!' "

The *amen*s and *yessah*s began with a few adults—staff mostly, then some teachers—and cascaded quickly to the seventh graders. Everlena and I and a few other well-known malcontents joined in, just for the hell of it, raising our voices with the others. Mr. Coleman was on a roll:

"Yes, I told him, come ahead with your visit. You will find that we know how to read. We know how to write. And we know how to do arithmetic!" Everybody hung on his words. We began to feel blessed—like a chosen people. Even old Jaybird Jackson, who was eighteen years old and had been left back in the sixth grade for more years than I had been in school, applauded wildly, tears falling around his snotty nose. Mr. Coleman paused to acknowledge the ovation. "Come ahead—we welcome your visit! Come ahead—because you will find that this school, Stone Street School, is bringing forth the Colored Leading Class of Tomorrow!" The applause was deafening.

"Now—" Mr. Coleman stepped back behind the podium and turned his charisma down a notch. "After this assembly, I will ask you all to meet back in your homerooms and have each teacher select the best reader from each class. These class champions will then give a reading to me, and I will select the best to represent Stone Street in a special program for our very important guests next Monday."

What Principal Coleman didn't say, but what was very much on his mind and on the minds of most of the teachers in the room, was a rumor that had been circulating during the last few months —that since the Supreme Court had ruled in *Brown v. Board of Education* that public school segregation was unconstitutional, Mississippi's schools might have to integrate. Years later, Mama claimed she'd known about the suit—she called it "dat Brown mess"—but she was sure that "white an' coloreds ain't gwine never go t' school degether in dis here Delta." But for the most part, we kids and our families didn't know a thing about desegregation, or we would have been as scared as Mr. Coleman. Having anything to do with whites —outside of serving their meals and washing their dishes—was dangerous at best, suicidal at worst.

But the question that was really on Mr. Coleman's mind, as it was for lots of black principals, was, What were they going to do with piddly black schools like his if the students went off to the better white schools? What would happen to the black principals and teachers? What white family was going to let its children be taught, helped, and touched by black teachers? Understandably, Principal Coleman and our teachers were anxious to show the school board that our school was doing just fine—and we were happy to stay in it.

Of course, at that time none of us really understood how great a difference there was between white schools and black schools, since none of us had ever been inside a white school. Some of us naïvely imagined that the only difference was the color of the students' skins. We thought that we were all receiving the same education, and attributed white students' greater success after graduating simply to the fact that they were white.

Since the past was all we knew, it was all we could imagine. Our dreams were limited to our sad and slight experience. We had been dreaming of freedom for centuries, but it was a dream that came only in installments, like a Saturday matinee serial at the Walthall picture show. Each new adventure left us breathless and hanging from a cliff, but none of us could imagine what would happen next, or how it would end. (Even now, when I visit Greenwood and talk to younger blacks who graduated from "all-white" Greenwood High, I stumble for a moment in disbelief.)

We marched from the auditorium to our homerooms. Our teachers held a hurried conference outside the door, then went from room to room selecting the best reader. My classmates could be divided into three categories: unprepared, unqualified, or uninterested. I fitted into the last box. I wasn't allowed to read my magnum opus, "Casey at the Bat," but instead was given some stupid story about a white boy's dog that got lost on a family vacation. I stumbled over the first few words and was disqualified before the damn dog got out of the car. Everlena's reading was even worse.

We all knew that Queen Oliphant would be selected from our room. Worst of all, Queen knew it herself. She was the teacher's pet, who never played hooky and read everything the teacher assigned. Today she read from "The Creation"—and I had to admit, she read it like the teacher herself, without stumbling or missing a word. She took her place with the other winners—Eddie Leach, Big Fat Maybell, and a new girl named Lorane whom I hadn't met —in the freshly waxed hall. They pivoted like soldiers and marched toward Mr. Coleman's office.

We could tell from the dejected look on Eddie's, Lorane's, and Maybell's faces when they trooped back past our classroom door that they hadn't been chosen. A few minutes later, Queen Oliphant returned, beaming and smug. Our teacher told us to clap for her, and we did. But the longer we clapped, the heavier my hands and heart became. Once again, someone else would be out in front of our parade.

By the time I got home, the news of our forthcoming visitors— and our champion reader—was the talk of the town. Mama was waiting for me on the porch.

"Now, gal, you jest tuck yore lip back in, and don't be draggin' no long face 'round here," she scolded, skeeting a stream of snuff juice into the coffee can I placed half-heartedly by her rocker. "You see now, Ida Mae, 'f'n you stop playing hooky, dey mighta put you up t' read—can't nosomebody cite better den you. But you is smellin' yore pee—done got all grown and 'omanish 'fore yore time. You done brung dis on yore ownself."

I knew better than to argue with Mama, so I just hung my head.

"How many times do I gots to tell you, Ida Mae?" she had warned me over and over again, when she heard about me playing hooky. "You gots to git out in de sky—up high—an' fly wit' de birds. De white folkses was gwine put our education in de sea 'til somebody say dat us colored folkses be strong 'nough to swim out dere to git it! Den some old ugly Colored Man in de co'ner—he raise up and beg dem white folkses to put education in books, 'cause I done swimmed in de ocean an' sea—but I ain't never read nane book, he say, an' don't 'tend to neither!"

I tried to follow the lesson Mama was trying to teach me, but I was getting lost.

"De story, it don't end dere," she went on. "De white folkses b'lieve dis man, an' went 'head an' put education in de book. Den us colored people start being de teachers an' lawyers an' doctors. Dats when de white folkses got degether some mo' an' say dey done made a great big mistake by puttin' education in dose books. Dey say dey been fooled by dat ol' nigger in de woodpile."

THE NEXT morning, I got up early and met Everlena near the railroad tracks.

"Don't worry, Cat—you kin read better den Queen," she said. "Dey jest pick her 'cause she be real light!"

"Don't care. I knows it oughta be me," I said. But even the cigarettes we smoked all the way down, without rationing them for once, didn't improve our morale.

On Sunday morning, Queen's mother, Miss Sue Willie, and Sue Willie's husband, Mr. Bo, brought Queen to Turner Chapel in a Blue Dot cab driven by Mr. Sims himself. He owned Blue Dot's "fleet" of a half-dozen beat-up cars. They'd take you anywhere in Greenwood for four bits, but for special occasions or emergencies, Mr. Sims drove personally, and he didn't charge a fare.

Mama's legs had been stiff and sore that morning, so she had decided to stay home. But it seemed like everyone else in town, even the drunks, had turned out to wish sassy Queen Oliphant good luck. She was escorted to the curb like royalty, supported under each arm by her parents. Their daughter was the talk of the town, and they wanted to make sure she got her propers from the community. People cleared out of her way, and she glided past us with a smug look on her face, head held high as any majorette. She was wearing one of the two new dresses presented to her by Kornfeld's department store.

"I swear, Everlena," I whispered, "dat girl's nose turned up so high she gonna *drown* 'f'n dere be rain." I was glad Mama wasn't there.

Preacher's sermon that morning was dedicated to the Oliphants. The theme was "keeping your light hid until the time is right." The sermon ended on an old refrain, about the joy obedient children bring to their God-fearing parents and their community. From the look on Queen Oliphant's face, it felt mighty good to have a "hidden light," something that made you feel real special. I thought I might have a light, too, but at the moment it seemed to be very well hidden.

Monday morning dawned bright and springy, with the smells of Mama cooking grits, gravy, salt meat, and coffee. She laid out my last year's Easter dress. "I wants you t' be clean and 'spectable in front of all dem big-shot white folkses," she said as she poured hot and cold water into our rusty tin bathtub. "Never will dey say Ida Mae Holland's gal be stankin'! 'Course now, dey kin say dat you ain't got no sense. I say dat my ownself. And dey might say dat you pee-de-bed—"

"Didn't mean to do it, Mama," I said, sopping my grits and gravy. "I be dreamin' dat dere bad dream. Didn't mean to pee-out yo' tick."

When I got to school, the VIP's were just arriving. Their car was surrounded by a caravan of shiny black official-looking cars. The caravan was led by the Greenwood Colored Marching Band, and the band was led by the majorettes, high-stepping out in front to the rocking cadence of the tubas, trumpets, clarinets, and drums.

There were no truants from Stone Street School that day. All the students were present and accounted for and wearing their best clothes.

"Hurry up, girls and boys," said Miss Robertson, shepherding us into the auditorium. "Take your seats—and no talking!"

She and all the other teachers were wearing expensive suits from Abide's department store. You could see right away that the lights at Miss Gardner's Beauty Shoppe had burned long past midnight, floating an odor of fried hair over Gee Pee and Gritney.

Gradually, the auditorium filled up. Students and teachers from all-black Broad Street High School had come to Stone Street, along with a small number of parents, members of the Eastern Star and Elk organizations, and a few white politicians, who sat up front in a roped-off section. The majorettes from the high school sat in another roped-off area along the side of the auditorium, short skirts flashing against shapely legs, giggling and tossing their long, straightened hair.

"Didn't I tell you, Cat—dey's all bright," Everlena whispered.

"You oughta take your hair down, Everlena," I whispered back. I wanted to see those bright girls stare when they saw the length and thickness of the coil she wore on top of her head like a thick, jet-black rope.

We arose as one, clapping loudly as the visiting white dignitaries, led by Mr. Coleman, were seated on the dais, with the black staff standing behind them. We clapped even louder when Queen Oliphant arrived on the arm of the captain of the football team himself, followed by the coach. Queen, though, looked like she was about to vomit. She stood awkwardly before her seat at the front of the auditorium, with a sickly smile on her face.

While we were still standing, the preacher from Friendship Baptist Church led us in the Lord's Prayer. Mr. Coleman then said the Pledge of Allegiance and the Wesley Chapel Children's Choir sang "Amazing Grace." Mr. Coleman introduced the superintendent, a fat, balding white man with a hawk nose and eyebrows like an eagle's. He looked out over the crowd, smiling painfullly. A hush fell over the room. He said he was happy to be here and told us the names of the dignitaries, then launched into a long-winded speech about cleanliness.

Suddenly he fell silent and stretched his hand toward Queen's chair. We clapped as the captain of the football team led her to the bottom step of the dais, where she stumbled and almost fell. But she recovered and, trembling slightly, accepted a book from Mr. Coleman. She opened it to "The Creation" and began to read.

Her voice was tiny, and the more she read, the weaker it got. Even the people in the first rows were straining to hear. Her delivery was flat, and full of hesitation. Then she paused, repeated a line, stumbled on a word, repeated the word, stumbled again. I wondered why Queen was trying to read the poem, when she knew it by heart. For Stone Street's best reader, she was not doing a very good job.

Suddenly she stopped and looked out into the assembly. Miss Sue Willie Oliphant slumped her shoulders and bowed her head; she could see that something had gone wrong. She clicked open her purse and began a frantic search for her best nylon handkerchief. Then she began to sob, her shoulders rocking to and fro, and murmuring broke out. Seeing her mama cry, Queen began to slobber and heave, holding back her own tears. In a choking voice she said, "I'm sorry," then threw the book on the floor and ran from the stage.

The entire auditorium gasped. Mr. Coleman's eyes bulged as he stared out at the assembled students and teachers, looking whiter than the superintendent. Then Mr. Boone, the music teacher, raised his baton, and the band launched into a rousing march.

Suddenly, a voice seemed to reach out to me over the trumpets and drums, saying, "G'won, Cat—you kin do it!" I don't know whose it was—Mama's, Everlena's, or my own—but it told me to get up and go to the stage. So I did.

"Ida Mae Holland, siddown!" my teacher shouted, but my feet had a will of their own. I moved past my classmates, who sat glued to their seats, looking stunned. Another teacher motioned me back, but I kept walking toward the dais, like a quarterback on his way to the end zone. I didn't rightly know what I was going to do when I got there, but I knew somebody had to do something.

I stood on the platform and looked out at the sea of faces. In the back rows, my classmates bent double with laughter. Mr. Coleman stared at me as if he wished the floor would open and swallow us both up. I picked up the book that Queen Oliphant had thrown down. My palms were sweaty as I righted it and casually turned the pages. At random I settled on one, cleared my throat, and announced, " 'Casey at the Bat,' by Ernest Lawrence Thayer." The auditorium went stone silent.

I held the book with one hand, the way our teacher had taught us was proper. " 'The outlook wasn't brilliant for the Mudville nine that day; / The score stood four to two with but one inning more to play.' " I paused for emphasis, the way Leroy Harper had taught me. " 'And then, when Cooney died at first' "—my hand went to my heart—" 'and Barrows did the same' "—my hand flashed down like an umpire's "you're out" sign—" 'A sickly silence fell upon the patrons of the game.' "

My heart was pounding like a hummingbird's. I was Shirley Temple, Tarzan, and Mama all wrapped in one. I felt the adrenaline course through my body, and my voice took on a commanding roar. It slapped the walls and bounced around the room like a basketball.

Halfway through the poem, I had the entire assembly hanging on my every word. By the time Casey came to bat, teachers and students alike were rooting aloud for him.

"Kill him; kill the umpire!" I bellowed, and the superintendent jumped as if he'd been shot.

The final pitch came on a crescendo, then I modulated into a strong, sad voice—" 'But there is no joy in Mudville—mighty Casey has Struck Out." I lowered my hands, hung my head, and let the weight of Mudville, Gee Pee, Greenwood, the Delta, the whole South sink onto my little shoulders. Then I closed the book and bowed to each person on the stage.

After an instant of silence, the applause erupted. I saw Everlena jump up and down, tears streaking her face. Mr. Coleman shook my hand and hugged me. Then the superintendent was back at the podium.

"I see that Stone Street Elementary School is doing a mighty fine job of teaching our colored boys and girls," he said, swabbing his face with a handkerchief. He stilled the pandemonium with raised palms. "A lot of troublemakers from the North come down here saying that our good colored children are not getting a good education. They want to send you boys and girls to the white schools, and start a lot of trouble. But I said to them: Our colored boys and girls know how to read! Well, now we can say to them, just look at"—he paused as Mr. Coleman whispered my name in his ear —"little Ida Mae Holland, if they want to know how well our colored children can read!" He sat down with a big smile on his face, and the football captain and other players helped me down the steps, ignoring the smirks on the majorettes' faces. I felt like a queen.

Afterward, everybody, even the good girls, talked to Everlena and me. In the girls' restroom, we smoked a cigarette in my honor with the seniors from Broad Street. By the time school was out, word of my triumph had spread all over town. People stopped me on the streets and shook my hand. When I got home, Mama was actually dancing, so jubilant that she forgot to low-rate me for my cigarette smell.

The news of my reading for the school board spread across Greenwood like a fire burned out of control. It was the kind of story that sometimes raced through Leflore County and the entire Delta, assuming a life of its own—the kind of story that the Delta's black people love to embroider and retell. By the time it reached the coast, it would have grown to mythical proportions—I would be depicted as a mere child with the thunderous voice of the angel Gabriel himself. The storytellers would say I'd been given to Mama for just such a time as this one—in order to save the day and make black people throughout the state proud. Even Jean got caught up in the glory—in my honor, she managed to drink free for an entire month.

The memory of that morning sustained me through a lot of Mama's lectures over the next few years. "Ida Mae, chile, you is makin' tracks but you ain't gittin' nowheres," she'd say, or, "It look t' me dat you can't make tracks in self-risin' flour." It sustained me, too, through a lot of speeches from Mr. Coleman over the next few years, lamenting how such a promising young girl like me could turn out to be such a disappointment, such a hoodlum. After a while, I thought Everlena and I were the only ones who remembered how I'd once showed up Queen Oliphant and saved the school, all at the same time—how the same principal who was chewing me out and calling me a loser had once hugged me on a stage in front of everyone and whispered, "Thank you, Ida Mae— we needed you!"

Did they forget about the speech? Did they forget how the band played just for me? How our preacher talked all about me in his sermon the following Sunday and didn't even mention Queen Oliphant once? How people went out of their way to pass through Gee Pee, just to be able to see Mama and say, "Aint Baby, you sho' 'nough must be proud of Cat!" and how she said, "Das de gospel truth!"

Didn't Mama remember that?

NOT LONG after my recitation, we moved to 119 East Gibb, a double-shotgun house that sat catty-corner from 114. It was just across the street, but it was a big step up for us. It had an extra room for sleeping or renting out, electric lights instead of coal oil lamps—even if they were just bare bulbs hanging from the center of the tar-paper ceiling—and gas for heat and cooking, instead of the wood stove that kept Mama cursing. We had an indoor toilet, too, that we shared with a neighbor.

As soon as we moved in, Mama went to Wall's furniture store and bought, on credit, a four-burner gas stove. She was so proud of that stove, she'd sit for hours looking at its shiny porcelain front. It didn't improve her cooking, but it sure improved her temperament. We had a bigger icebox now, too, one that swallowed up our five-pound block of ice and barely kept the RC's cold.

But for me the pièce de résistance was the battery-powered clock one of Mama's white ladies gave her. I led a steady line of children into the kitchen to point it out where it hung over the stove. I didn't mind that its hands moved spasmodically and were always at least an hour fast. It was a beautiful clock.

But even the nice house had its shortcomings. More space meant more roaches and rats, and Mama's swatter was busier than ever.

Bud was more enterprising. "I betcha a cat-eye dat us got a heapa roaches—and our rats be as big as Miss Millie's cat," he'd say to the other teenage boys.

"Aw, shucks, dat ain't nuttin'," said Cross-Eye Jack, his best friend, lining up his shot with a translucent marble. "Us'n got rats dat's bigger den old Frisgo!" He shot and reached into the dusty circle to pick up the marbles.

"I wouldn't do dat, Chief—'cause 'f'n you touch dem marbles, you gonna draw back a nub!" Simon Jr. warned quietly from the porch where Mama had him tied to the railing. Simon was a deadlier fighter than Bud, but you wouldn't know it to look at him, lashed there in the dress Mama made him wear to keep him from running away.

Since my recitation and our move across Gibb Street, we had more kids to play with. Now everybody, except the real light-skinned kids, wanted to be our friends.

Mama's white folks got wind of our recent good fortune, too, from Miss Hall, a young white woman who owned several double shotgun houses in Gee Pee and Baptist Town. One day, Mama was at the home of Miss Victoria, the white lady for whom she did the most ironing, where many of Greenwood's finest white women were gathered for their monthly sewing circle. Miss Victoria called her out of the kitchen to the dinning room.

"Dem white 'omans be smellin' like a big bunch o' magnolias," Mama beamed. "My nose be itchin' 'cause o' dat 'spensive toilet water dey use." She started play-liking. "Dat 'oman, old lady Victoria, she took my arm and 'scorted me 'round 'mongst dem white 'omans. All de time, she be tellin' dem dat it be *my chile* who proved dat de colored chilluns is learnin' jest like de white chilluns.

"Old lady Victoria even gi'e me a seat t' set in." Mama showed me how her "First Sit-Down" in the presence of white women had progressed. " 'Fore I sot down, she put newspaper in de chair. I folded my hands in my lap while de sweat runned down my bosom from de ironin'. I tucked my footses underneath de chair an' I sot dere an' looked at dem jest like I done been settin' down wit' white ladies all de time." Mama raised her eyebrows and cast a scornful, defiant look all about her.

"Den Miss Clorine sashayed over to me. Lawdy, she smelt like my petunia bed!" Mama rose to her feet, play-liking Miss Clorine, the white lady whose family owned most of the Delta's gas stations. " 'Aint Baby,' she say, 'here, I done brung you some books to gi'e your girl, den she kin see 'f'n she wants to be a teacher.' " Mama stretched her hand forward to receive the imaginary books and said grandly, " 'My, my, I sho' does thank you and de Lawd, Miss Clory —Ida Mae is gwine a be some kinda glad to git dese books!' "

"Den Miss Lawrence, she come over to me and gi'e me a dollar for you. 'Aint Baby, I have a job for yo' girl—I wants her to babysit my grandchile, Miss Rebecca.' " Mama did a great job of play-liking Miss Lawrence, a stuck-up white woman who put on airs. " 'I sho' does thank you, too, Miss Lawrence—and de Lawd—for smilin' down on my little gal.' Den I got up, toted de books and de dollar in plain sight, so dat dey seed dat it was gi'e to me, dat I didn't steal dem—you know how white 'omens is. I th'o'ed my head back and marched to the kitchen jest like I set down wit' white ladies ever day. It must be a real good sign."

I thought it was a good sign, too, as I pocketed the dollar Miss Lawrence had sent me and paged through the cardboard box full of Perry Mason novels from Miss Clorine. I felt like the luckiest little girl in the world.

Five

According to Mama, Miss Lawrence and her husband had once been the "cat's meow" in the Delta. Now they were middle-aged, Mr. Lawrence was an invalid, and they had lost most of their money and status. But they still lived in a big, beautiful, plantation-style house in North Greenwood.

The Lawrences had a daughter, who had been a beauty—a catch you might say, leastways that's what her mama, Miss Lawrence, thought. Hadn't she carefully groomed her daughter—who had been a lead majorette of the Greenwood High School marching band, a cheerleader, a Cotton Queen, and a Cotillion queen—to marry, to fetch or catch or be caught by some big fish? But instead of being caught by a doctor or a lawyer as her mama had hoped, the Lawrences' daughter had been caught from below, pulled down to the bottom of the lake, "trapped," as the ladies in her mother's sewing circle used to say, "by a worthless gambler" with whom she had a daughter, Miss Becky Ann, who now lived with her grandparents.

I'd been to the Lawrence house a number of times, when Miss Victoria loaned Mama out to help Miss Lawrence with her sewing circle. At first I had to sit out on the back porch so I wouldn't be any trouble. Later, I was allowed into the kitchen, to be an object of distraction for little Miss Becky Ann. It was on those occasions that I learned the ways of white folks. I never so much as glimpsed a sewing needle, but I did see the quick shuffle of cards and heard the gossip passed back and forth in loudly hushed tones, followed by peals of most unladylike laughter. As the afternoon went on, the words slurred, thanks to the nervous gulps of whiskey drunk from the tall silver glasses that Mama kept brimming with ice—glasses sweating with moisture, quite unlike the ladies themselves.

My job was to keep Miss Becky Ann out of Mama's and Miss Lawrence's way. She was five years old and spoiled, even for a white girl. I'd play ball with her, and when she got tired of playing ball, we'd play dolls. I'd sit and wait while she brought her dolls down to me, one at a time. She had one special doll she always held just out of my reach. It was so lifelike, with the whitest skin and long, long blond hair. But what fascinated me most was that when you tilted her head back, her hard blue eyes would flash open and catch you in her gaze, then shut tight, as if she'd captured the image of your soul behind her eyelids. It was that trick with her eyes—the seductive batting, the flirtatious, knowing look—that always made me catch my breath.

But this Saturday I was going to the Lawrences' by myself, to babysit Miss Becky Ann. It was my eleventh birthday, and Miss Lawrence had promised me two dollars as a birthday bonus. I was looking forward to playing with Miss Becky Ann's dolls again. Maybe this time she'd let me play with the special doll with the amazing eyes.

When Miss Lawrence's big red car pulled up outside our house and honked its horn, I could see Miss Becky in the backseat. "Ida Mae! Ida Mae!" she shouted at me through the window.

"Ida Mae! Ida Mae! Hurry up, gal, Miz Lawrence dem is here!" Mama dismissed me with a nod.

"How y'all feel, Miz Lawrence, Miz Becky Ann?" I said, wrestling with Becky Ann for control of the door handle.

"Well, howdy do, Ida Mae," Miss Lawrence said. "Say howdy do to Ida Mae, Rebecca Ann. Now you behave yourself and move over so Ida Mae can get in. And remember to say happy birthday to her, like the sweet little thing you are!" Becky Ann finally gave up the fight and slid over. I got in and slammed the door just as Miss Lawrence found first gear and peeled away in a big U-turn back toward Fulton Street and the Keesler Bridge.

I knew how you were supposed to ride in white folks' cars. I'd seen black cooks and maids getting picked up and carried to and from white folks' houses. Meek as lambs, they climbed into the backseat and sat straight and tall like arrows. I was no arrow. I bent forward in a curve as I leaned out the car window, waving to all my friends as we passed. I wanted them to see me being "chauf-feured" in a white woman's car. Everybody got a wave and a smile so they wouldn't think I was full of myself—what with my saving Stone Street School and all, and now my own white woman and a babysitting job.

Miss Lawrence brought the car to a jerky stop in front of her house.

"Now Rebecca Ann, you be nice to Ida Mae," she warned as we got out of the car. "She came to play with you. You hear me, Rebecca Ann?"

Miss Becky dragged me out on the front lawn to play kick ball —which meant kicking me as much as the ball. I would pretend that I was going to throw it back as hard as I could, but somehow the ball always tumbled from my hand in the softest and slowest of motions, only to be caught and returned again to my bruised stomach and face. Playing with Miss Becky Ann was hard work.

Before long, Miss Lawrence appeared at the front door. "Ida Mae! Ida Mae, come over here."

"Yas'm, Miz Lawrence, here I come." I had knots all over my shins and was grateful to be saved.

"Ida Mae," she said pleasantly, "come upstairs. Mr. Lawrence wants to see you and wish you a happy birthday."

This, I thought, was truly a red-letter day for me. Smoking

cigarettes in the bathroom at school, I'd heard other girls talk about being "called upstairs" in a white employer's house. Since upstairs was where the family lived, I assumed being called there was a high honor. The girls always bragged about whose white family had the finer things and fantasized about what it would be like to live in such houses ourselves.

I'd been especially taken with the stories I'd heard from Percy Mae Palmer. Percy Mae was our chief orator, entertainer, and object of admiration. She had a big booty that stuck out a long ways and sat on great big legs, and short hair that she greased every night so that it would curl around her plain round face. She also had the whitest, prettiest, straightest teeth we'd seen, and she never shut her mouth so as to show them off full-time.

While her mouth was open, Percy Mae told stories about her times upstairs in white folks' houses—stories so magical that to us they were like fairy tales. She told of rooms in white folks' houses where bearskin rugs covered the floors—rugs with whole bears' heads, their mouths wide open, waiting to catch you between their teeth.

Now I was going upstairs and I could see for myself whether what Percy Mae had said was true or not. I stepped slowly, careful not to put my wide feet down flat because I didn't want to mark up the prettiest floor I'd ever seen. And I didn't want to miss a thing. I was looking for that bear; I knew if anyone could get a bear to lie still upon the floor, the Lawrences could, because they were at the top of white society in Greenwood.

At the top of the stairs, Miss Lawrence took my hand and led me into the master bedroom. After the slick, shiny hardwood stairs, the deep pile carpet in the bedroom made me stumble. When I recovered my balance, my eyes went immediately to the big four-poster where Mr. Lawrence lay, with the covers pulled up to his chest.

Mama had done the washing for Mr. Lawrence's mama when she was alive, and she'd been at the white ladies' sewing circle the day Mr. Lawrence collapsed at work.

"Chile, I was dere when de law come," she said, play-liking on the front porch on a Saturday night. "Mr. Big Smitty, de high sheriff, he come in and whisper in my ear. 'Get some wet towels for Miz Lawrence, Aintie—'cause I got some bad news for her!' " Mama could roar just like Mr. Big Smitty.

She showed us how she ran to the bathroom to get the towels and made it back just as Sheriff Smitty announced to the sewing circle that Mr. Lawrence had had a heart attack. Miss Lawrence had fainted, and it took Mama a long time to tell the story because she had to fall to the floor, too, then pull herself back up, using the outstretched arms of our neighbors. It took Mama a long time to tell any story involving Miss Lawrence, for that matter, because she liked to imitate Miss Lawrence's airs. She held her head high and turned up her nose like she smelled doo-doo. She jutted out her behind like Miss Lawrence's did, and walked on her tiptoes, swishing her hips.

I'd seen Mr. Lawrence a few times before he took sick, peeping at him through the thin crack of the kitchen door when he came home from work. One time he almost came into the kitchen, but Miss Becky Ann ran to meet him and he bent down to hug and kiss her. He didn't notice me, perhaps because I stood way back, making myself invisible. At ten I had already learned the secret of invisibility all black folks knew.

The sheets and covers on Mr. Lawrence's bed were purest white, soft and silky as new-fallen snow.

"Yassuh, Mr. Lawrence," I said, grinning. "Here I is." I expected two dollars to appear from beneath the bedspread in his gnarly old hand.

Instead, Miss Lawrence pushed me forward and tore back the

sheets. Underneath, they were piss-stained—filthy as my outney mattress, and stinking worse than me before my bath. Mr. Lawrence pulled up his nightclothes to reveal his old shriveled *thing* — a slimy white penis asleep on his pasty leg.

I had glimpsed Bud's and Simon Jr.'s penises before—we called 'em thangs and dingalings—when we got up from our beds in the morning. I didn't know much about them, except that I always thought they were like fuzzy worms. But I had never seen a white man's dingaling before. It wasn't a soft, fuzzy worm, it was a slug —a white slug, wet and leaving tracks. I knew that if you poured a little salt on a slug, it would melt and die. I looked at Mr. Lawrence's penis. I could kill it if I had some salt, I thought. But I didn't have any salt.

Next thing I knew I was lifted into the air, Miss Lawrence's strong hands under my arms, and then I was on top of Mr. Lawrence. His hands pulled down my shorts and snapped down my panties and something began rubbing where I went to the toilet. I remembered how Mama told me how *nobody* was supposed to touch me down there, so I looked back all panicky for Miss Lawrence to help me, but she wasn't there.

I looked back at Mr. Lawrence and he had a funny look on his old face. His dingaling was hurting me bad now. How could that be? Before it had been all shriveled—just an old white slug.

"MAMA, HE HURT ME! MAMA, HE HURTIN' ME SO BAD! MAMA, HE BURNIN' ME UP!"

I beat my hands against the wall, grabbing and pushing at the same time, looking for something to hold on to. The walls were covered with cloth, soft and smooth except where embroidered flowers rose up. I tried to catch at the petals, but I couldn't get a good-enough hold of them.

Once I'd spied on Simon Jr. and his girl through a keyhole. Simon Jr. was on top of her, talking to her in whispers that seemed to brush across his skin. Whatever he said and whatever he was doing to her must've made her glad, because she kept saying things back—things that didn't make no sense but sounded like some kind of happiness. I remember her throwing her head back, over and over again, and I could see her eyes flashing like Miss Becky Ann's doll.

How come she liked it, I wondered now, this thing they were doing—how come it felt so good to her and made her so happy, when it felt so bad to me? Maybe it was because she was doing it with a colored boy, I thought.

I remembered Simon Jr. saying, "Do you like it?"

"Yes, I like it," she'd said to him, and he'd kissed her.

Suddenly I heard Mr. Lawrence speaking to me for the first time that afternoon. "Do you like it?"

My voice emerged from somewhere. "Nawsir," I said. "It hurts!" I hoped he didn't try to kiss me.

Now he was on top of me. I wondered when it would end—it seemed like a lifetime to me. I began to think I was dying. I'd heard old folks say when you die your life passes before your eyes. I thought my eleven years were passing before my eyes. Then I realized that what was passing before my eyes was another pair of eyes, the saddest eyes I'd ever seen. I realized I must be looking into the eyes of Mama Lena, because Mama Lena had the saddest eyes I had ever seen.

Mama Lena was a woman whose children had abandoned her to go up North, to Chicago, I think. Mama Lena had no home of her own anymore, so she lived by going from house to house in our community begging food and shelter. Women in the community would pass their old clothes on to her. Their too-big dresses hung on her bony old body and billowed in the wind, and she stank so bad I turned up my nose to her more than once. But when Mama

Lena knocked on your door, and you opened it and looked into those sad eyes—well, you just couldn't turn away.

One day she came to our house and Mama took her turn by taking her in for the day and night. Mama Lena couldn't feed herself, so Mama told me I had to feed her. I didn't want to feed her and got mad, but Mama said, "G'won and feed her." Mama Lena was holding a fork in her hand, and as soon as Mama turned her back, I snatched that fork out of Mama Lena's hand and started shoving food in her mouth as fast and as hard as I could. I thought she'd say something, call out to my Mama and tell on me, but she didn't, so I just kept shoving it in. When I stopped, Mama Lena didn't say anything—not to me, not to Mama. I looked at her and she looked at me, and her eyes seemed even sadder.

It was those eyes I was seeing now. They seemed to be speaking to me, saying something no words could say. I felt something deep inside of me, in a place even Mr. Lawrence could not reach. It wasn't pain, it was regret. I felt regret for what I'd done to Mama Lena.

Folks used to tell how, in the South, no white man wanted to die without having sex with a black woman. It was just seen as a part of life, and if you were white, there was so much on this earth in between the birthing and the dying. Only God had power over your life. But if you were black, you were always at the mercy of white people, and all you had in life was the hope of heaven. If you were white, dream and desire were possibilities, not madness or fantasy like they were for black people. And what was the white man's great dream, his burning desire? To have sex with a colored woman.

Mr. Lawrence had finished at last. He rolled off me and slid me down his furry old dog leg until I found myself standing back on the floor.

I felt a wetness between my legs, as if I'd peed on myself, or as if someone had poured clabbered milk on me. I looked at Mr. Lawrence and he still had that funny expression on his face. He said something to me again—something I don't remember or didn't hear, "Happy birthday," maybe—and handed me a five-dollar bill. Then he lay back on his pillows. I crinkled the green bill tight in my hand and ran out of the room.

Miss Lawrence was waiting for me in the long upstairs hallway. She didn't say anything, just looked at me without expression, as if she'd gone somewhere else. I looked back at her from behind my eyes, careful to give nothing away. But I knew that she knew that the bull had thrown me.

Going downstairs, I memorized every detail of the long carpet runner, the dark mahogany banister, and the newel cap carved like a bouquet of tiny roses—leaves and petals all the same blood-red color. The big house, once alive with busy servants and magical furnishings, seemed now like an ornate tomb—all big, empty, and dead. But like a reminder of bygone days, everywhere in the house were colored folks holding up things—some of them so big they looked real.

I became aware of the five-dollar bill I was clutching and stuffed it deep into a pocket of my shorts. But try as I might, I couldn't get excited anymore about treating Everlena to the Walthall picture show, or even the picture show itself. Becky Ann was all over me to play dolls. The prospect seemed absurd now. *I'm a 'oman now,* I thought, and it did not feel the way I wanted. After all was said and done I felt they had exaggerated, Percy Mae and the other girls in the bathroom at school; it wasn't all that beautiful upstairs, leastways not to my way of looking at things.

I stood in the backyard, near the car, supervising Miss Becky Ann but not really playing with her, waiting to go home. A hot poker sat between my legs and belly, but I was determined not to cry. I only wanted to see Mama. I didn't care about my birthday. I didn't even want to have another birthday. If this was what it was like to turn eleven, I didn't want to live to be twelve.

After an hour or two, Miss Lawrence came out and told Becky Ann it was time to take me home. I decided then and there not to tell Mama what had happened. What was the point? So we could both feel bad? So Bud and Simon Jr. could get themselves in trouble coming up here one night to vandalize the house and get even? My somber mood must have been infectious, because neither Miss Lawrence nor Becky Ann said much on the drive back to Gee Pee.

A few days after I'd met the bull at Mr. Lawrence's, I was in Miss Robertson's class at school, thinking and stinking. I hadn't bathed well that morning. I was late and it still hurt to put Mama's lye soap between my legs. No one had been around to check me before I left. Bud and Jean had gone off before dawn in Mr. Walter Foreman's truck to pick cotton. Simon Jr. was now living with his stepmother in Chicago. And Mama had gone to the Health Department to take her midwife's class.

As the morning heat increased, so did my odor. Finally, Miss Robertson stopped talking and opened all the windows. I noticed Junior Boy James across the aisle, trying to act like he didn't smell my funk, sitting up straight and breathing through his nose. Queen Oliphant started sniggling and sniffing the air like a hound. Other girls behind me threw spitballs at my back. Soon I had enough moist paper wads at my feet to build a snowman. I tried to bluff it out—to make it look like I, too, didn't know where the smell was coming from. Inside, I vowed to wash every inch of me with that awful soap, no matter how bad it burned.

Miss Robertson's lesson on the Louisiana Purchase now turned into a sermon on the virtues of regular bathing, laundered clothes, and clean fingernails. "You're growing up into fine men and women," she said, walking up one aisle and down another, eyeing each one of us suspiciously. "As far as you young ladies are concerned, you must pay special attention to your hygiene as you get older."

She stopped beside my chair but didn't look down.

"Now," she concluded, "I'm going to stand in the doorway. I want the person who didn't take a good bath this morning to get up and march off to the bathroom and clean yourself up."

Naturally, nobody budged. We might have been uneducated, but we weren't stupid. Time seemed to stand still. The room got hotter and I could feel sweat running down my neck. Every time I shifted in my seat the odor got worse. Eventually, God took pity on me, even if Miss Robertson didn't. I was saved by the recess bell.

After a split second, the students jumped to their feet, slammed shut their books and hinge-topped desks, and scuttled from the room under the nose of Miss Robertson, who was standing by the door. I fussed with my books and pencils until everyone had gone, then tried to slink out, knees pressed together.

"We didn't take enough time to wash ourselves this morning, did we, Ida Mae?" She stopped me with a hand to the shoulder. Without making eye contact—in fact, while gazing at the ceiling —she added, "Your sickness is all over the back of your dress."

I yanked my dress around quickly, to see if I'd sat in vomit. A big red splotch stared back at me like a gunshot wound and I realized suddenly that the sticky goo between my legs wasn't just pee and sweat, but my own bright blood. I dropped my books and ran hollering from the school, back toward East Gibb Street and Mama.

Solemnly, Mama explained the " 'oman's curse" while she tore a clean white rag into strips. "Dis sickness you got, it come every month 'til you is a old 'oman. You gotsta stick dese here rags in yo' panties to sop it up. Now, when you *not* bleedin', you gotsta stay away from boys. 'F'n you fool wit' boys now, you kin git bigged. Dats what a granny midwife does—helps de 'omans who git bigged."

That evening, instead of whining and complaining about staying up a little longer to read my Perry Mason, I went to bed as soon as the sun went down. I still didn't know how bleeding from my bottom and getting bigged were connected, so I gave the whole matter to God with my bedtime prayer. For weeks afterward, well after I'd stopped bleeding, I examined my stomach to see if it was getting larger. I wasn't sure what "being with boys" meant exactly, but I suspected it had something to do with what Mr. Lawrence had done to me. That really didn't count, though, I was pretty sure. He was a white man, after all.

Stone Street School never seemed the same after my shameful "stinking day." The boys continued to make fun of me, as they always had, but now it was because of my embarrassing bloody dress as well as my family. The worst came at recess, when the teacher took her break. Some of the boys pinned red paper streamers on their pants and ran around bowlegged, drawing hoots and cheers. Everyone seemed to forget the time I saved their honor and their school. Now, like mighty Casey when he struck out, I was just a joke.

My refuge during all of this was the girls' restroom, where three or four of us womanish girls continued to meet, smoke our furtive cigarettes, and complain about the world. Percy Mae continued to impress us with her experiences "going upstairs" in her white employer's house, but I heard them differently now.

"We was done wit' de kitchen so den I went upstairs," she said one day, preening in the mirror. She was deciding whether to leave the top button of her blouse open.

"Wow, what was it like?" one girl asked. "Did you see de white folkses' bedroom?"

"Naw," Percy Mae replied, "I didn't. Didn't want to, neither." Something about the way she said it set off a bell in my head.

"*Sheeeet*—" the other girl said, "I ain't *never* gonna see no pretty thangs like that. My daddy say I cain't never work in no white man's house. You's so lucky!"

When I went to the girls' room next I told my own story about going upstairs, skipping around the part about the rape. I was disappointed that I had no bear to talk about, but I found myself stretching the details I did remember to the ends of the earth. Percy Mae was jealous. Our eyes met in the mirror and we both knew; I knew she had been upstairs, and she knew I had been upstairs. It brought us together and it kept us apart.

Do you think it's possible to feel pride and self-pity all at once? That's how I felt, becoming a woman on the horns of the bull. Half of me was proud that I could at least boast about "my white folks" who liked me so much they gave me a five-dollar bill, even if I had to leave out the rest of the story. My other half was raging jealous of the girls who had daddies who knew the score about white men and kept their daughters safe by refusing to let them work in white households. I figured later that about half the girls my age in Greenwood—maybe the whole Delta—lived without fathers. Out of those, maybe three-quarters had been thrown by the bull like me. And we didn't have to be sitting babies or cleaning houses to fall victim to the white man's lust. We could just as easily be picking cotton or walking to the store or spending money in the white man's store when the mood would take him and he'd take us —just like that, like lightning striking. No longer any one man's property, now we belonged to everyone.

Part of the code of having known a man was that you never talked about it openly—even with your best friend. Even girls who lost their virginity "naturally"—to a black boy their age, even to a football star—never came right out and admitted they'd had sex. You could only let the fact be known to a select audience, to fellow travelers who'd gone your way, through sly innuendo, knowing glances, and telling silence—the way outcasts in any society identify each other.

That's why Everlena and I, close as we were, saw less and less of each other, and Percy Mae and I became closer and closer. We walked to school together, smoked together, played hooky together. Sometimes we just sat together in bored, long-suffering silence, watching the "children" who still acted their age. Our friendship even survived graduation to Broad Street High School, where we spent our first year trying desperately not to look like freshmen. Then Percy Mae's family moved to Greenville. Although it was less than sixty miles away, it might as well have been on the moon.

S i x

MAMA AND I HAD DIFFERENT IDEAS ABOUT
WHAT IT MEANT TO BECOME A WOMAN. "IDA MAE,
chile," she'd say, "you's crowin' even though you still be lost in de
woods! You gots to make somethin' o' yo'self, gal! Now, I know
you ain't de pretties' girl in town. Your hair ain't long an' you got
big lips. You's stout and yo' legs is real little. But dere ain't nobody
'round here kin turn a stick or read or make dem marks better den
you!"

"Yas'm, Mama," I'd reply. She usually made these speeches when
I was in the bathroom fixing my hair or trying to read one of my
books instead of doing my homework. Mama's white ladies were
still sending me their old Perry Mason novels—they never sent any
other kind—but I was glad to have them because we couldn't
afford to buy books from Chaney's drugstore, and black people
weren't allowed inside the county library.

I'd close my book or turn away from the mirror reluctantly, but
the truth was, it always pleased me to hear Mama praise my good
points. Sometimes she got me to join her on her knees.

"Sweet Jesus, Lawd," she'd bray in the direction of heaven,
"bless my chile so dat she kin keep her footses turned t'ward de top
o' de ladder—so dat she kin walk 'mongst de best o' folkses, wit'
her head up real high, on her journey through dis here hard life."

It was Mama who'd introduced me to Jesus in the first place. As
a child, I thought he lived somewhere up in our tar-paper ceiling,
because Mama always looked up when she talked to him. Then at
church Mama pointed out the stained-glass window where Jesus

was pictured with the lambs, and a statue of him with his hand just below his heart. The heart glowed red to indicate blood, or maybe flames. And then one day the heart was gone—or rather, it was still there, but it wasn't glowing. In came Miss Lizzie Bell, who went right up to Jesus, reached inside of him and pulled out a lightbulb that was painted red—and I saw that was all his heart was, just a lightbulb that had burned out.

Jesus himself was always white, no two ways about it, a white man with long blond hair and blue eyes. But Jesus reminded me of angels, and I thought angels were probably black. I had an angel, my own personal angel, and she was stout. On nights I didn't pee in the bed, I was convinced it was because she had shaken me awake just before I had to go. I had no doubt about it.

But I was older now, and I had more doubts. I never sassed Mama or told her what I really thought: that her dressed-up prayers to Jesus on my behalf seemed more threadbare than any of the cheap polyester jumpsuits or double-knit dresses and skirts her white ladies sent me after they had about worn them out. We'd say "Amen" together, then I'd get up and go back to my book or my primping. But I was annoyed at her mention of "the best o' folkses," which to her meant white folks. More and more I viewed them as the source of all my troubles. It was getting harder and harder for me to see why I should court their favor. All I cared about at the moment was making my short hair prettier, my big lips glossier, my stout body shapelier—and getting my skinny legs to move better when I practiced "walkin' my walk"—my womanish, wide-legged stride, slinky and seductive, in front of the Broad Street boys. Didn't Mama know there was more than one way to make a name for yourself?

My nemesis in this battle for independence was Dossie Ree Johnson. When we moved across Gibb Street, Dossie Ree had moved out of our house and into her own shotgun house right next door. She had a way of knowing when I was late to school or hadn't shown up at all, where I'd been and who I was with, and what brand of liquor we'd been drinking. Her motto was "a heap sees, but a few knows" and she was always one of that all-seeing, all-knowing few.

"I hears dey be dancin' to dose Elvis Presley records," I over-heard Dossie Ree tell Mama one hot night when they'd left the screen door open. "Down yon'er at Sam Ciroe's joint in Gritney. Drinkin' whiskey and playing records—"

"Well, dat pishy, pee-de-bed, 'omanish lil' gal!" Mama said. "Can't nosomebody in dis town say I didn't do right by Ida Mae. Didn't I send her to de schoolhouse?"

"You sho' 'nough did, Aint Baby—I be a livin' witness!"

"Didn't I nurse dat chile when she be run over by dat white 'oman's car?"

"Yes'm, you sho' did—"

"An' don't I pray to de Lawd ever' day to save dat chile from de street?"

"You do, Aint Baby. I hears you my owndearself!"

"I jest wants Ida Mae to be Somebody, like I is."

"Den you oughta know what dey be sayin' 'bout Cat down at de church house." Dossie Ree's voice dropped to a whisper. She sang in the choir, and so caught up on both the young and old folks' gossip during weekday practice. "Dey say dat Cat is walkin' de streets—sellin' herownself to de mens! Ol' lady Lizzie be over yon'er gittin' money for de church, an' she seed Cat goin' in de roomin' house wit dat old ugly scound, Scarecrow!"

"Lawd amercy Jesus!" Mama wailed. "I try to make all my chilluns be Somebody, an' what does I git? I gits mannish boys who quit school to shoot marbles all day wit' Cross-Eye Jack. I gits 'omanish Jean, who dranks mo' whiskey den Son Boy Brown! Ain't no wonder I puts all my hopes on de baby, li'l Ida Mae. Dat's how come I keep her from de fields, even though I send Bud and Simon Junior and Jean. Dat's how come I make her stay in de schoolhouse. Dat's how come I works my fangers to de nub an' try an' set a good 'xample for her—gittin' my midwife 'tificate. How come dat pishy gal don't 'preciate nothin'?"

"Now, don'cha cry, Aint Baby," Dossie Ree said. "You jest gwine make yo'sef sick. I shouldna told you. But dat's what de folkses be sayin' 'hind yo' back."

It was bad enough that Dossie Ree had upset Mama, but she had her gossip a little confused. To the older generation, "streetwalking" meant prostitution. But to us younger women, streetwalking was another thing entirely. It was about strolling, trolling, and strutting your stuff, showing off from table to table, counter to jukebox, joint to joint. Your stride was your signature. Street-walkin' girls might have sex, or they might not, and everyone knew it was their choice. A man's job was to entice them—with drinks, flattery, slick manners, and tall talk—to make that choice their way. Merely trading sex for money—that was what whores and hookers did. But Dossie Ree couldn't tell the difference, and Mama didn't want to know.

My one ally at home was Bud. He hated school more than I did, but he was a lot better at avoiding Mama's wrath by finding work. When he couldn't get hours at the chicken slaughterhouse, he collected garbage or did other casual labor for the city, in the course of which he met an older man we called Old Zeke. Bud introduced me to him one day when they stopped by after work.

"Oh, so *you* be de Cat—Bud's lil' sis!" he said. He was a good-looking man in a kind of beat-up way, and very soft-spoken.

A week later I saw Old Zeke again at Sam Ciroe's, where I was hanging out with some of the older kids from school. With my woman-sized body, it was fairly simple to talk my way into the juke joints, even though the owners knew I was underage.

I said hi to Zeke and he said "How do," and he watched us kids dance. After a while, he came over to my booth, sat down, and handed me a paper bag.

"Here y'go, Cat gal—dis here gone wet yo' whistle."

It was an unopened half pint of Old Crow. This made me real popular, so I doled out drinks to my friends in little paper cups, two fingers at a time. Boys who had never before paid me any attention started asking me to dance, including Wilbur Tee, whose usual partner, a girl named Johnnie Mae Wade, was to bop what I was to streetwalkin'—simply the best there was. We danced to Elvis's "Blue Suede Shoes" and I tried to imitate all of Johnnie Mae's moves, but that Old Crow was beating its wings and I went back to my booth with a spinning head.

When the first half pint was gone, Old Zeke produced another, and we again drew a crowd. The jukebox kept blasting and more people drifted in and out and somehow it got dark. I was bopping in my seat, laughing at how I could feel so light-headed while my butt felt made of lead, when I noticed Old Zeke's hand was on my thigh. I put it back on his and went on like nothing happened.

Old Zeke chuckled and took a deep drag from his cigarette.

"Say now, Cat girl." He strained to be heard above the music. "I gots three dollars in my pocket. What says we gits up an' go." The hand was back on my thigh.

"What you mean, dere, Mr. Zeke?" I played dumb and moved the hand back. "Go where?"

" 'Round de corner to Black Mary's."

My vision was blurry but I could see real clear where this was going. Everyone in Gritney knew that Black Mary was a moonshiner and a madam.

"Three dollars!" I joked. "Sheeet—dat ain't enough for dis ol' gal!"

"All I gots is seven, Cat baby. An' I gots to give three o' dat to Black Mary."

"She don't charge no three dollars for no room!" I said. After all, my mama had been in the business before we'd moved across East Gibb Street, and I knew that the average room went for fifty cents a night. The most Mama'd ever charged was seventy-five, to those who could afford to pay more—like the preachers and teachers—and riffraff she wanted to discourage.

"She do 'f'n it be de bride's room!"

I hadn't been negotiating so much as stalling, but Old Zeke had me there. Black Mary's "bridal suite" was as well known as her home brew. It cost more, but the folks who paid extra said the punch was worth it. My curiosity was piqued, but I couldn't sound too anxious.

"Five dollars," I said.

"Say what?"

"What does I care 'bout de bride's room?" I said, trying to sound blasé. After all, I'd already seen upstairs at the Lawrences' house. " 'F'n you wants me to go wit' you, it gonna cost you five dollars."

"How 'bout I gi'e you fo' dollars now and one dollar come Satiddy?" Old Zeke put my hand on his thigh and began to move it around.

"Gi'e me four dollars now, and when Satiddy come, I'll go wit' you." I couldn't believe I said that.

Old Zeke stuck his cigarette in his teeth and fished for change in his coveralls. He counted out what he had, but it wasn't enough.

"Say, Bro,' " he shouted across the room to a natty man at the counter. "You takes my marker till Satiddy?"

"How much?" the man asked.

"Sawbuck."

"All right."

Zeke scooted out from the booth and close-talked to the man, a well-dressed gambler I'd seen in there from time to time. Then he put his *X* on a piece of paper, the man unrolled a wad of bills, and Old Zeke returned with his money, which he put in his pants, not in my hand.

"Let's go."

WE WALKED around the corner to Black Mary's double-sized shotgun house and Zeke knocked on the door. Just as her home wasn't really a whorehouse (she rented to travelers and migrants, mostly), Black Mary wasn't really that black: more honey amber and West Indian–looking than African. She recognized me at once.

"You's Aint Baby's chile, ain't you? De one dey call Li'l Cat." Out of respect for my mama, she wouldn't let me in until Old Zeke's three dollars overcame her scruples.

Old Zeke led me into the bridal suite like a proper groom. In place of the usual canvas cot or wooden palette was a huge double bed with box spring and mattress topped with a frilly white quilt and satin pillows. Overhead, a painted bulb cast a seductive light around the room. The walls were covered with velvet paper and a couple of framed pictures. Half of me was enthralled. The other half, the bottom half, wanted to run like hell.

Before I could do or say anything, Old Zeke had his overalls off and laid across a chair. Through the opening in his BVDs I could see his tarry flesh and the big earthworm nestling in his crotch.

"Ain't you gonna git outta dem closes?" he asked.

I had run out of ways to stall. "Uhhh, I's gone let you do dat, honey," I said, smiling limply.

I half expected Old Zeke to pass out as he fumbled with my zippers and straps and snaps, but he didn't. He unwrapped me like a present on Christmas morning and went right to work. I was on the bottom this time and just hung on for the ride. When it was over, Old Zeke rolled off and fell asleep. And that was how I accidentally made an honest woman of Dossie Ree.

I lay there awhile, taking in the surroundings, pretending I was a queen in my royal chamber. Then the place between my legs got itchy and Zeke started snoring louder than Bud and Mama combined. I plucked the five-spot from his trousers and made my getaway. I have to admit, I didn't feel like a fallen woman. All I knew was that I was five dollars richer and didn't have to spend a day picking cotton or plucking chickens or doing any other damn thing besides lie on my back for ten or fifteen minutes.

It beat babysitting by a long shot—the most a girl could make if she babysat for a black family was seventy-five cents a day. Or if she stayed in school until eleventh grade, she could become a teacher at one of the black schools and make about five dollars a day. Or her family could receive welfare, which nobody admitted to. All in all, I thought I had done pretty well for myself.

The next morning I went to Kroger's and bought two jars of mayonnaise, which Mama loved, a loaf of white bread, a pound of bologna, and a jar of Garrett snuff. I plunked the whole sack in Mama's arms and pressed the change—two moist greenbacks and some coins—in her hand. She peeked into the sack, put it down by the sink, then stared at the cash. She couldn't have looked sicker if I had smeared shit from a public toilet on her palm.

"Where in de Lawd's name did you gits dis here money, chile?" she asked in a breaky voice.

"Say, ra—babysittin', Mama," I said.

"Dat's a babysittin' *lie*, Ida Mae!" she said. "You's been havin' mens! An' after all I tries to do fo' you!" She threw the money onto our peeling linoleum floor. "I guess I gots no choice but t' git J.K. over here an' whup yo' ass, gal! No choice a-tall!"

When Mama's wire strap failed to tame us, she'd call over our elderly widowed neighbor, Mr. J.K., to give us a man's touch. Usually, the mere threat of calling him worked. But now I was as big as Mr. J.K., and probably stronger. I could certainly run faster than he could chase. So instead of begging for mercy, I just glared at Mama defiantly. I knew what I had done was wrong, but it wasn't *that* wrong—and I had food and money to show for it.

"An' I thought Dossie Ree be lyin' when she say you be street-walkin'," Mama sniffed. "Can you 'magine Susie's gals doing such a thang? Never inna hunnert years!"

Miss Susie Brooks and her five children, four girls and a boy, lived two doors down in an immaculate house with a regular husband and daddy. Her older girls, Velma Lee and Queen Ella, sneaked me food over the back fence: fried chicken, roast potatoes, and lye hominy, which was kernels of corn washed in lye to take off the husks. Miss Susie dipped snuff like Mama but was a stern disciplinarian. Her older daughters were the neighborhood Goody Two-shoes; they took piano lessons from Miss Blumenberg, always went to church, and never played hooky. Mama never ceased comparing them to Jean and me. "Now why can't you chilluns be mo' like Susie's chilluns?" was her standard way of ending an argument.

"Here I is gittin' ready to send you down yon'er t' Campbell College, jest like Susie's girls," Mama was saying, "but I can't do dat now! Naw sirree! Dey not be wantin' no drunkards or pee-de-bed, hooky-playin', juke house gal whats be common wit' de mens! You ain't grown up as you thank you is, Miss pishy-tail, 'omanish Ida Mae Holland!"

I picked up my money and ran out of the house—straight to Mr. Fred's dollar store, where I bought two pairs of Red Fox stockings; then to Stanley's department store to put a sexy blouse with matching skirt on lay-by. If I was doomed to be nothing more than a pishy-tail, 'omanish chile, at least I would look good in the part.

A MONTH later, I was expelled from Broad Street High School. The way it happened was a surprise, although the reason for it wasn't.

The better I made myself look outside, the worse I felt inside. I took real pride in hiding or disguising my feelings, acting angry when I was sad and sad when I was mad. Even better, I learned to act any old way that would get me noticed. I got wilder and did dumb things, including babysitting a pistol belonging to Pole Cat Pogue (and almost blowing a hole in my neighbor, Pearlie, by accident), and turning my second trick, with a white truck farmer north of town, while Bud and Jean and a dozen neighbors picked melons in his field. He called me "Little Britches" and paid me ten dollars, which became my white man's price. That meant Mr. Lawrence still owed me for what he'd done—a debt other white men would pay.

Now you may wonder how such a nice girl like Little-Leg Cat came to be so low-down and spiteful as to turn tricks with white men and spit on her mama, who was trying her best to put me on a godly path. At the time, it just seemed to me that trying to walk the straight and narrow, like Miss Susie's girls did, only made you older and poorer and respected by all the wrong folks: those who had nothing and weren't likely to have any more, or those, like white folks, who didn't care much for you anyway. In other words, I figured that if the bull was going to throw you, you might as well get something for your pains.

At school I had become leader of my pack—largely because I

had begun sneaking whiskey wrapped in a newspaper from Sam Ciroe's onto the Broad Street campus, where I doled it out on the playground. Not only did this make me popular with the kids, it shut Mama up, too, since my attendance went from terrible to perfect. Of course, my luck didn't last. A half pint of Old Crow slipped out of the paper one morning and shattered on the concrete. The odor on my dress alone was enough for the playground monitor to send me straight to the principal's office.

While I waited for Mr. Threadgill, I rehearsed my defiant speech. I was tired of kowtowing to Mama and teachers, and I didn't care about detention, extra homework, more lectures, or make-work punishment like collecting litter and washing windows. Those would only make me a better martyr for all the other kids who understood how our teachers and parents were wrecking their lives. By the time the principal finally called me in, I was ready to give as good as I got.

"Well, Ida Mae," he said, his voice full of resignation, "you seemed to be making some progress, but bringing alcohol on campus is a very serious offense." He put on his glasses and looked at my file. "I see unexcused absences, tardiness, low grades, smoking in the restroom, fighting with other girls, petty theft. It looks like you're not very interested in being a member of our student community here at Broad Street. I've sent several letters to your mother, but I don't see any answers. I can only assume she hasn't had much luck with you either. And, I have to say, I've heard some disturbing reports about how you spend your time away from school. If I thought we had the slightest chance of turning you around, I'd fight to keep you here. But truthfully, I don't think you fit in—*want* to fit in—with the other students and the decent Negro families here in Greenwood. And, frankly, my first duty is to them. As a result, I have no choice but to declare you expelled, here and now, from this school. If you attempt to come back on campus for any reason, we'll have to call the police. Do you understand what I've just told you, Ida Mae?"

My eyes watered with hurt and surprise. The retort I'd prepared stuck in my throat. I said something, but it wasn't cool and defiant, then stormed out of the office. Expelled, expelled, well, I don't gi'e a damn, I thought. But I did!

I'd only stomped half a block before I turned into the Broad Street Cafe, which catered to a younger crowd than Sam Ciroe's. Being close to school, it was favored by dropouts from all over Gee Pee, Baptist Town, and Gritney, including the baddest delinquents in town: Rosemary Fitzpatrick, who carried a gun; Snake Samuels, who wore his namesake as a belt; Trick Greene, who was as crazy as Cross-Eye Jack and a lot meaner; and Trick's aptly nicknamed brother, Goggle Eye, who drank anything that had alcohol in it.

To my surprise, Rosemary Fitzpatrick invited me over as soon as I came in.

"Yeah, I knows about de Cat," she said, offering me a smoke and a drink. She dressed wild, in clanky jewelry and sexy clothes that hugged her thin body and drew attention away from a face that, while it wouldn't stop a clock, would sure make you lose interest in the time. She asked if it was true that I'd been run out of Broad Street by the *police* and that I knew how to handle a gun. I didn't know what to say, so I said I'd be a fool to sit at her table and call her a liar. She thought that was real funny, and poured me a drink from her paper bag.

I could tell Snake didn't like me, but Trick did. He slid close and asked if I knew how he got his nickname. I said I supposed it was because he was tricky, and he said, no, it was because the whores in Gritney always gave him a ride for no fare.

We partied like this for some time. Never before had cigarettes been so plentiful; beer and whiskey flowed nonstop. People came and went, and Fitzpatrick or Trick introduced me, saying, "Dis be de Cat—she be de one dat de cops kicked outta school!" I decided not to correct them, because now I had a reputation and was somebody who shouldn't be messed with. I met the white man who owned the liquor store and cafe across the highway. He had a soft spot for black women, and I had heard he was in love with a black girl who attended Broad Street School. I was uncomfortable when Fitzpatrick cursed him out—I'd never heard a black person talk to a white person that way—but he just laughed and thrust more money in her bosom.

I met Pigeon Williams and her followers—a bunch of nice-looking girls who dressed like white girls, in neck scarves, ankle bracelets, hoop skirts, and saddle shoes. They had all stopped going to school about a year ago, when they started running in a pack. Most of the guys were afraid to approach them because the rumor was they were lesbians. They were also said to gang up and fight with whatever weapons were handy, like bottles and knives. Pigeon herself was like Fitzpatrick—homely with a great figure. "Yeah, she be a fox from de back," Trick said while we were slow-dancing, "but she be 'nother kinda zoo bird if you catch her from de front!"

About nine o'clock I got a hootch headache and said I had to go home. Being with Fitzpatrick's gang was a lot of work. You could never really relax, and you had to be careful about what you said and how you said it. Everyone else decided to go home, too, so we all spilled out onto the sidewalk, laughing and hooting and pawing each other and saying good-bye. I thought Trick would walk me home, or at least offer to, but he got busy with Snake under a street lamp so I just waved good-bye and headed west.

After a few blocks, though, I got the feeling I was being fol-lowed. I squinted back down the street but Old Crow was still doing the looking. When my vision cleared, I saw someone who looked like Trick—same clothes and slouchy build—running to-ward me. I smiled and started to meet him, then stopped. Something was wrong—bad wrong. He could've yelled something friendly, to stop or hold up, but he didn't. He just kept running, like a bobcat after a rabbit. Then he let out a shriek and I turned to run, but he slapped me to the sidewalk. We fell together and rolled off into the weeds. I tried to get up, but he had me by the hair. His foot went back and I shut my eyes. I felt his shoelaces hit my face and my head snapped back and all the lights went out.

When I came to, my hands were on my face and my fingers were wet and my teeth felt loose. Black blood was all over, and I was screaming bloody murder. Through half-shut eyes I saw Trick running away. Then Pigeon and her girls were helping me up, leading me to the streetlight, blotting my face with their hankies.

"Dat Trick done lost his mind!" Pigeon said. "Dat's jest his way, honey."

With Pigeon's flock as an escort, I headed home as fast as my aching legs would take me. We passed McDonald's Funeral Home, then the underpass where Main opened into Gibb Street, and we were in my neighborhood, where Pigeon's girls got nervous and left me. I limped the rest of the way home.

The house was dark. Mama was snoring gently in the front room. I felt for the dangling electric switch and listened to the roaches rustling in the dark. I always made a little bet when I switched on the light: Which side of the room would the roaches favor—the left side, with the picture of Jesus, or the right, where Mama's big frame lay anchored like a battleship? But that night I left the light and roaches alone and felt my way to the second room, where Bud lay snoring in a whiskey fog.

He moaned and smacked his lips and turned over, and I decided not to turn on that light either. If Bud saw my face, he'd want to know who beat me, and there would be hell to pay in Greenwood. He now had a reputation as the fightingest boy in Gee Pee, having been trained by the previous champ, Simon Jr., before Simon went

to Chicago to live with his daddy. Unfortunately, he had all of
Simon Jr.'s cussedness as well as his fighting technique. If he found
out it was Trick and got him alone, one of them would wind up in
the morgue, and the other in state prison.

Feeling my way in the dark, I stumbled onto my cot and tumbled
down. My face throbbed like a thumb hit with a hammer, but it
hurt too much even to groan. As I lay there, the roaches resumed
their parade, foraging and creeping and dragging their hulls across
the floor, across my arms and neck. I didn't even have the strength
to shoo them away.

I let my mind topple into my "someday space." It was a blurry
place, but it wasn't the same as being asleep or dreaming. I could
feel the mattress on my back even as I floated above it, light-limbed.
There, I could round up all my scattered and shameful thoughts
and put them through their paces, follow them over waterfalls as
they cascaded one after another. I could undo mistakes and misfor-
tunes, reliving them or living them some new way. I could wish-
travel anywhere I wanted to go.

I'd discovered my someday space on the night of my eleventh
birthday, after the bull had thrown me at the Lawrences'. Since
then, I'd use it to think about my daddy, whichever one he was, or
to write poems in the air. It was a hard place to stay in, to
measure or map—teetering between here and there, then and now,
something and nothing, wishing and forgetting—but after a while
I got good at it. In later years I'd call it up without thinking
whenever I sat down to write.

Tonight, I had a lot of work to do in my someday space. I had to
get out of the Delta: that was my plan, my dream, the destination
for which I set my mental compass and trimmed my sails.

As my body got lighter, the light behind my eyes got brighter.
Suddenly, I was hot, burning hot, but I couldn't see the fire. I
floated pass Mama; she was waving and hollering, trying to get my

attention. "All dat shine ain't gold," I heard her say. "Make yo' way to de cen'er o' de stage."

"Yas'm, Mama, I will!" I shouted back.

And indeed there was a stage. The crowd parted, and there was Trick on center stage. He held out his hand for me to join him. My body pressed forward but my bruised, swollen head held me back. Finally, my head got so big and so far behind that people in the crowd had to help me hold it up. Like some delicate piece of furniture, I was slowly passed forward and lifted to the stage. There was Trick, sliding farther away, reaching out, beckoning—

I woke up to a moist rag cleaning my face and the sound of Mama sobbing. Light streamed through the window and I saw Bud's angry face hovering over Mama's shoulder.

"Who done dis t' you, Cat?" he asked.

"Trick," I managed to whisper.

"I'm gonna git dat sucker!" Bud swore. I heard his fist slam into his palm. "I don' care who he be or where he be, I'm gonna make him pay fo' what he done to yo' face!"

"You ain't gwine do *nothin'*," Mama said, sniffing back tears. "You gwine go to yo' job an stay outta trouble, das what *you* gwine do."

"But Mama—das de Li'l Cat! Look what he done to her face!"

"You wanna hep, Bud?" Mama turned and looked him up and down. "Den you talk t' Ida Mae here like a daddy. You tell her where she oughta go and who she oughta hang wit', 'cause she sho' 'nough don't lissen to me."

I didn't hear Bud's answer, only the sound of the screen door slamming behind him.

Mama put salve on my split lip and cuts and scrapes, then sat with me the rest of the morning. We talked and cried and I didn't say anything more about who I was with or what I'd been doing, least of all that I'd been thrown out of school.

Since I had no place to go and was ashamed to be seen in my sorry state, I was content to stay home and be cared for. The term was almost over anyway, so after a week or so all the kids were out of school and the subject never came up. By the time the next term started, I would have other, bigger troubles on my plate; and Mama would understand, if not condone, the reason I stayed out of school.

A few hours later, Bud came back, but he didn't look like he'd been in a fight. He said, "Trick ain't gone bother you no mo' " and I hoped he was right, though I had no real plans to go back to the Broad Street Cafe and find out. Later, Pigeon told me that Bud found Trick at the cafe, surrounded by his gang. Even though Bud was all alone, he walked right up to Trick and said he was my brother. He said Trick owed me and my family an apology, and he could give Bud one now and save a lot of bother, or he could give Bud one later, assuming he'd be able to speak. For some reason, Trick thought that was funny and laughed like hell. Maybe he admired Bud's bravery. Maybe he just thought Bud was so crazy and stupid that he wasn't a threat. Either way, Trick said he'd been so drunk, he couldn't remember what happened, except he kind of liked me. "You tell de Cat she kin come back to de Broad Street Cafe any ol' time—we be glad to see her."

That was the closest thing Bud was going to get to an apology, so he took it. Trick and Bud shook hands and that was that—at least according to Pigeon. Bud told a slightly different story.

"I'd a tore up his head," Bud sniffed that night at supper, " 'f'n Simon Junior had been here. Thing was, Goggle Eye an' ol' Snake Samuels be easin' 'round 'hind me while we talkin.' But ol' Trick, he not dumb. He know if he don't beg pardon, I be back with Cross-Eye Jack and Simon Junior next time Simon come from Chicago. An' Cross-Eye Jack, he fight wit' a *dutch*. Naw, ol' Trick be nasty, but he ain't dumb!"

The truth was, our young black men didn't need a reason to fight, or make peace. They all felt the same frustration at living in the barless prison we called the Delta. They had the pride of any natural man, but what good did pride do them? Their violent ways, like my own rebellious spirit, were just an equal and opposite reaction to the forces that held them down. With no way to strike back at the things that mattered, they passed time striking out at each other.

I finally asked Pigeon if she thought it was safe for me to go back to the Broad Street Cafe and see Fitzpatrick. She said sure, but I never went back. The Broad Street gang had too many rules I didn't understand; and the rules I knew about, I didn't like. Getting away from the things I hated—getting out of the Delta—would take more of a journey than a walk across town. There had to be a way to get there. All I had to do was find it.

Seven

A few days after Trick beat me, Mama made me do the family washing. I guess it was a way of punishing me. She poured boiling water from the stove into the tin washtub that sat in our backyard. Then she brought an armload of soiled clothes that she stuffed down into the tub. I could see Turner Chapel through the high-grown bushes and tall weeds, and I made a vow: If the sunflowers that grew in our yard bent double before twelve o'clock, I would join the church again and become a good Christian.

Around eleven-thirty the sunflowers bent double and kissed the ground. And so I went where most people go when they don't know where to turn: back to church.

The preacher welcomed me back, and so did most of his flock, which was a mild surprise. This was the first time I realized what the church meant in our community: a place where fairness and goodness—in short supply everywhere else in Greenwood—flowed freely. It was a place where black people could behave with dignity and fill responsible roles we could usually only dream about. Outside we might be laborers or mammies or drunks, but inside God's house we were deacons and choristers and Mothers of the Church.

I got myself rebaptized and joined the choir. This was partly to please Mama, who scraped together enough money for me to buy a white robe. But it was also to please me. New baptisms made a good show on Sundays, as did our choral singing, and I missed being center stage. Besides, Miss Susie's daughters played the piano and sang with the choir, and it pleased Mama no end to see me up there in the best-ironed robe in Greenwood and to hear my big contralto alongside their prissy high notes.

At home, we started getting ready on Saturday for church on Sunday: the girls washed, oiled, and plaited their hair while the grown women straightened theirs, and we all ate homemade pork skins and drank RC's while they gossiped and play-liked.

"Y'all knows dat old drunkard Son Boy Brown, don'cha?" Mama began one evening. "Y'all know he use ta have a wife, Sweet Chile, she be dead and buried now." Every head nodded.

Although Miss Sweet Chile Brown died when I was a baby, I had heard this story so often that I could finish telling it. Sweet Chile had been married to Son Boy Brown, Gee Pee's resident drunk (he could get drunker than anybody in town; and he was drunk even when he didn't have a drink). Sweet Chile wanted a baby bad, but Son Boy was never around or sober enough to put her in the family way. When she finally did get pregnant, she was so proud, she put on her maternity suit in the first month. After seven months, though, complications set in. She was bleeding so bad they sent for Gee Pee's "ambulance"—the Century Funeral Home hearse—to take her to the Leflore County Hospital. When they got there, the white nurse said they were out of beds, which meant they didn't have any room left in the colored ward, though there was plenty of space in the white. Good thing she was riding in a hearse, because by the time they got home again, Miss Sweet Chile had bled to death.

Bro Pastor went around the whiskey houses on McLauren Street to track down her husband, and when he heard the news, Son Boy came running. He didn't drink another drop until after his wife's funeral. But Mama hated losing babies, and she hated losing mothers more. Ever since Miss Sweet Chile died after being turned away from the hospital, Mama stopped going to the hospital to wait on white women and vowed to help out whenever and wherever else she could.

"I 'cided rat den an' dere dat I wouldn't let nane other 'oman die 'f'n I knowed how t' he'p her live." When the white nurses realized she wouldn't come help them with the white women at the hospital anymore, "Dey got mad an' say dat I ain't got no permit nohow. I be 'fraid dey gwine th'ow me in de river, but den I say t' myself, dey kin keep de five dollars dey gi'e me—an' I jest learn how t' drank dat river water!"

Somehow Dr. Feinberg found out about Sweet Chile Brown and raised a ruckus. " 'F'n Dr. Feinberg be at the horsepital," Mama grunted, "dat li'l gal be nursin' a new baby 'steada bleedin' to deaf in dat car." Mama and Dr. Feinberg had put each other on pedestals. He was one of the few white doctors who could get things done to help black people, and he recognized Mama's talent for catching babies. He spoke for Mama to get the county to grant Mama's permit to practice even though she couldn't read or write. By then she'd been delivering babies so long most people thought she already had her permit, if they thought about it at all.

One hot Saturday while Mama was ironing my choir robe, Man Son Matthews ran up to our porch in a lather. Man Son was the teenage boy of Miss Sweetney, who lived with her seven children at the Buckeye, a small community west of town, where the oil mill was located. Mama had delivered Miss Sweetney's last two babies and was now coaching her on the eighth.

"Aint Baby! Aint Baby!" Man Son shouted. "Sweetney call you! Her belly hurt *real* bad!"

Man Son stumbled on our front steps and Mama dropped her iron to catch him. He was a sweaty, dusty mess from taking a shortcut through the sandpile out back of Will Huggins's place, and salt tears ran south of both eyes. Mama held him close and rubbed his cocklebur head.

"Whoa, boy," she said, "hold on a minute. Settle down now. Take a seat an' catch yo' breath. Ida Mae!" she shouted over her shoulder. "You git yon'er and brang dis boy a big drank o' water. An' git him one o' dem tea cakes. He jest 'bout fried in dis heat."

I'd heard Mama complain to her friends, "I ain't gwine wait babies no mo' fo' dat 'oman Sweetney. Ever'time she gits down, she 'spect me t' use my 'spensive doctor tools and she ain't never pay a dime on her granny bill from de last two chilluns!" But if the truth be known, she had nothing to worry about. Mama might complain about money, but it wasn't her master. More often than not, when she got paid at all, she took her fee in goods—eggs, butter, clabber milk, even furniture. If a woman was in labor, Mama was there to help. She once told me, "Ida Mae, you kin look over folks when you is pickin' in low cotton, an' you kin look over folks when dere ain't no cotton t' pick. But can't never look over nosomebody when de cotton is high. Howbe ever, you gots t' do whatsonever you kin."

Like the midwives she'd learned from, Mama was called for at any time of the night or day to help Delta women deliver their babies. She always knew just what to do. When the medicine in her doctor bag failed, she had her "nature sack"—a little bag of folk remedies and charms she wore around her neck—to evoke the "hoodoo" some people preferred to the white man's medicine.

Man Son drank his cool water straight down, then headed back to tell Miss Sweetney that the cavalry was on the way. While Mama gathered her things, I ran to Mr. Sims's cab stand to book a charity ride, but he wasn't there. Instead, I had to flag down Buddy Boy, a freelance driver so fat that his rattletrap old car had a permanent tilt to the driver's side. He didn't haul Mama for free like Mr. Sims, but he didn't charge much either, and he never turned down a fare.

"Hey dere, Buddy Boy," Mama waved, shambling out of the

house with her doctor bag as the cab pulled up out front. Buddy Boy rolled out of the driver's seat and helped Mama in, then off they went. I had begged and pleaded with Mama to let me accompany her to a delivery, but she said I was too young to see "all dat a 'oman hada suffer." So I had to be satisfied with filling out the birth certificate at home when she was done.

While Mama was at Miss Sweetney's, I smoked a nickel's worth of Camels, then stretched out under our old chinaberry tree and read my latest Perry Mason. Before long, the print got blurry and I was somehow in the dock being charged with the murder of Trick. I sent for Perry, who immediately got me out of jail on *habeas corpus*. Then the sound of Mama's voice woke me up. She was thanking Buddy Boy and paying him for her ride.

I ran to meet her. "What she got, Mama?"

"Sweetney got hersef' a burr-head boy," she replied, plowing right by me, looking tired. She went into the house and put on the kettle so she could boil her tools. "Ida Mae," she called over her shoulder, "git dat pencil over yon'er and write dat 'oman's baby name on de birth 'tificate 'fore I forgits dat crazy name she come up wit'."

The birth certificate had to be filled out within three days after a birth. Mama would study the form like she could read and then she'd make her *X* mark and I would sign her name and mail the certificate to the Department of Records in Jackson. I felt proud to use my school skills helping Mama.

"How come de name be crazy, Mama?" I asked.

"It crazy 'cause dat 'oman losin' her mind, dat's why! 'Magine goin' through dis world wit' a name like Gene Autry 'Merica Flame Matthews! Yeah, you laughin,' gal, but dat ain't no joke! An' dat li'l cuss jest lucky to be here."

"How come? What happen, Mama?"

Mama opened an RC cola and collapsed on her bed.

"When I gits t' Sweetney house, she be hollerin' somethin' terrible. I wash my hanes an' 'xamine her good an' see dat de baby head be pokin' out. But den it don't come out, 'cause it be hung up on somethang. I be 'fraid dat she gwine strangle de poor baby to deaf. I don't say nuttin'—I jest git in de bed wit' her an' rub her belly 'til she be relax. I knows dat she needs de Lawd an' a steady voice to give her ease, so I say to de angel: you kin brang de li'l baby on now. An' I say to Sweetney, 'C'mon, push easy, 'cause here it come!' An' Sweetney kinda huff an' den push, an' den Man Son done got hisse'f a new baby bro."

I was in my early teens the first time I saw Mama in action as a granny midwife. Like Simon Jr., Jean had gone North to live with relatives, and the cotton was high. Mama, Bud, and I went to the corner one foggy morning to meet Mr. Walter Foreman's truck, which would take us to the fields. But because of her great weight, her lack of exercise, and the dampness of the morning, Mama was having trouble climbing into the truck. She'd been having "dizzy spells" more and more often lately; she'd laugh when she fell and claim to be play-liking, but she didn't fool anybody.

Bud got up under the tarp to pull while I stayed on the ground to push, but Mama was going nowhere. Mr. Walter was getting more impatient by the second. At just that moment, a frog-eyed pickup with headlamps boring holes in the mist pulled up beside us. Mr. Walter started to cuss the driver for parking so close, but when he saw who it was, he shut up. Nobody cursed Straw Boss and lived.

Straw Boss was close to seven feet tall, blacker than the bottom of Mama's teakettle, and covered with scars left by knives and razors. They said he'd killed nine people, including two women, though he never spent a night in jail. As soon as the police discovered Straw Boss was a suspect, they stopped the investigation. If they didn't, they'd get a call from his employer, a wealthy white planter near Cruger, who'd say, "Better not touch a hair on my nigra's head. I want that boy back here 'fore sunup. He's got plowing to do!"

Straw Boss got out of the pickup, walked around the hood, and stood by Mr. Walter's tailgate. It was then that I saw what up till now I'd only heard about: his trademark four front teeth—all made of gold, inlaid left to right with the aces of spades, clubs, hearts, and diamonds.

"I is lookin' for de granny 'oman dey calls Aint Baby."

"I be Aint Baby," Mama said. "Who dat be axin'?"

Straw Boss stepped up and took Mama by the arm. "Bob Johnson sont me," he said. "Mag—she be in labor."

"Lawd amercy!" Mama squawked. "Ain't dat jest like Magnolia to git down wit' me on my way t' the fields! How does dat gal 'spect me t' pay my rent?"

"Old Bob say he gots money dis time. Say I's 'sposed to fetch you back."

Mama lowered her foot from Mr. Walter's bumper. "G'won yon'er, Ida Mae, and git my grip; hurry up, gal, 'cause Mag done sont for me. Bud, you g'won t' de chicken house an' see 'f'n dey kin gi'e you a day—"

"But Mama, I's—"

"You *git!*" she said, and that was that for Bud. She turned back to Straw Boss and said what I'd been waiting years to hear: "My gal chile gots t'come wit' me, she kin fill out de birth 'tificate."

Straw Boss only shrugged, and I ran to get Mama's bag. We slid onto the pickup's bench seat, with Straw Boss behind the wheel, Mama on one side, and me in the middle. I was so close to Straw Boss I could smell the breakfast on his breath and had to dodge his big elbow as he spun the wheel, pulling out onto the highway to

Cruger. I figured I was the closest anyone had ever been to Straw Boss and lived.

After what seemed like forever, we turned down a rutted road to the sharecroppers' quarters and slid to a stop, scattering chickens, on the soft dirt before the house. Straw Boss got out, leaving the motor panting, and helped Mama down; I bounded after.

Bob and Magnolia Johnson already had thirteen kids. Dr. Feinberg had told Miss Mag she would die if she had another, but that didn't stop her from getting bigged. She said she would go when the Lord called her, not before. I guess she wanted a little insurance, though, so she sent for Mama.

Bob Johnson met us at the door, his children running around behind him like geese.

"Now, Ida Mae," Mama said, "fus' thang you do be t' take dese chilluns outta here t' de yard. When I gits ready t' write de birth 'tificate, I calls you."

"Yas'm, Mama," I said, disappointed I couldn't stay with the women, but determined not to let that stop me from finally seeing what birthing was all about.

As soon as I got the kids outside, we all ran back and lined up along the window. Inside, Miss Mag was lying in bed, whimpering like a dog. Sometimes her arms and legs would jump, but Mama just sat there.

"Ain't you gonna do nothin', Aint Baby?" Bob Johnson asked in frustration.

"Sho 'nuff," Mama answered. "I's gwine have me a RC."

He brought her the cola and she scuffed her chair closer to the bed. She half-shut her bronze eyes and had a swallow of RC, rocking and humming quietly. All at once, Miss Mag screamed and spit blood, and shit from her bottom all over the bed. Mama just grunted, put her drink down, and cleaned her up, and Miss Mag just shit and bled some more, panting between screams that the baby was going to kill her.

"Say dere, Johnson," Mama said, turning to him, "y'all gimme dem pances you got on."

"Say what?"

"I say gimme dem nasty overhalls you be wearin'—we ain't got time t'chat 'bout it."

Without delay, Bob Johnson took off his bib overalls and handed them to Mama. He just stood there, bony legs sticking out of his boxers. The little kids giggled and I told them to shush up.

"Here now, chile," Mama laid the pants across Miss Mag's belly. "Dese'll he'p you wit' de pain."

Gradually, Miss Mag stopped whimpering. Mama looked over her shoulder. "Well, Johnson—what you doin' standin' 'round wit' yo' arms crossed? C'mon over here and hold dis gal's hane."

Mr. Johnson knelt on his bony knees and took his wife's hand. "It gwine be all right, Magpie," he said in a low voice. "De Lawd gwine make a way."

Mama grunted, "Johnson, de Lawd he'ps dose what he'ps dey-selves. Now put dat ironin' board down underneath Mag's back—dis ol' mattress 'bout t' swaller her up."

Together they eased the ironing board under Miss Magnolia, who began to chant, "Lawdy, Lawdy, Lawdy—you knows I needs you now, Lawd. He'p me, merciful father!" Spittle foamed at the corners of her mouth.

"You sho 'nuff be right 'bout de Lawd, Mag," Mama said, getting up and bending over the foot of the bed.

"What be hap'nin', Aint Baby?" Mr. Johnson cried.

"Why, y'all be havin' a baby, Johnson," Mama eased one little black foot out from Miss Mag's bloody slit. I could see tears streaming down Bob Johnson's face. Miss Mag screeched like a cat and rose up.

"Hol' dat 'oman down t' de bed!" Mama commanded. She knelt between Mag's knees, eyes bulging in concentration, the cords on her neck popped out. Then she pushed that little black foot back into Magnolia's distended belly.

"Whatcha doin', Aint Baby?" said Bob Johnson. "Talk t' me! Talk t' me!"

"I gots t' turn de baby 'round, Johnson," Mama answered, brow knotted, elbows flying. "Now dat be all I gots t' say."

She flattened her hands as if to pray, then inserted them into the birth canal. Miss Mag moaned so loud I thought the roof would fall in, but it didn't. Then she passed out.

I thought she was dead, so I shooed all the kids from the windows. Big old Baby Brother, the next to oldest boy, looked like he was going to faint. The oldest girl's—Bobbie Ann's—blouse was soaked with vomit. Just then, Straw Boss returned in his pickup.

"Y'all c'mere, Bobbie Ann," Straw Boss called. He gave her a plate covered with a white cloth. "Dis here some-teet be fo' y'all t' eat 'til yo' mama feel better."

"Yassuh, Mr. Straw Boss," Bobbie Ann answered, taking the plate.

Then, looking directly at me and smiling with those four aces, Straw Boss put a second, smaller plate on the first.

"An' dis here be fo' dat gal Cat over dere." I lifted the cloth and was surprised to see two crispy chicken legs between two slices of bread. But at the moment, food was the furthest thing from my mind.

Inside, Mama now had both arms up to the elbow in Miss Mag's belly. They twisted and turned while Mama talked in a low, steady voice. Miss Mag was panting shallow, like a sick animal. Mr. Johnson was in the rocker, hands over his face.

Then, something really strange happened. Mama pulled out her arms, all red as if she'd dipped them in a bucket of paint, and stared at that bloody slit. She said something in a low voice, I couldn't hear what. Then she began to rock, repeating the same words over and over, in a language I had never heard before. She rose up like a mammoth barge and began talking; she backed into the corner closest to the window and did a war whoop, the way I'd seen Indians do at the Walthall picture show; she made a clicking sound deep in her throat and waved her arms like Mr. Monroe, the choir director. Maybe she'd gone crazy, I thought.

Then she seemed to float back to the bed. She leaned forward and the top of a black ball appeared between Mag's legs. Her slit became a circle and the black ball got bigger: an orange, then a cantaloupe, then a perfect baby's head. Mama had turned a breech birth around in the womb!

Mr. Johnson rolled from the rocker to his knees, sobbing and praying out loud. Mama scooped up the baby and held it by its heels. She spanked its slick behind till it cried, then tied the navel and cut the cord with her stainless-steel scissors. From her doctor bag she took some drops, which she put in the baby's eyes, then hawked up some spit for Magnolia's navel and mixed in something from her nature sack, stirring it around with her dog finger.

"How dose critters doin'?" Mr. Johnson asked from the door, grinning like a polecat.

"Say, ra—dey done et." I didn't know what to say.

"Now, you chilluns kin come mere," he said, "but jest two at a time, an' say 'how-do' t' number fo'teen. Y'all gots a brand-new li'l sis!"

"Y'all gits one look, den skeedaddle!" Mama shouted from beside the bed. "Ida Mae, you set here in dis chair an' put down de baby's name. Hey, Mag—what you gwine call her?"

"I's gwone name her Mercedes!" Magnolia beamed.

"Now how you gwine spell dat?" Mama asked, looking over my shoulder. "You know how to spell dat, Ida Mae?"

"No'm. But I hears it on de radio."

"Hey, Mag," Mama shouted again. "Bence my gal can't spell dat, you gwine hafta git 'nother name! Y'all don't want no baby to go through life wit' a name nosomebody kin spell! Hey, Johnson— kin you spell dat?"

"Can't cipher, Aint Baby."

Mama scowled at him. "Den you gwine hafta come up wit' 'nother name, or settles for whatsonever Ida Mae here kin write down. An' put yo' pances on, man! You gots chilluns runnin' 'round here now lookin' at yo' 'hind end!"

Mr. Johnson dutifully put his children down and fished his overalls from the bed. I asked Mama, "How come you thro' Mr. Johnson's pants on Miss Magnolia?"

She made a sour face. "Don't dey teach you nothin' at de schoolhouse? 'F'n dat baby be his, de pain go rat down. Now cut out all dat gigglin' and finish up wit' dat birth 'tificate. And de rest o' you chilluns—shoo! Scat! G'won—git outta here!" She chased them like chickens out the door. "Now you, Mag, gi'e Johnson de baby so's you kin squat on de slop jar and git rid o' dat afterbirth. C'mon now, up you gits."

While Mag was squatting, Mama cleaned the bed. When both were done, Mag climbed back in and Mama gave me the soiled laundry to put it to soak in the backyard tub. She took a dip of snuff and sat heavily in the chair. "Okay, Johnson. Now dat you gots yo' britches on, go tell de Straw Boss we's ready to gwone home."

I sat next to Straw Boss on the long drive back, the bloody images of the morning replaying themselves in my mind. If this was what the ultimate womanly mystery was all about, I wanted no part of it.

• • •

NEWS OF Mama turning little Mercedes around while she was "still in the garage" spread like hot oil over town. Miss Maddox, the grand midwife, gave Mama a new pair of surgical scissors to commemorate the event; Miss Miller, a Gee Pee midwife, gave her a bundle of clean white rags. Everybody made 'mirations over her. Everybody in Greenwood suddenly had their own Aint Baby story: from her prowess at starching and ironing to how she picked cotton like a whirlwind to how she saved half of Gee Pee's newborns from "de clutches of de devil!" Miss Sweetney told how she had "talk t' de baby 'til it come out." All the women on the plantations around Cruger started asking her to wait their babies, which was a real compliment, seeing as how plantation folk were always suspicious of us folk who lived in town, where life was supposed to be easy and the cotton always high.

Dr. Feinberg and the other folks started calling Mama the Second Doctor Lady. Instead of her old outney smock and open-toed slippers, she began to wear a white uniform when she made house calls, complete with stockings, cap, and white shoes like a Leflore County white nurse. But she still kept her nature sack around her neck, because some folk still trusted "conjure doctors" better than those with stethoscopes and pills.

"I sho 'nough be somethang t' see, Ida Mae," she said proudly the first time she went out in full regalia.

"You be pickin' in high cotton now, Mama!" I agreed.

"You see, gal? You gots t' grab dat ol' bull by de horns 'f'n you gwine be Somebody. 'Less'n you wants to be Somebody, can't nosomebody make de way for you, nawsir!"

My own reputation improved somewhat, now that I'd given up the Broad Street gang and taken up the choir. I started getting invitations to young people's events and other church-sponsored gatherings. But I attended reluctantly. I felt like a grown woman now, and I needed a new hangout.

Before long, I got hooked up with a group of gamblers and night people. At Dillard's Fish Market on McLauren Street in Gritney, I met Clyde Jones. Clyde was a tall, thin, older man who always dressed well. He hung out with the best-dressed man in town, Mack Gilmore. When they walked down the streets, they were a sight to behold, in their fine snap-brim hats, brightly colored shirts, well-fitting suits from Star Tailors (the finest men's store in town), and soft leather shoes. They had plenty of money, too; whatever game you were playing—pool, cards, dice—they did, too, and they never lost.

Clyde lived in a room over Dillard's Cafe. I had my own key, so I had a hideaway where I could do as I pleased. He had interesting matchbooks from Chicago and St. Louis; I liked to squeeze them and make wishes. Clyde's sheets were soft and silky when we "made love"—the first time I ever heard sex referred to that way.

Because Clyde slept most days and went out after dark, I would go to his room early in the morning and get into bed with him. Sometimes I would take an armload of Perry Mason novels, so that I could read without being disturbed. We had bottles of whiskey and beer to drink whenever we wanted to, and when we got hungry, he'd order us a meal from Booker's Cafe, or we could run downstairs to get the best fried catfish sandwich in Greenwood at Dillard's. That's where I was coming from the night I saw the mortuary's ambulance pull up to the house of Miss Rosebud Julia Dupree, thereby ending the unhappy saga of Son Boy Brown.

Miss Rosebud had come to Greenwood about the same time Mama had, at the beginning of the Great Migration of rural blacks to the North. Her husband died during World War II, when the big green John Deere tractor flipped over on Mr. Ludlow's plantation. It was said that when she received the news, she put on her black dress and wide-brimmed hat and went to the Century Funeral Home to make arrangements. After that, she stopped by the church to schedule a memorial service with Bro Pastor, then she picked up her teenage son, RL, still a second-grader at McLauren Street School. Right after the funeral, Miss Rosebud packed RL a hog's-head souse sandwich and moon pie and took him down to the bus station to catch the Greyhound for Chicago—to finish the migration she and her husband, like my Mama, never had time to finish.

Since then, Miss Rosebud had seldom left her porch or her window, let alone her house. Her main occupation was sitting in her window or on her porch, day after day, night after night, watching her water meter. It was mounted under an iron plate a few inches from the sidewalk, just inviting passersby—especially kids—to step on it and make it clang. That was the object of her vigilance: to keep children, drunks, sinners, and strangers from using her water meter as a toy.

Those of us who were her neighbors knew she meant business. She had a stack of bricks by her chair that she flung down on any intruder foolish enough to invade her territory. My friends and I had tested her marksmanship many times ("Cat, you slew-footed cow—git off'n my water meter!") and knew it to be true. Betty Ann Wilkinson, who was a good girl, once stepped on the meter accidentally and was chased down the street by a brick-throwing Miss Rosebud.

All of Gee Pee knew she was addle-brained, so the women fixed her plates of food and carried them to the steps of her front porch. That was as far as she allowed anyone to come. When she got sick, the women could go only as far as the front door with their medicines. Nobody had seen the inside of her house for many years.

Of course, the water meter belonged to the city. Every so often a crew of white workmen in orange jackets would set up their traffic cones and do something or other to the rusty pipes beneath.

I took to sashaying past their trench, my Lucky Heart perfume arriving just before I did. One by one, their heads would pop up and they'd smile and I'd smile and begin walkin' my walk, all the time thinking about what ten dollars a head would buy: dinners at Dillard's, a new dress from Kronfield's, part of Mama's rent.

Their supervisor was a one-armed white man named Big Jim Smith. He was the one who put the bug in Miss Rosebud's ear about keeping folks off her meter. It seems Miss Rosebud had been Mr. Big Jim's mammy, and his mother's before him. As a teenager, he'd run away to Greenville to join the army, then lost his arm in an accident at boot camp. He was welcomed back like a hero, and Miss Rosebud was invited to sit near the white folks for the parade in his honor. Mr. Big Jim always gave her special treatment when the water workers came to work. He'd go out with the crew in person and talk and laugh with Miss Rosebud, and that's when the trouble started.

One day Mr. Big Jim said to her, "So you watch out now, Aintie Rosebud. Don't let none of these colored folks step on your meter or your water bill gonna go sky-high!" Then he threw back his head and laughed and laughed, nudging the man closest to him with his nub arm.

"Yassuh, Big Jim!" Miss Rosebud said. She was the only black person in the Delta who didn't have to address him as Mister. "I gwine be on de lookout!"

It had started like a game, but all of Gee Pee knew Miss Rosebud never played it with a full deck. So when Son Boy Brown, who had gone back on the bottle, came weaving down Walthall Street one morning, she yelled to him, "Y'all be mighty careful, Son Boy—don'cha step on my meter!"

"You crazy ol' 'oman!" Son Boy yelled back. "Dis here ain't yo' meter!"

"Dis here be my meter, fool!" Miss Rosebud armed each hand with a brick. "I knows you be jest a pissy ol' drunk, but keep messin' wit' me, and dey gwine tote you off in de ammulance!"

"Sheeet—" Son Boy answered with as much dignity as a headful of sploe whiskey allowed him. "Ain't gwine set footses on dat meter!" He ambled past as if stepping on that meter just to spite her was the last thing on his mind. Nonetheless, Miss Rosebud kept him in her crosshairs until he had safely turned the corner, then went back to her chair.

That evening, Son Boy was carousing at Miss Lussie Bee's juke house when Big Red Parker brought up the subject of Miss Rosebud's famous water meter. It wasn't that people disliked Miss Rosebud, or delighted in causing her grief; only that Mr. Big Jim's joke was all over town and that damned iron plate had become forbidden fruit.

"I bets dis here half pint o' Old Crow," Big Red said, "dat nosomebody in dis room be bad 'nough to g'won rat now an' step on Rosebud's meter!"

Faced with his last drink and empty pockets, Son Boy replied, "Aw, shoots—I ain't 'fraid o' dat ol' 'oman! 'F'n y'all throws in a quart o' beer, *I* be de one who steps on dat ol' meter!"

Miss Delie, who could outdrink and outfight most men in the room and who had her eye on Son Boy since Miss Sweet Chile passed away, said, "Don'cha do dat, Son Boy! Dat 'oman, Rosebud, her ain't right in de head!"

But Son Boy was as determined as he was thirsty. "Don'tcha worry none 'bout me. Dat ol' 'oman be fast t' sleep dis time 'o night. I go tromp on dat meter and be back in a flash—den we g'wone ball de jack, gal!" Son Boy swatted Delie's behind and staggered out the door.

Normally, Miss Rosebud was a sound sleeper. But this night, she had been tortured, as she was from time to time, by dreams of that big John Deere spinning its wheels and grinding its gears. In her sleep she strained her old arms to pull, once again, the mangled body of Mr. Dupree from that tangled wreck. She'd taken so many BC powders, in fact, that though her head had stopped aching, her stomach hurt so bad it woke her. She went out on the front porch to rock in the cool night air.

So there she was when Son Boy drew near in the darkness, on the other side of the tracks. He had stopped to take a pee and noticed Preacher Magee (who wasn't a real preacher, but a jackleg) following at a discreet distance, to witness for the crowd back at Lussie Bee's. Son Boy zipped his pants, squared his shoulders, and marched off into battle.

Miss Rosebud quit rocking and watched the slovenly figure shuffle toward her down the sidewalk. Silently, her right hand went for a brick. The figure weaved back and forth, coming closer and closer to her lawn. Her left hand went for a brick.

Then, like a torpedo, Son Boy went straight for that meter and clanked it with his foot. Before the second foot could follow, his head split open and a big glob of brains flopped forward onto his shirt. He hit the pavement hard, along with the first gush of blood and Miss Rosebud's spent bricks.

Or at least that's how Preacher Magee told the story to the crowd that quickly gathered. I pushed my way to the front just as the ambulance pulled up. Poor Son Boy was curled up over the curb like a bloody newborn. As they put him on the stretcher, somebody started to pray; then another person started to sing; and then Big Smitty, the Leflore County deputy sheriff, led Miss Rosebud out of her house to his waiting squad car, lights a-flashing. She was wearing an old-fashioned black dress and a wide-brimmed hat.

"Dat ol' devil thought I be 'sleep!" she said to nobody in particular as she got into the backseat. "But de Lawd gi'e me de stren'th t' sen' dat debbil t' hell!"

Big Smitty spoke on the two-way to a scratchy voice at the station. Then everybody waited till an orange city truck pulled up and Mr. Big Jim Smith got out. He took a long look at Son Boy's body on the stretcher, then went over to the squad car to talk to Miss Rosebud. We couldn't hear what he said, but he looked like a kid explaining a broken window to his mama. She never looked at him, or back around at us, just kept her eyes fixed forward like a queen.

Gee Pee buried Son Boy two Sundays later, in Potter's Field. The delay was on account of his kinfolk having to come from out of town. After the funeral, Miss Tut Vaughn went up to Whitfield, where Miss Rosebud was confined in the mental institution. She reported that Miss Rosebud was doing real fine and had asked about her water meter.

Mama told Dossie Ree that white folks had given poor Rosebud the wherewithal to throw those bricks—a crime, given the old woman's brains were addled to begin with. Mama called me out of the house many times to tell the tragic story to our neighbors, which I did, just like "Casey at the Bat." Each time my stomach felt worse, though, like it was full of maggots trying to hatch out. Finally, I stopped telling the story at all, and people stopped asking. All that was left was the hot summer air, a few stains on the sidewalk by a boarded-up house, and the rattly iron cover to the water meter of Miss Rosebud Dupree.

Eight

SOON AFTER SON BOY'S DEATH, I QUIT GOING TO CLYDE JONES'S ROOM. ALL THE THINGS THAT HAD seemed wondrous to me there now seemed ordinary. The matchbook covers no longer excited me; the silk sheets no longer felt soft; I no longer needed a hideaway to read Erle Stanley Gardner's books, because Perry Mason's cases no longer interested me. And on top of all this, Clyde had gotten a new girlfriend. He said I had changed ever since Son Boy Brown got killed.

Indeed, Son Boy's death had awakened feelings that I didn't know I had. I'd begun thinking about life and death: how precious life is, how final death is. I was determined to live my life to the fullest, and not to be buried in an overgrown field among makeshift headstones. I quit visiting my "someday space" and started living for the moment.

I didn't go back to school. When Mama found out, she fussed at me. "Ida Mae, gal, you don't see yo'self now, but I does. I sees a whole lotta chilluns; a 'oman dat de mens done used up; a ol' drag dat nosomebody wants," she said. "When my head be cold, you ain't gwine have nuttin' t' 'pend on. You oughta g'won back t' de schoolhouse an' beg Mr. Threadgill pardon, so dat you kin be 'mitted—'cause you ain't no mo'e den fo'teen years ol'."

But I didn't intend to stay in Greenwood long. I was determined to go North and be Somebody. I had decided I was going to be a famous singer who would make Mama proud. I'd gotten the idea from the posters I'd seen advertising a minstrel show that was coming soon to Greenwood. I'd stood for the longest time looking

at the singers in their fancy gowns painted on the posters. I wanted
to join the show. I was ready now.

The biggest show was the Big Show itself, the Silas Green and
Rabbit Foot Minstrels show—featuring comedians, blues singers,
and pop musicians—that came through the Delta every few years
and performed in a big lot near Stone Street School. People came
from all over—Grenada, Lexington, Cruger, Tschula, Itta Bena,
Ruleville, Indianola, Belzoni, Pugh City, the hills and the plantations alike—to see it. I had been too small to see the last one, but
this year I was waiting with bells on. Mama had other ideas.

"Ain't no need a you gwine out yon'er to lissen to dat mess!"
she said, powdering her nose and rouging her lips. My womanish
behavior was bad enough, but flaunting it in front of Mama's
friends, at a place most older folks viewed as their refuge from the
young, was something else.

The afternoon before the first performance, three of us dropouts
followed the music to the biggest tent and slipped under the side.
Inside, a dozen people pranced back and forth in front of a silk
curtain, rehearsing the show's finale. Even without their costumes,
they were the grandest sight I'd ever seen. We snuck out the way
we came in, too excited to sit still and afraid of calling attention to
ourselves.

That night, we went back dressed in our best. The white folk
entered first and took up all the best seats in the center and front,
which had been roped off for them. Then the black people filtered
into the sections that were left. I sat next to Adele McCaskill, Bud's
new girlfriend, for whom I managed to ruin much of the show,
thanks to my inside knowledge of what came next. Still, it was hard
to take the thrill out of all the colored lights, sequined costumes,
heart-thumping music, and performers smiling so wide we could
hardly see their rouged cheeks and long eyelashes. I especially

admired the master of ceremonies, who wore a ringmaster's top hat and got to be on stage before and after every act, sharing the applause.

After a while it occurred to me that these people were my true brothers and sisters: showing off in front of the crowd, getting noticed and being loved. Besides, what was a show tune except a poem—like "Casey at the Bat"—set to music? I could see myself up there, singing and dancing and taking my bows—and best of all, traveling to Jackson and Memphis, even to Chicago and beyond.

After the final curtain, the crowd filed out. I ditched Adele and melted around the back to where the performers were taking off their costumes and gripmen packed away the props. I overheard that most of the cast was going to the 82 Bar and Grill for ribs, potato salad, and drinks. For the moment, though, I had to find the MC, to ask what I had to do to join the show. I looked for that big red top hat from one end of the group to the other, but never saw it. Finally I got noticed by a friendly face, a black janitor leaning on his broom and giving me the eye. I sidled up to him.

"So, how long you work for de show?" I asked, smiling prettily.

"I been *in* de show since Jackson," he said proudly. "See, my brother, he de manager. I be jest heppin' out till we gits to Memphis."

"What does you do?"

"I be a singer!"

"Oh—" I tried to sound more impressed than skeptical. "Well, I kin sang, too!"

"Is dat right?" He grinned. "Well, what be yo' name, sweet thang?"

"Ida Mae. But everybody call me Cat."

"Well, dat's a good name—Cat," his eyes narrowed. "I likes dat. You know, we be lookin' for a new gal what kin sang." He stared at my chest, but I don't think he was imagining how much air my lungs could hold. Before I could do anything, his hands followed his eyes. Still, I didn't flinch while he fondled my titties.

"Dat'll cost you," I said.

"Hell, gal," he replied, grinning, "I gits my bro right now! His name be Arv. I tell him to lissen to y'all sang, and 'f'n he like you, we take you wit' us when we pulls outta here."

"Well, dat's fine," I said, "but whats you got in mind still gonna cost you five dollars." It occurred to me I probably wasn't the first girl he'd sweet-talked about joining the show.

"Fi' dollars!" he said. "Why, gal—I ain't never paid dat much for no poon-tang an' ain't 'bout to start payin' it now!"

"Den I gi'e you some for three dollars, but you gotta fetch yo' bro soon as we done."

"One dollar. Den I fetches my bro."

I was running out of time, so I settled for a dollar. An hour later, Arv came back, with barbecue sauce on his chin, puffing a cigar. For my audition, I sang:

Why don't my goose
Sing as well as thy goose
When I paid for my goose
Twice as much as thine?

I danced the bootie green each time I sang "goose," but it didn't make any difference. Arv just stared in disbelief and walked away. I gave my dollar lover a hard look.

"You know any jokes, gal?" he said. "Sometimes dey hire gals what kin tell stories."

"I knows 'Casey at the Bat.' "

"Casey who?"

I put my feet in motion, and by the time I got home my anger and embarrassment had turned to despair. If the minstrel shows didn't want me, my only recourse was the carnival, like the one that put down stakes every year in the same pasture, as part of the Leflore County Fair. It wasn't as classy as the Silas Green and Rabbit Foot show, but it had games and thrill rides and belly dancers.

But it wasn't carnival season yet, so I killed time watching TV over at Miss Lizzy Bell Strong's. Miss Lizzie's white folks had given her the set at a time when very few black people had one, and there was always a crowd gathered around it, laughing and talking back to the performers.

I had outgrown the kiddie shows, and now preferred "The Lucky Strike Hit Parade" and westerns like "Gunsmoke." I began to pay attention to how the actors acted and what made a story good. None of them were black. Occasionally, Simon Jr.'s letters told about a TV appearance by Nat "King" Cole or Leontyne Price, colored singers respected even by white people. But even though Miss Leontyne came from Mississippi, her shows were blacked out in Greenwood. The white TV station managers had also spared us the newscasts showing black students trying to enroll at Little Rock High School, and the Arkansas governor, Orval Faubus, mobilizing his militia to resist them.

When the carnival came back to town, I was ready for it. I no longer cared about Dipping for Ducks or shooting like Annie Oakley or pitching pennies at glass dishes or breaking balloons with darts. I didn't want to be amazed by the Elephant Man or the Alligator Woman or the midget with three heads. I didn't even want any cotton candy or candied apples. All I wanted was to get to the little tent at the back of the lot where Howlin Wolf sang the blues and Miss Candy Quick, Queen of the Exotic Dancers, stole the show.

Candy Quick danced two times each night, at eight and eleven o'clock. I arrived near the end of the eight o'clock show. I gawked at the big color picture of Candy painted on the tent outside, then dug in the pocket of my borrowed pink pedal pushers for a pair of quarters and went in. The men stopped cheering for a minute; they had never seen a woman watch the show before. Then they resumed chanting—"Candy Quick! Candy Quick! Go on, Candy! Candy Quick!"—so loud I could barely hear the phonograph record that accompanied her.

Their eyes were glued to a toffee-colored female writhing half-naked on a little roped-off stage at the far end of the tent. She had a pot belly and saggy breasts, but I saw at once that for the men watching, at that moment she was for them the only woman in the world, Eve and Pandora rolled up in one. I imagined my face on the portrait out front, luring men by the hundreds to worship me with their quarters.

When the music stopped, the applause shook the tent. I hung back while the men filed out, smiling and laughing, and waited for the great woman to appear, accompanied by Nub Arm Preacher, who took tickets at the Walthall picture show and was acting like her bodyguard, and a fat white man, who acted like the boss. She accepted her 'mirations, then quick-marched through the carnival looking for her supper. I followed.

I screwed up my courage. "Say, ra—Miss Candy?"

"How you doin', li'l gal?" Candy flashed me a wide smile. "Ain't you de one dat come to de show?"

"Yas'm. You be de greatest, Miss Candy. You know, I be a dancer my ownself"—I cut a step or two I'd learned from Johnnie Mae and Pigeon at the juke houses, but Miss Candy barely watched—"and I wants to go wit' you, th'ow in wit' you and de carnie!"

Miss Candy looked annoyed. "Now you shoo on home, chile. You don't know nothin' 'bout nothin'."

But I wouldn't give up. I dogged her every footstep, pleading, whining, lying about my age, showing off my best streetwalker's walk.

"Aww, Candy," a deep male voice came from behind. "Why don'cha gi'e li'l Cat a chance?"

It was Nub Arm Preacher.

"Sheeet—she be jest a baby!" Miss Candy said, wrinkling her nose.

"Maybe she is." The fat white man leaned closer. "But that's how they like 'em, ain't it?"

Miss Candy wrapped her shawl tighter around her shoulders, thought a minute, then said, "All right, chile, you come 'long and we talk 'bout dis bidness. You see what you gittin' into and you gone run back to yo' mama *real* fast!"

But I didn't change my mind, not after we talked; not after we went back to the tent and I saw her whole act; not after I went home and dreamed about my stardust tour—north through the Delta all the way to Chicago.

FOR THE next few days, I met Miss Candy in her room next to the 82 Bar and Grill and took some lessons. She said there was nothing about "exotic dancing" that most women weren't born knowing. The trick was just letting yourself use what you knew in front of a crowd.

"You been wit' a man 'fore, ain't you?" she asked.

"Yas'm," I said. At least I didn't have to lie about that.

"Den think like you got dat sucker up front of you, and you be makin' love to him, but you can't use no hands—you hear what I'm sayin'?"

I heard. I thought about making love with Clyde Jones, and that did the trick. It was all so much easier than I'd expected. Miss

Candy gave me long, loving glances as I danced, although sometimes she cussed and said, "No, gal, do it like dis——" and then
she'd get up and show me. I imagine that I looked a lot like she did
at the start of her career.

When I had mastered fifteen minutes of slides and slithers,
bumps and grinds to her scratchy old record, Miss Candy finally
said, "Okay, Cat—you be ready to warm up de crowd. But you
ain't never gonna be no star less'n you got somethin' special to
gi'e."

I didn't know what that could be, so she gave me a suggestion
—a trick that had made her famous from Baton Rouge to Memphis. She'd had to give it up after too many men and too many
babies.

The carnival closed on Saturday, the night Miss Candy scheduled
my debut. I packed my pasteboard suitcase in secret and at dusk, I
blew a kiss to Mama's sleeping form and tiptoed out the door.
Outside, I gave Frisgo a big hug and made tracks down the cool
dark street without giving 119 East Gibb and my old life in Greenwood a parting glance.

"I'm gonna be famous, I'm gonna be known all de way to
Chicago, I'm gonna be Somebody!" I mouthed the words all the
way to the fairground.

I ARRIVED just in time to put on my makeup and get
into the costume I'd made from the odds and ends in Miss Candy's
trunk. A big crowd milled around our tent. As I passed through, I
heard the men grumbling.

"Say man, you hear de news?" Old Man Baker, who owned the
shoeshine stand, asked Mr. Cornell, the shoemaker. "Miss Candy
—she ain't dancin'!"

"What? Awww, man!"

"Naw, dey gots somebody I ain't never hear tell o'—de Delta Queen. Any y'all ever hear tell o' de Delta Queen?"

They all grumbled, and Nub Arm Preacher looked none too happy either. He got a dime for every dollar he brought in, and the pickings tonight looked slim. Fortunately, he had a brain under his hat—and he was my friend.

He stomped out his cigarette and waded into the crowd. "Now looky here, y'all," he said. "De bossman gots a suprise fo' y'all, dat's all. Miss Delta Queen be de most famous dancer in Chee-cago! Looka here, Elroy—you been to de nawth, ain't dat right?"

"Sho' thang!" Mr. Elroy answered proudly.

"Den if you beens to Chee-cago, you knows all 'bout Miss Delta Queen, ain't dat right?"

"Well, er, I—"

"C'mon now, man," said Nub Arm, "don't tell me you done made up dat whole trip!"

Mr. Elroy looked at all the eyes pointed his way and made his decision for Jesus. "No suh! I knows all 'bout de Delta Queen!" he said with great authority. "Oooeeee—dat's some gal!"

"Awright, den," Nub Arm said. "Now y'all git in dere while we still gots de seats. Dat's right. C'mon. Make it snappy. You gon' tell yo' grandsons 'bout dis night, I guaran-damn-tee it!"

The house filled up while Miss Candy helped me glue down my eyelashes and pin on the flame-red wig she hadn't worn in years. I puckered my lips and smeared on a whole fingerful of rouge.

"Okay, Miss Candy, Miss Delta," the bouncer said, pulling back the curtain. "Y'all gots a full house. Any time you is ready."

A thrill shot up my spine even as my stomach sank to my knees.

"Okay, honeybun," Miss Candy said. She stood back, admiring her work. "Break a leg!"

"Say what?"

"Dat jest mean good luck. Dat's how we show folk talk. Y'all gits out dere and dance yo' tail off. An' don't forgits yo' smokes!"

Show folk! I patted the gauzy scarf around my waist where I had stashed my Camels. I tied my wispy cape around my neck. Now it was all up to me.

The phonograph music started. I took a deep breath. Miss Candy's bouncer mistook my tremble for a nod and the curtain flew open. I was instantly blinded by the lights. A big hoot went up from the crowd.

I sashayed around the roped-off square, squinting at the crowd. In front were Mr. Elroy and Mr. Baker and Preacher Magee. I knew all three could recognize me, despite my wig, but who was looking at my face?

Almost on their own, my hips began to sway. My feet started sliding and my streetwalker walk took over. The row of dark faces passed—all gleaming smiles and big Mantan Moreland eyes. The biggest were on Reverend Booker, whose jaw dropped open as I sidled by. Finally someone had recognized me—but somehow it didn't matter. I wouldn't be around tomorrow to face Mama's recriminations.

The music swelled, and so did my audience. Off went the gossamer cape. Off went one flimsy scarf; off went the other. The cheers kept coming. The applause got louder. Suddenly, I realized they weren't clapping for a tittie or a flexing buttock or a glimpse of snatch: they were applauding *me*—all of me—for getting out there, for giving them something they needed, something no wife or girlfriend would dare. For ten wonderful minutes I was the only woman on earth. They deserved something extra.

I plucked a Camel from my sash and approached the front of the crowd. I put a cigarette to my lips and asked, "Now who gonna light my fire?"

A dozen lighters and matchtips flared. I picked one held by a scrawny little gent, sucked in the flame, and blew smoke back in his face. Bedlam.

"Lawdy, Lawdy—dat's my Delta Queen!" Mr. Elroy shouted. "I's gwone *marry* dat gal!"

Mr. Baker poked him in the ribs. "Dat's what you say 'bout Miss Candy Quick, Elroy. Y'all can'ts marry dem all!"

"Well, I kin dream, brother—*I kin dream!*"

I moved to the center of the stage and shimmied down to my knees. I lay back on my haunches, real sexy-like, waving my arms like branches in a storm, then leaned forward and took a drag on the Camel. That was the bouncer's cue to lift the phonograph needle. The music stopped. I opened my thighs and pulled back the little patch of fabric that covered my privates. The ragged cheers gave way to stunned silence. Carefully, I pushed that cigarette half its length into my vagina. As Candy taught me, I tightened my stomach until the red ash glowed. Then I relaxed, and a blue cloud billowed.

Gasps—laughter—the canvas walls shook with applause.

I puffed a few more times, then constricted my whole abdomen. I plucked out the cigarette with two fingers, lay back again on my haunches, spread my legs even wider, then relaxed and tightened my muscles in pulses. Magically, perfect little ovals of smoke emerged.

Screams of delight broke out, and the chanting started: *Del-ta! Del-ta! Delll—ta! Delll—ta!*

I rocked forward quickly and snapped my cloth back in place. Bouncer dropped the phonograph needle and the music blared. In one smooth motion I was back on my feet, holding the half-burned cigarette overhead like a trophy. I made one circuit of the stage, wriggling and grinning and winking, just out of reach of the clapping, groping hands. When I got to the rear of the stage, the curtain magically opened and I ducked through it.

Miss Candy, glowing in the dark, gave me a hug. Then she spun me around and gave my behind a shove.

"Curtain call, gal!" she shouted above the roar. "*Dey loves you!*"

Suddenly I was back in the spotlight. I bowed deep, the way I remembered Miss Candy bowing—a drop-down curtsy, one taut bare leg outstretched—then made another big circle of the stage, waving, and disappeared while they were still clapping. The phonograph needle ripped across the record. The lights snapped off. The show was over.

I took my time taking off my makeup. I put my street clothes on very slowly, savoring the moment when Miss Candy had said how great I was and how great I would be in Memphis and Chicago. *I was in show business.*

When the bouncer came backstage, he was all business. A couple of men behind him started striking the tent over my head.

"Gotta hit de road, gal," Miss Candy said. She had on her traveling clothes and was stuffing her costumes and makeup into a trunk. "Dat's half o' dis bidness, chile—packin' and unpackin'. You see mo' trains den a conductor and mo' miles den a teamster. Better gits used to it."

The bouncer said a small group of patrons wanted to make 'mirations over me outside. Miss Candy grinned and said, "Oh, all right. Y'all gwone and greet yo' new fans. I'll finish wit' dat."

I stepped into the crisp night air behind the bouncer and a half-dozen black faces lit up. I held up my hand like a princess, but nobody reached out to shake it. Mr. Elroy looked ashamed, and slipped out of the crowd.

"Dere, you see!" Mr. Cornell said. "I tol' you it be de li'l Cat —Aint Baby's Cat! Y'all de biggest fools 'round here—goin' on like she be from Chicago. Sheeet."

I ran back inside what was left of Miss Candy's tent. At least I'd never have to look at those faces again—not till the carnival came back. By then, I'd be a star with my own painted poster. Then I really *would* be from Chicago.

"C'mon, chile." Miss Candy helped me finish dressing. "I almost forgits—if you gonna hit de road, you gots t' have paper." She meant the contract I had yet to sign, which the carnival manager was supposed to have ready if Miss Candy agreed to take me with her.

We threaded our way through the maze of collapsing tents, stacks of scaffolding, and miles of coiled ropes and cable to the bossman's office, a little trailer at the center of the grounds. Outside, an older white man in a leather jacket was having a serious discussion with a strapping black man and two security guards. When we got closer, I saw that the black man was my brother.

"Bud!" I exclaimed brightly, but my spirits were sinking. His eyes were red, and he had one hand in the jacket pocket where he usually kept his razor. He reeked of liquor, and the two beefy guards at his elbows looked twitchy and nervous.

The bossman turned to me. "This boy here claims to be your brother. True?"

"Yassuh," I said meekly. "Dat's my bro. He name be Bud."

"I know his name, sweet pea. He says you're underage—too young to sign this contract. Is that right?"

"Mama gon' skin yo' hide!" Bud spat.

"That's enough, boy," the bossman said. The security guards edged closer. "Well, gal, are you eighteen or not?"

"Not yet," I said in a tiny voice.

"What'd you say?" the bossman bellowed. "I can't hear you, gal!"

"I say, nawsah, I ain't eighteen yet."

The bossman dug out his wallet and produced a five-dollar bill, which he tossed at my feet. "Now get them the hell outta here!" he barked at the guards and went back in the trailer.

I picked up the money, told Bud I'd meet him at the gate, and went back with Miss Candy to get my suitcase. She didn't say anything as we walked. I couldn't believe how fast the carnival had been reduced to a jumble of crates and boxes. When we arrived at the place where Miss Candy's tent used to be, my suitcase was tied in with a mass of rolled canvas and steel bars on the back of a flatbed truck.

"Dig out de gal's grip," Miss Candy told the bouncer. "She ain't goin' wit' us."

The ratty suitcase bumped at my feet. Nobody would look me in the eye except Miss Candy, and all she said was, "You take care o' yo'self now, Cat." She shook my hand and walked away.

I dragged myself and my suitcase to the main gate, where Bud was pacing furiously.

"I's sorry, Bud," I said meekly. "I jest—"

He slapped my face hard. He grabbed my suitcase and jerked me by the elbow down the road toward our house.

"You gon' git it now, Li'l Leg Cat! Mama fit to be tied—*fit to be tied!*"

Back on East Gibb, which I had not planned on seeing again for several years, our house lights were the only ones burning. Mama's eyes were as red as Bud's, but from crying, not from whiskey.

"Thank you, Bud," she said evenly, solemnly, as he slammed out of the house.

Mama just sat there looking at me, crying that silent cry. I wished that she would rant and rave, but she didn't. I took the suitcase into the middle room and hung my few things back on their nails. I felt a hundred years old. I washed my face and lay on my bed. I heard Mama rummaging around in the other room. I guessed she was looking for her wire strap. I waited awhile for her to come in and whup me or cuss me or do something, but she never did.

Instead that big old woman just shuffled up to the light cord and said, "Good night, Ida Mae. We talk 'bout dis in de mornin'."

She snapped off the light, and the room plunged into darkness.

N i n e

MAMA WHUPPED ME GOOD THE NEXT MORNING AND LOW-RATED ME FOR A WEEK. EVERY TIME SHE thought about me dancing, the tears began to flow and she'd get out her wire strap. "Dis ol' gal o' mine," she'd moan, "she done got on de wrong road, Lawdy, Lawdy."

Naturally, I didn't spend much time at home, but outside was even worse. I no longer had to worry if I was the talk of the town —I was. People passing me on the street seldom looked above my waist. Boys hooted and jeered and made grinding moves with their hips. Good girls turned up their noses and looked away. I wanted to be noticed, but not like that.

"Dey's actin' like dat 'cause you done come common wit' de mens," Mama said, "dancin' at de fair wit' yo' closes all up and showin' yo' tail to de whole world!"

One Saturday morning I was feeling especially sorry for myself, drinking RC and reading a Perry Mason at a back booth in Miss Lussie Bee's juke house. The only people who treated me decent these days were the juke house regulars. Greenwood's greatest gambler, Big Red Parker—who was five feet tall and black as a crow—swatted my behind and bought me RC's. Natty Mack Gilmore, the closest thing we had to a gangster (in Greenwood, a gangster was a man who owned a fancy car, dressed in the latest fashions, and drove slowly down the streets with his car windows rolled up against the Delta's heat and dust) whispered in my ear that he had connections for a brave girl like me. And Straw Boss dared the others to talk bad about me, saying, "Cat be my gal, even 'f'n she gits bigger!"

The cotton crop had been brought in, and this morning the place was filling fast with sharecroppers and wage hands from the plantations. Miss Lussie Bee was selling Falstaff and homebrew beer, Old Crow and sploe whiskey hand over fist—but covertly, in old RC bottles. Miss Lizzie Bell Strong and her Mothers of the Church were on one of their periodic visits to the juke joints. They all dressed in white and huddled close, sipping RC's and giving regulars the evil eye.

The plantation people kept the music going, with their hard-earned nickels and dimes. They especially liked the blues, which started from field hollers, after all. The closer they got to the record player, the more animated they became: dancing and prancing and acting and learning again how to enjoy themselves after a season of backbreaking labor.

The townspeople had a good time, too, because now they had an audience. Mr. Big Red Parker, Mack Gilmore, and Straw Boss rolled dice on the floor behind the long bar where Miss Dobbs, a white lady who was an outcast among her people, sat on her reserved stool. Miss Fanny Sims, who sipped her whiskey so daintily, was stretched out on the sawdust floor, drunk as a skunk, with her dress hiked above her moth-eaten bloomers. Her friend Old Dell, whom nobody messed with because she carried a razor, did the Camel Walk, to the delight of the country folk; she'd been known as Miss Odell until she got so nasty, and she was still deemed the best dancer in Mississippi. And Miss Crying Shame, an actress who always made 'mirations over me, play-liked she was the Queen of Sheba. "Dis here young'un jest wants to be in show business," she said as she patted my cheek. I was enjoying myself so much, it seemed to me if only I had some popcorn, everything would be perfect.

To get hot buttered popcorn, you had to go uptown, across from the post office, which sat catty-corner from the J.C. Penney and the army recruiting center. Not too many black people wandered this far uptown, especially not many black girls. Because the popcorn stand was whites only, we had to stand outside to be served, and while we were standing there, the white soldiers from the recruiting center would jeer and snicker and make obscene gestures at us—and sometimes feel our behinds, when they could get close enough. But today I bought my dime bag of popcorn without incident and walked quickly back. It wasn't that I was afraid of white men, I just didn't want them to get a *free* feel.

When I crossed Howard Street, I noticed a crowd of people— mostly church women and street kids, plus some teenage girls like me—surrounding a black soldier. He was a sight to behold: We had seen many white soldiers and a few black ones, but never a black Master Sergeant. His uniform was adorned with several stripes and gold braids on the sleeves, red cords on the shoulders, medals, and a big American eagle on the khaki chest. His spit-shined boots were so bright they made my patent-leather choir shoes look dull. Though he was only five feet tall, his pride made him stick up like a flagpole.

Without thinking, my feet propelled me to his side of the street. I dropped my popcorn and held my Perry Mason book up higher so this worldly soldier would know I was a cultured woman— a "different breed of Cat," no matter what he might have heard about me.

Our eyes met above the children's nappy heads. I have to tell you, it was love at first sight. I forgot about turning tricks and began thinking of wedding bells, shoes, and rice. As we stood there talking, a white army officer passed and returned the sergeant's snappy salute, proving he was a man to be reckoned with. We began walking toward Gritney, past Miss Lussie Bee's juke house to Spriggin's Cafe.

The Master Sergeant talked a lot about the army and not much about himself. To tell you the truth, I didn't care. What mattered to me was that he was clean and important and that given his career, he was bound to travel. If I couldn't be Somebody, like Mama, then I could surely marry somebody who was.

We stayed out late that night and visited a few of the juke joints. I couldn't go back to his quarters, he said, because women weren't allowed. So we made love under the trestle, and he promised to meet me the next evening.

"So, 'f'n you be engaged, Cat, where yo' ring at?" my friend May Liza teased me the next day.

"I didn't say I *be* engaged, girl," I answered testily, "I say I be goin' to *git* engaged."

Nothing comes between girlfriends faster than a new boyfriend. As the week wore on, my friends' jokes became some serious signifying, and I knew I'd have to make progress with my beau or get some better excuses. I invited him home to meet Mama, but for one reason or another, he thought that was a bad idea.

"Dat ol' scound don't mean you no good," Mama said when I told her he wasn't going to come visit. "I knows de Pigeon Drop when I sees it. Any kinda man dat mean some good woulda c'mere t' see yo' mama. Dat man y'all be callin' de Master Sergeant be lyin' t' you, Ida Mae. I betcha a fat man, he ain't even now in no army!"

By now Mama's complaints about me and my dreams were like wind rattling the windows. All I could think about was getting my diamond ring to flash around Miss Lussie Bee's and make May Liza and Pearlie and my other friends choke.

"Where yo' ring be at, Cat?" they asked in a singsong whenever they saw me.

"Oh, de Master Sergeant gone git it from Barranco's Jewelry Store," I'd answer.

Even though I lacked a ring to make it official, the juke house gang gave me an engagement party. Miss Crying Shame played like a bride, and we both got all teary when she said, "I do." Old Dell dedicated a new Camel Walk to me, Miss Fanny offered me a drink of her precious whiskey, Miss Dobbs gave me an old head scarf, and Miss Lussie Bee gave me five dollars. Mr. Big Red Parker even patted me on the back instead of the butt, and Mack Gilmore whispered his good wishes until Straw Boss growled and called them back to their card game. The only dent in my happiness was that the Master Sergeant couldn't attend; he was "O.D."—on duty —he explained.

Meanwhile, the Master Sergeant and I courted all over town, holding hands. He always helped me over the curb and pulled out my chair when we sat down. When it rained, he called a cab and Buddy Boy drove us around Greenwood. Some of the townspeople, including a few of my so-called girlfriends, told him that I was a " 'ho' who gits nekkid 'fore de mens," but he ignored them. He already knew what he needed to know about me, and what he knew, he liked.

Three weeks after we met, I finally maneuvered him into promising me a ring. I invited May Liza and Pearlie to sit with me on my porch and bear witness on the Saturday afternoon when he was supposed to present it.

"You be some kinda lucky Cat," May Liza said, stuffing a wad of snuff into her bottom lip. "You done kotch a big fish—bigger den ever be kotch by us Greenwood wimmens." She looked to Pearlie for agreement.

We killed time by planning my wedding. Pearlie volunteered to make my wedding dress, and May Liza said she'd curl my hair. We talked and laughed about what food to serve and who would come and who wouldn't be invited, and before we knew it, it was dark.

"He be here directly, Cat, don't worry," May Liza said, but she didn't sound as if she believed it.

"Yeah," Pearlie added, "you know how dem white folkses be when dey see a colored man come in to buy a diamond. Dey think he musta stole de money and try to keep him busy till somebody kin check wit' de police. It ain't nothin'. He be 'long in a little while."

"I sho' 'nough hope he ain't sick uptown," I said, trying to sound like a worried wife. "Or in de jailhouse."

In truth, I was mostly worried about being humiliated. Dinner time came and went, but we didn't eat. Bud went out to drink and Mama went to bed and put out the lights. Still, we sat on the darkened porch like three hens locked out of the coop, waiting for my prince to come. By midnight we'd run out of excuses and encouraging words. My friends went home and I went inside to count the roaches.

The next morning Mama dished up harsh medicine for breakfast. "I knowed he be up to no good," she said. "Dat ol' skunk—you be gon' marry somebody a whole heap better den him. Good riddance, I says." She swept out the kitchen with great angry swings. "He come back 'round here, I go upside his head wit' dis broom!"

For the next few days, I nursed the hope that he might show up, but I never saw him again. I didn't want my friends' pity, so I just stayed inside and moped. Finally, Miss Lussie Bee stopped by to give me a report on her own investigation.

She had stopped by the army recruiting office downtown. She said a man in an army uniform had come to Greenwood and made promises to a local girl, then left her "seduced and abandoned." The white soldiers on duty listened patiently, then laughed.

"We ain't got no nigger Master Sergeant at any post 'round

here," one of them told her. An older soldier at a desk farther back flipped through some papers and called out, as if Miss Lussie Bee wasn't even standing there:

"What'd that gal say the boy's name was?"

"She don't know his name, Cap'n," the young soldier answered.

"Us'n jest call him de Master Sergeant," Miss Lussie Bee said, now feeling about three inches high.

"Sounds like that old boy they had over at 'lanta," the captain said, closing his folder. "Remember? Georgia Guard sent out a letter on some nigger runnin' 'round impersonating a Master Sergeant."

The young man grinned up at Lussie Bee. "You heard the Cap'n, Grandma. It's against the law to pretend to be in the army. So if you gals get your hands on him, make sure to leave somethin' for us."

I had been embarrassed before, and I was willing to take my lumps. But this was something different: a slap in my face as a woman. It was also another setback to my plan for escaping the Delta.

It was a month before I ventured outside, even to go to the store, and again as long before I dared show my face at Miss Lussie Bee's juke house. As it turned out, I needn't have worried.

The plantation workers and sinners and drunks and regulars welcomed me back like a long-lost sister. Nobody made fun of my mistake, even after all my bragging. Instead they blamed the "Master Sergeant" for tricking us all, and making us look the fool. They invited me to "do my callin' " on the sawdust floor, a high honor I couldn't refuse. But even as I gave them my patented rendering of "Casey at the Bat," I knew this would be my last recitation, especially when I reached the "okey doke" and Casey had to strike out. Something told me I had been associating myself with this loser just a little bit too long.

I needed a new source of inspiration, and it came in a roundabout way. Irving Neal and Johnny B. were inseparable buddies who were a little bit older than me. They had watched me recite from the doorway of Miss Lussie Bee's (they were too nice to go inside) and waited for me on the sidewalk. They said how great I was and asked if I would like to dance and drink beer with them at the Big 25, a truly hep place I had visited on the arm of my Master Sergeant.

Big 25 was somewhere between a juke joint and the big-city club it aspired to be. Johnny B. spun records there on weekends and drew a more mature crowd that included fewer drunks and gangsters. I spotted a girl I knew, Jackson Street Cat, and her boyfriend, Joe Lewis. I had no interest whatsoever in hanging out with two nice boys, so once we were there, I went strollin'. I was open to turning tricks (after staying home for three months, I was flat broke), but what I really wanted was somebody to take the sting of the Master Sergeant from my soul. I didn't have to hunt long.

One of the first men I spotted was a sharp dresser a few inches taller than the Master Sergeant, but with hazel eyes and much better looking. After Jackson Street Cat introduced us, I had no trouble holding his attention and getting him to buy me a drink. What happened after that took on a life of its own.

His name was Ike. He was from Rome, Mississippi, and worked for the Butane Gas Company driving a service truck. This was a prestigious job because most days he rode around checking out people's gas cylinders, not even wrinkling his uniform. He was single and seemed to like me, so right away an angel who looked like Mama popped up on my shoulder and whispered, "Now be careful, Ida Mae—don'cha mess dis one up!"

Later that night, Ike and I piled into the backseat of Joe Lewis's car, with Joe and Jackson Street Cat up front, and the four of us headed for the juke houses that sat across the road from each other at the Buckeye. When Joe swerved to miss a hole in the road, I was thrown into Ike's lap. He kissed me, and I kissed him back. I had never felt so warm and protected and loved before.

Every weekend afterward we went for long rides in Ike's car, a green late-model Chevrolet. He drove proudly and slowly through the Delta's small towns—Money, Wyonia, Pugh City—as we talked about love, death, responsibility, family, and marriage. He was kind and respectful to me, and he seemed to be honest. When he asked if I'd go to a roominghouse with him sometime, I took a few moments to review my social calendar and said yes, and we set a time for him to pick me up.

So there I was again, sitting on May Liza's porch across the street from my house with May Liza and Pearlie, eating watermelon, trying to quiet May Liza's baby, waiting for my prince to come. This time, I set my sights lower: He didn't have to marry me and take me from the Delta and make the rest of my life perfect. I just prayed to God he'd show up.

"Set down, Cat," May Liza said, hunting around for her mama's spittoon (she was still trying to learn to dip snuff). "You be makin' me nervous."

"Never you mind, Cat," Pearlie reassured me. "He be comin'. Yo' luck *gots* t' change. Here—have a piece o' dis here melon."

That's just what I needed to make sure Ike would come—spill watermelon juice down my dress! And if that didn't drive him away, there'd be May Liza's bawling brat, wailing like a siren. He'd probably think it was mine. Still, both May Liza and Pearlie had husbands. They knew about men. They knew about *getting* men. They knew it was my turn.

"From what you been sayin', Cat, it sound like he really likes you," Pearlie said. "But don'cha worry. Once we see him, we smoke him over. We kin tell rat off 'f'n he mean you some good."

I was still too nervous to sit down. I wobbled back and forth on my borrowed high heels, recalling Mama's last words on the subject:

"He jest wanna git you in de bed, Ida Mae," she'd said. "He jest playin' 'round wit' you. He done heared how big a fool you be from de other mens—taking up wit' any stranger dat hit town and have on a uniform—army or Butane Gas Company, it don't make no diff'rence." Mama talked like I was the only girl in Gee Pee to ever get jilted, though what she meant was, I was the only girl of *hers* to get jilted—what happened to me reflected back on her. At least she closed on a hopeful note—"Well, we gwine see, we'll see"—rather than her usual, "Ida Mae, chile, you is on de fast track to nowheres!"

And sure enough, there was Ike's beautiful green Chevy, turning the corner off Walthall and pulling up in front of my house, the eyes of the toy dog in the back window lighting up as he put on the brakes. May Liza's and Pearlie's jaws dropped open. "Cat—you done hit paydirt!"

Ike sat in his car, smiling like a polecat, while the neighborhood kids made 'mirations over his Chevy. It was all we three girls could do to pretend we didn't see him. After a minute, he got out and stretched like Tarzan. His short-sleeved sport shirt was crisp-ironed —no cat-faces—and I hoped Mama was looking. His trousers hung just right over his alligator shoes.

"Looka dere at dem shoes!" May Liza said from the corner of her mouth, eyes straining sideways in her head so Ike wouldn't notice her "smokin' him over." I looked around and noticed Miss Susie's and Dossie Ree's faces peeking out of their windows, too.

When I thought enough time had passed, I pretended to notice Ike for the first time, waved, and ran across the street.

"Hi dere, Ida." He grinned at me. "You be lookin' great!"

"You, too," I said, beaming. I noticed a grocery bag in the front seat. "What be in de sack?"

"I brought your Mama some cold RC's."

Mama stood in the doorway of our house with the expression of a child on Christmas morning.

"How do, Miss Ida Mae," Ike said, nodding politely and smiling his most charming smile. "I hope you be thirsty this fine day!"

Mama's grin got so wide it spilled off her face. She shook hands with Ike and made a big show of inspecting each bottle as she took it from the sack. "Well, Lawd amercy!" Her eyes clouded with tears. "Look-a-here, my son-in-law done brung me some snuff."

I had to go pee, so I ran inside, taking the risk of leaving them alone. When I came back, Mama and Ike were laughing and chatting like old friends. From that day forward, no matter what he did to me, Ike could do no wrong in Mama's eyes.

That night, Ike and I danced cheek to cheek at the Big 25. After that, we went for a snack at Booker's Cafe and shared from each other's plates. We held hands and kissed at Sam Ciroe's and went to Black Mary's to make love.

"I loves you, Ida," Ike whispered. "I don't care what you done 'fore we be's degether."

"I loves you, too, Ike—more den I ever love anysomebody!"

We courted hard and heavy. We were separated only when Ike went to work. We even wore matching clothes. We became an item. People started going to the same juke houses that we went to, because they wanted to be in the same place we were. I tried to distance myself from my old reputation. I gave up my wide-legged stride for slow, measured steps that often tripped me up. I no longer had to turn tricks because Ike was giving me money every two weeks.

Months after Ike and I started going together, Mr. Charlie, an old man who was my "sugar daddy" from Baptist Town, sent a boy to our house with a crudely printed note summoning me to his house. Before I met Ike, I would slip into Mr. Charlie's house by the back door every week and we would have "dry sex"—meaning we'd paw and fondle each other on the bed for hours and then he'd mount me, clothes still intact, and grind and wiggle until he fell off me with a satisfied cry. Sometimes he cried like a baby, and sometimes he gave me fifty dollars and some food. But all of that was behind me now.

Still, I decided I owed Mr. Charlie an explanation. I went to his house reluctantly, knowing it was the last time I would visit him. I decided to go in the front door. His next-door neighbors were sitting on their porch, fanning to keep the heat and mosquitoes away.

"You done made up yo' mind, Cat?" Mr. Charlie asked, after I told him about Ike. " 'Cause I ain't takin' you back."

"I be in love," I told him. "I don't want nosomebody else. But we kin be friends." I wanted to keep the door open, just in case.

We talked awhile longer and I felt Mr. Charlie's eyes boring into me in the dim room. I heard him weep softly and hawk and spit and blow his nose.

"Charlie—uh, Charlie—who dat you got in dere?" a woman's voice called out, laughing all the while.

"Dis ain't yo' bizness, 'oman, tend t' yo' own self bizness," Charlie hollered back, laughing and wiping his eyes. I could tell he was pleased to have her ask.

We hugged our good-bye and he saw me to the door. The neighbors were still on the porch, and I realized I knew one of them, a woman I'd seen and spoken with at the Big 25.

"I know you, too!" she said. Her name was Eva Mae, and she introduced me to her mother, Miss Gertrude Brown, the woman who had called out.

"Charlie, you be sixty-odd years old, and foolin' 'round wit' dis young gal—you oughta be 'shame of yo'self, old man." Miss Gertrude chastised him fondly. They hollered back and forth, exchang-

ing quips and playfully signifying. "Come on in, Cat," Miss
Gertrude said to me, "and have some of these greens." Eva Mae
invited me in and fixed me a plate of the best candied yams, fried
chicken, cornbread, and greens I'd ever eaten.

From that day, Miss Gert welcomed me to her house and table
and treated me like a daughter. She was a tall, big-boned woman
who had several children, of whom Eva Mae was the only one left
at home. She lived well off a pension her husband had left her.

Eva Mae was about the same height and build as her mother,
with short hair, a round face, and a kind, gentle disposition. She
wore the most beautiful clothes I'd seen, and she didn't have to
work outside the home. Her only job was taking care of her baby
girl and Miss Gert. Eva Mae and I became good friends, almost
like sisters, the way Everlena and I had been. But Eva Mae didn't
smoke, and she had an easygoing nature. She let me look through
her closet and choose whatever I wanted to wear, even if it was
brand new.

I would walk into the Big 25 on Ike's arm, wearing Eva Mae's
clothes, which looked just right on me. I even gained a few pounds
so that they would fit me better. We introduced Eva Mae's boyfriend to Ike, hoping they would become buddies so that we could
double-date. But although the men were cordial, they never became
real friends. When the bar closed, Ike and I would take Eva Mae
home, if her boyfriend wasn't there. Then we'd go to the closest
roominghouse to have sex.

A few months later, around Halloween, I was out in the wood-
house, vomiting up my breakfast.

Bud stood in the yard and watched me, smirking, then ran to
tell Mama.

"Ida Mae, gal." Mama loomed over me like a thunderstorm in
the wood house. "You finally done it! You got bigged!"

"No'm, I ain't! I swears it!"

Mama started to cry, and for the second time ever, I heard it—a low gurgling like the sound a drowning person might make. "I wants mo' for you den you wants fo' yo'self!" she moaned. "I wants you to go down yon'er to Campbell College in Jackson wit' Susie's gals. I wants you to make Somebody outta yo'self. But you —you be satisfied wit' any Tom, Dick, or Harry dat come down de street! Whose it be, anyways? Who done got you in de family way?"

"Ike," I said hopefully. If I had to throw a bomb, it might as well be that one.

Mama recoiled, covering her mouth like she was going to throw up herself, and fumbled for a chair. She acted so stunned, she would've put Miss Crying Shame to shame. Never mind that none of her own children ever had a regular daddy.

"Well," she said finally, " 'least I know everthang gwine be all right. Dat Ike—he be a real man, he gwine do de right thang by you. Tell him I wants to see him."

"Tell dat sucker I be watchin' him, too!" Bud piped in.

I told Ike in the backseat of his car, after a heavy petting session. "Ike, I be bigged," I said. "Gon' have yo' baby."

I was braced for him to cuss, jump out of the car, or hit me. But instead he just grinned.

"Well, I be," he said. "I's gonna be a daddy! *Hot damn!*" He hollered into the night, "I's gonna be a *daddy!*"

Not long after that, Ike and Mama had a long, private talk. Afterward, Ike and Bud drove off to have their own talk, man to man. Even though I was going to be the mother, I was not deemed mature enough to take part in either of these discussions. All I knew was that every Friday, like clockwork, Ike called for me and took me out. On Saturdays, when he used to hang with his friends, he parked his car out front of our house and washed it, or worked on the engine. On Sundays—most Sundays, anyway—he went to his cousin Sammy's house in Dixie Lane alley and went to sleep until we came back from church. He was the most visible man any of us in Gee Pee had ever known. And he was mine.

Now, you might think all this was just what I wanted—and you'd be right, as far as it goes. But what occurred to me after a few months of this, as the days got colder and longer and my belly got bigger, was that with a local boy who had a good job and was respectful of my mama, I wouldn't be going anywhere—least of all out of the Delta.

Ten

BY THE TIME I STARTED SHOWING, IKE HAD
MADE HIMSELF SCARCE. AND WHEN HE WAS AROUND,
he wasn't fun anymore—just dutiful, distant, and aloof. The only
time he smiled was when he felt the baby kicking in my stomach.

This change in him, along with the changes going on in me, gave
me a scare. I had seen other girls my age who had "grown up" too
fast. Weighed down with crying babies and dirty diapers, they
searched the juke houses for their children's daddies to beg for
milk money. They seemed doomed to the Delta. I had laughed at
them, vowing I would never let the same thing happen to me. But
here I was. The townspeople looked at me scornfully, saying, "Dat
Cat, I tol' you she be no good."

I couldn't dance. I couldn't run. I couldn't borrow Eva Mae's
pretty clothes anymore. I couldn't even sit in one place for very
long to read my Perry Mason novels.

I took to visiting Miss Gert every day and crying and telling her
about my dream of getting out of the Delta. She listened patiently
and cried with me.

"Now, Cat, ain't no need to cry now," she said kindly. "Jest
don't git wit' no mo' chilluns. G'won in yon'er an' git some-teet
to eat." Even Mr. Charlie relented and began bringing greens
and other vegetables for Eva Mae "to cook up for dat bigged gal,
Cat."

I heard Ike was dating a girl from the local college. Enraged, I
asked Mr. Charlie to drive me to the outlying juke houses to see if
I could spot his car, but I never found him. I felt like a trapped rat

—and anybody who'd lived in Gee Pee very long knew what those critters were like. Something had to give, and it did.

I became a thief.

My friends Coot and her sister Big Sis, Miss Tillie Mae, an older woman who was married to a much younger man, and my sister Jean, who was now housekeeping with a man named Eddie and living on Big Egypt Plantation, helped get me started, but it didn't take much of a push. I was tired and cranky and angry all the time —as if I'd been robbed myself.

We met on Saturday mornings at Miss Tillie Mae's house in the alley behind Howard Street. None of us, except Miss Tillie Mae, had ever stolen from the big department stores. We were awed by her knowledge and nerve in "gittin' back whatsonever b'long t' us," as she preached, quoting from the Bible to back herself up (at least it sounded like the Bible). She taught us how to distract the saleswomen, how to steal clothes, where and how to hide them, and how to look and act completely innocent. One girl from Gritney, Doot, said Miss Tillie Mae didn't know as much about stealing as she claimed, and that we'd end up in jail. So she stomped off, and Jean almost followed. But the lure of pretty clothes kept the rest of us there.

For the next two Saturdays, we stole clothes and trinkets from the department stores in the colored areas uptown. I even managed to steal a diamond ring from Barranco's jewelry store. We each kept our own loot. Jean and I had to slip ours past Mama, into the middle-room closet and the wood house.

On the third Saturday we ventured downtown to the stores in the white area. We decided to try the Stork Shop, a maternity shop on River Road. Coot and Big Sis kept the white saleslady busy while Miss Tillie Mae and I stuffed clothing under our skirts. Jean shielded us by holding up dresses against her fat body—colored girls weren't allowed to take clothes into the fitting rooms, lest we

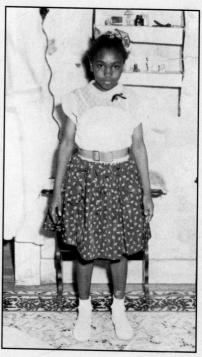

Me, three years old.

Me, age nine and a half.

(Courtesy of the Holland
Family Archives)

(Courtesy of the Holland
Family Archives)

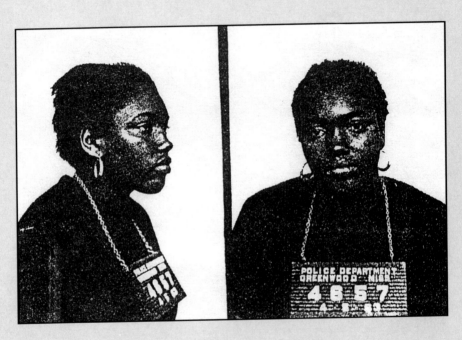

My mug shot, from the 1960s.

My family, the
late 1950s:
Mama.

Simon Jr.

Bud.

Jean.

Greenwood: 114 East
Gibb Street—my birth
house refurbished.

McLaurin Street, Gritney.

(Courtesy of Habibi Minnie Wilson)

Ike, my first husband.

(Courtesy of the Holland Family Archives)

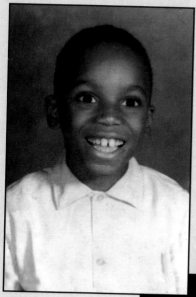

Cedric in Greenwood,

eight years old.

(Courtesy of the Holland Family Archives)

Me, Cedric, and

Mary Davis

(Muh Dear, Ike's

mother), 1985.

(Courtesy of the Holland Family Archives)

Easter Mae,

Greenwood.

*(Courtesy of the
Holland Family
Archives)*

May Liza and Pearlie,

childhood friends.

*(Courtesy of Habibi
Minnie Wilson)*

Horace Laster, M.D.,

my esteemed mentor.

(Courtesy of the Laster
Family Archives)

Everlena, my childhood friend.

(Courtesy of the Holland Family Archives)

With my New York
host family,
the Childses, and
Cousin Mabel
on a SNCC
speaking tour.

*(Courtesy of the
Holland Family
Archives)*

With my first cousin T.C.

(Courtesy of the Holland Family Archives)

Street life in Minneapolis, early 1970s.

(Courtesy of the Holland Family Archives)

In Buffalo with the poet Amiri Baraka, nearly thirty

years after the premiere of his play <u>The Dutchman</u>.

(Courtesy of Baba Simba Mlee)

Graduation Day. I accept my Ph.D. from

the University of Minnesota.

(Courtesy of the Holland Family Archives)

Manning a mock polling place with other

civil rights activists, Greenwood, 1963.

(Courtesy of Matt Herron)

March following Medgar Evers's

funeral, Jackson, Mississippi.

With Oprah Winfrey and Bob Moses.

steal them. When we'd stashed our fill, Miss Tillie Mae and I walked out, followed shortly by our accomplices. When we got nearer to Goldberg's shoe store in Gee Pee, we laughed like hell and took out the prizes we stole from the best white maternity store in town. We low-rated the white folks for being so gullible and stupid and made 'mirations over each other while we walked back to Johnson Street.

That's when the patrol car pulled up. The saleslady, sitting like a fussy bird on the edge of the backseat, pointed us out. I'd made the mistake of stealing the most expensive maternity dress in the store, so she'd noticed it missing right away. Jean broke and ran toward Kornfeld's, but the owner ran and locked the door. Coot and Big Sis ran toward their house on the low end of Johnson Street. Miss Tillie Mae made an abrupt turn into the Dixie Theater. And I just strolled down the street like I didn't see the police beckoning to me.

After booking us at the Greenwood police station, the police chief and two officers took Jean and me back to our house in handcuffs. Mama let them in without a word; she just started those silent waterworks. The police ransacked our house front and back and found every bit of loot Jean and I had pilfered.

"Coot an' Big Sis an' Miss Tillie Mae be wit' us!" Jean hollered, although I was begging her with my eyes to say nothing.

"Well, I be damn," one cop said, emerging from the back room where Jean and Eddie slept on the weekends, when they visited from the country. He held up a satin jewel case. "Here's a watch from Barranco's!"

"Uh-huh," said another, from the doorway behind him. "Chief —y'all oughta come an' looka here."

The police chief took off his sunglasses and squinted at the evidence. "You li'l gals in a heapa trouble. This here's a Ninety-nine Fifty—grand larceny."

"Barranco's! Barranco's! As de Lawd be my secret judge, Chief," Mama wailed, "dese here fast-tail, 'omanish gals done took de white folkses' stuff on dey own. I ain't got *nothin'* t' do wit' it!"

"Well, dey be goin' to jail, Aintie," the Chief said. "Can't help that none."

"Jail!" Mama wailed. "Lawd, Lawd, Lawd—y'all can't put my baby gal in de workhouse! She gon' have a baby herownself real soon!"

I pushed out my belly even farther and tried to look ten years old.

"Aw, hell, Aintie—that don't matter none to Cap'n Arterberry. He knows how to handle gals that 'bout ready to foal." The officers laughed.

Mama clasped her hands. "Y'all don't need to take both my chilluns. My gal Jean—dat big-un dere—she ain't never done no harm to nosomebody. I ain't sayin' she never gits drunk, but she ain't never 'fo' now be stealin' from no white folkses!"

The chief faced her. "I'm sorry, Aintie. Truly. But it's outta my hands now."

They loaded our loot into a police van, then led Jean and me out through a gauntlet of our silently staring neighbors and back to the patrol car that brought us. As we pulled away from the curb, I saw May Liza and Pearlie waving and shouting, " 'Bye, Cat! 'Bye Jean! Don't worry—we loves you!"

Well, I thought, at least we're leaving in style—this looks like some kind of parade.

THE NEXT Monday our gang—except Miss Tillie Mae, who the court decided was too near her delivery date and gave probation—were sentenced to thirty days in the Leflore County Penal Farm, known as "the workhouse," and fined a hundred dollars each. The Leflore County Penal Farm was a country club compared to the state penitentiary at Parchman, I would learn later. Where you were sent was determined by the severity of the crime. Most often, if the offense was against another black person and you had a white person to speak on your behalf, you'd serve "easy time" in the city or county jails. If you were found guilty of a minor infraction involving whites, like stealing less than a hundred dollars or prostitution, and you had a white person to speak up for you, you'd land workhouse time. If the misdeed involved murder or armed robbery or a considerable theft and you had no white spokesperson, you were sent to dreaded Parchman.

Given the amount we'd stolen, our sentence was a slap on the wrist and everyone knew it. The judge was one of Mama's ironing customers, and he didn't want to get any cat-faces in those fine linen shirts he wore under his black robe. And we had two white people, Mr. Pete and Miss Ellen, the white storekeepers, to speak up for us.

We rode to the workhouse in pairs. I rode with Jean, which was something of a comfort. Actually, I wasn't scared at all—at least until we got there. We turned off the highway onto a bumpy dirt road marked "Property of Leflore County." In the distance we could see several white frame buildings surrounded by well-kept fields. Here and there, colored work gangs in striped uniforms chopped weeds and hoed the rich earth. But most convicts, I knew, were leased out to private companies to maintain the railroad lines and levees.

Jean exploded in tears. "I ain't got no business here! I didn't git nuttin'!" She rocked back and forth on the seat. "Y'all gotta tell dem white folkses dat I ain't knowed y'all be stealin'!"

"We done tole dem dat you ain't no rogue—you be de blocker!"
I said. "Dey don't lissen. Now we gots t' look after our owndearself."

Jean was spooked by the place, but I was fine until the door to
the main building opened and a big guard dog came out, straining
on its leash. His coat was shiny satin—the kind of fur that comes
from eating lots of meat. He was half as tall as the person who led
him, a khaki-dressed white man who looked like Gene Autry, in a
ten-gallon hat and hand-tooled cowboy boots. The muscles on his
forearm rippled as he worked to restrain the dog, now barking to
beat the band and throwing flecks of foam all over the yard.

"Cap'n Arterberry," our deputy-driver informed us.

"I see," I grunted like Mama. "An' who be de one in de hat?"

"Hesh-up, dere, Frisk boy!" Cap'n Arterberry shouted. "Take it
easy, dere, big boy!" He pounded the dog on the shoulders until
Frisk shut up, panting and slobbering and wagging his tail.

"Howdy do, Cap'n," our driver said, handing him our paperwork. "Got two more for you. Shoplifters, so you better keep
your eye on 'em. 'Specially dis li'l gal here. She's got a belly full."

Cap'n Arterberry gave us the once-over through the car window.
"Okay," he said. "Git 'em outta there."

Jean and I scooted out and stood in the dusty compound in our
manacles. At the jailhouse, we'd heard all kinds of stories about the
workhouse and its keeper, but Bud and Simon Jr. had both done
time here and said it "weren't nothin'." The neighbor women
claimed that Mama had once served time here, too, for accepting
stolen sheets.

Cap'n Arterberry was sizing Jean up. "Well, this is a big one,"
he said. Then he looked at me. "An' this one's big. I'd say I got a
real big one and one that's real big, wouldn't you, Frisk?" The dog
barked and the Cap'n yanked his chain. That was the first and last
time we'd see Cap'n Arterberry smile.

I looked at the workhouse and saw Coot's and Big Sis's smiling faces pressed against the bars, welcoming us. I threw back my shoulders and fairly strutted into prison.

The women's dorm was a long, low room with half a dozen metal bunk beds along two sides. The windows were so dirty they looked frosted. Only up close could you see the wire mesh embedded in the glass. A half-enclosed bathroom separated the beds on the left side of the room: a row of doorless toilet stalls and two sinks without a mirror. The single shower room was as big as a carwash. When we arrived, there were no other female prisoners besides the four of us.

The men's prison was behind a fence across the hall. It contained several large cells with bunk beds that slept about fifty men. It was usually filled to capacity, but at the moment there were only about forty male prisoners. I'd hear later that our arrival caused a lot of talk; some of the colored men had planned to sneak into our facility after hours, when Cap'n Arterberry wasn't around. I gathered such visits weren't uncommon even for the one white prisoner, who had a cell to himself and didn't go out with the regular chain gang but instead worked around Cap'n Arterberry's house, raking leaves and doing other odd jobs.

Since I was pregnant, I got a nice lower bunk at the center of the dormitory, close to the bathroom. We spent the rest of the day talking about how fast our relatives and the public defenders were going to get us out of there, though nobody believed it, especially Jean. At six, we wheeled left out the door and marched in a straight line to the dining room. Inside was one long table—actually, a whole lot of tables slid together end to end—with clattery benches along the sides. The kitchen was behind a long serving window from which we drew our tin plates and plastic spoons (no knives or forks were allowed) before sitting down. A tough-looking, heavyset, very dark skinned colored woman with long curly hair passed behind us dispensing a slab of thick bologna, a big heavy biscuit, and a half cup of molasses on each plate.

"Which one of y'all be bigged?" she asked.

"I is." I held up my hand.

"Hmph." She waddled over to between Jean and me and dropped an extra biscuit on my plate. When she was gone, I gave it to Jean.

"Nug!" the woman shouted. "Nug—where you be? C'mere an' brang dese gals some buttermilk! Hurry up, man—ain't got all day!"

A thin, light-skinned black man clad in a worn service uniform appeared with two pitchers. "Here 'tis, Miss Laurel."

"Fill up dat gal's glass first," Miss Laurel commanded, pointing at me. "She gon' have a young'un."

As Nug poured, he kneeled on the bench and rubbed his leg against my thigh. I looked up at him and he winked back.

After dinner, we filed back to our building. The male inmates, who had now come back from the fields, whistled and called to us from across the hall. Suddenly Miss Laurel appeared in the dorm. Without saying a word to us, she headed for the bathroom, and the odor of a bowel movement assaulted our noses.

"Bence dis be y'all first time here," she said, washing and wiping her wet hands on the rough toilet tissue, "de Cap'n he done gi'e me 'thority to lay de rules out t' y'all."

"Yas'm," we said, trying to sound serious.

"De Cap'n, he be de bossman. Dere be three of us'n afder him: me, Nug, an' L.C. De boss done gi'e me de say-so over dis farm. I runs de kitchen, and I says when an' what y'all eat. Me an' Nug be married up—an' I sho' 'nough got de say-so over dat!" Miss Laurel paused to let this information sink in. "Now, L.C. be de trusty—dat dere means he still be a convict—but he be 'llowed t' go huntin' wit' de Cap'n an' handle Frisk. Nug an' L.C. be de onliest mens 'llowed 'round y'all gals." She looked each of us in the eye.

I could see that Miss Laurel wasn't used to making such a long speech, but seeing that she had our undivided attention, she leaned forward and said, "It don't pay to mess wit' L.C., 'cause he be some kinda ornery. He got drunk an' cut up his 'oman real bad. De white lady dat his 'oman work for had him sent here. He be lucky dat white lady didn't have him sent t' Parchman Prison." She hawked and spat into the balled-up wad of toilet tissue. "His 'oman, dat crazy fool, begged de jedge not t' gi'e him mo' den a year— dats de onliest thang dat keep him outta Parchman. I swear, 'f'n he hada done dat t' me, deyda be puttin' him in de graveyard!"

"I 'spect you woulda, Miss Laurel, 'cause you is some kinda lady —no man in his right mind would try t' cut you," I said, aiming to get on her good side.

"You kin bet yore bottom dollar on dat! How be ever, 'f'n I ketch Nug wit' anysomebody, dey be a dead duck—y'all git de pitcher?"

"Yeah," I said, "stay away from Nug!"

"You got dat right, gal!" Miss Laurel laughed and said good night, patting my stomach. She and Nug slept on a cot in a tiny room behind the kitchen that had once been the "hole," where any convict who broke a rule was placed.

Although I expected trouble from Nug, L.C. was the first one to bother us. Where Nug was sly, snaggle-toothed L.C. was just crude and dangerous. He had a thing for fat girls, which meant Jean was prime fish. He told Miss Laurel and the Cap'n that he suspected Jean of smuggling contraband out of the kitchen, so he searched her after every meal—a degrading ritual that let him run his nasty hands all over her while he whispered dirty trash in her ear. Nobody stood up to L.C. because Cap'n Arterberry liked him. L.C. had all kinds of special privileges, like going into the women's dorm when the Cap'n wasn't present. On one of these visits, he lined us all up in front of our bunks to "see if we had weapons."

"I betcha y'all gots somethang hid underneath dese titties," he said, feeling under Jean's big bosom.

"You better be gone, L.C.," Jean said, knowing there wasn't a damn thing she could do about it, or him. "You knows I ain't got no razor. Leave me 'lone."

"Y'all gots somethang, Big Mama." L.C. grinned. "C'mon now, drop dem drawers so dat I kin take a look!"

"She ain't gotta do none o' dat!" I snapped.

L.C.'s smile faded. "Well, she better, li'l mama, 'cause 'f'n she don't, she gon' git whupped."

"I gots my sickness, L.C.," Jean pleaded.

I didn't know if that was true, but I stuck up for my sister, "Yeah, L.C., she gots her sickness!"

"Well den, li'l Cat," L.C. circled to face me menacingly, " 'f'n big Jean don't drop dem drawers rat now, I'm gwone tell de Cap'n 'bout how yo' old man come t'see you when you be at de docdur!"

That knocked the wind out of me. Mama had tracked down Ike and told him of my situation. Because he couldn't get off work on Sunday—the regular visiting day—he had met me secretly at the infirmary, which was closer to the highway, when a visiting LPN gave me my weekly checkup. Nobody suspected a Butane Gas Company truck on the premises, so he could stay as long as he wanted. My only guard was Frisk, and Ike bought his friendship the first day by giving him a handful of crowder peas.

"How come you knows what old Frisk like?" I asked Ike after we embraced.

Ike grinned. "Bud told me all about old Frisk, and how to git to de infirmary, too. You ain't havin' no problem wit' L.C. Whitehead, is you?"

I would've given anything to have Ike here now—or even Frisk.

"Ain't gon' tell you no mo', big gal—drop dem drawers!" L.C. barked.

Jean hiked up her big smock dress, unpinned her big underpants, and let them fall, looking miserable. The panties were stained with menstrual blood. L.C.'s smile disappeared and he moved down the line with his "inspection."

Afterward, one of the girls told Miss Laurel what had happened and she said she'd report it to the Cap'n, but nothing happened. Cap'n Arterberry was not anxious to punish a trusty based on complaints from the prisoners, because a trusty had to be trusted: to keep order, not try to escape, and to be the jailer's ears and eyes. Better to let the prisoners suffer a little injustice and give them a reason to keep their noses clean than lose discipline in the compound.

ONCE A year, Cap'n Arterberry went out all weekend to hunt raccoons. He took L.C. with him, to set up camp and dress the animals he killed.

"We be goin' to Two Mile Trestle," L.C. bragged Friday evening as he drew some sandwiches from Miss Laurel. "I gwine be in charge o' Frisk—de best coon dog in de world!"

We were all surprised, then, to see L.C. back in the compound first thing Saturday morning.

"What be de matter?" Miss Laurel asked.

L.C. shook his long face. "Oh, it be some kinda bad, Miss Laurel. Last night, Frisk cotch dis big ol' coon at de trestle, cotched him in de switchin' rail. Now ain't nothin' mo' bad den a trapped coon, an' ol' Frisk he knows dat. So he jest be layin' back on de tracks, barkin' at dat ol' coon, waitin' for de Cap'n to come wit' his rifle. Den de *City o' N'awlins* come racin' down dat track and cut dem critters in two—both o' dem. I ain't never seed nothin' like dat. I tell you"—tears welled in L.C.'s eyes—"de Cap'n, he be cryin' like a new baby, holdin' ol' Frisk head in he lap, hollin' at me to git up de guts an' thangs. So I come up wit' ol' Frisk 'hind end, den de Cap'n, he jest haul off an' hit me—*pow*—like dat! Den he cuss at de Lawd and axe why God not let me git hit by dat train an' not ol' Frisk."

That afternoon, we stood around the compound watching as L.C. took off his shirt and got the whipping of his life from Cap'n Arterberry, who cried out Frisk's name with each lick.

"So you sow," Miss Laurel said in a low voice, "so you reap."

A FTER THIRTY days in the workhouse—days filled with washing, ironing, sewing, cooking, and tending the Cap'n's private fields—Coot and Sis were released because their family had raised the fine. I'd had an easy time of it, going to the clinic, shelling pounds of peas, and helping Miss Laurel in the kitchen. In the evenings, we'd tell stories and play-like—my rendition of "Casey" was a big hit—and watch my baby kicking in my stomach. Sometimes we got sad and cried, but most of our time we laughed and cursed Miss Tillie Mae for getting us into this mess.

Nobody I knew, not even Ike, had the kind of money lying around that we needed. On one of her Sunday visits, Eva Mae told me that Miss Gert would give me twenty-five dollars toward my fine. But there were no other offers forthcoming, so my thirty days stretched into sixty. The second month was harder, too, because Cap'n Arterberry assigned me to the garden. He'd gotten it into his head that a pregnant woman would make the cabbages grow faster. Jean was assigned to maid's work in the Cap'n's house.

After six weeks, Jean's husband had scraped up enough to get her out, but since L.C. wasn't bothering us anymore and I was getting pretty big, Jean decided to finish her sentence to look after me as she had never done at home. When my stomach hurt me and my left leg cramped up, Jean finished my chores for me, even when she was tired from doing her own work. My feelings were especially sensitive, and Jean was quick to low-rate anybody foolish enough to make the least little remark about me and my baby. She also kept Nug's roving hands off my stomach. It was in the workhouse that Jean became a real sister to me, and I promised myself that I would never forget how she'd stood by me.

Finally, it was the day of our release. I took a long shower, dusted myself with Evening in Paris—a gift from Miss Laurel, along with an ugly, ill-fitting maternity shift she'd made for me when my own clothes got too tight—and packed my strangely familiar but half-forgotten street clothes. Jean and I talked quietly on our cots, waiting for Eddie to pick us up. I had decided to have the baby on my own—not to bother or depend on Ike for anything. He had admitted to me on one of his rare visits that he was ashamed of me for stealing and that he had started seeing another woman, even though he said "she don't mean nuttin'—jest somebody 'til you gits free." But until you've lost it, you don't know how wonderful freedom is, and I relished getting mine back.

Eddie's old Cadillac arrived, and we waved good-bye to Miss Laurel and Nug. I could see the tears welling up in Miss Laurel's eyes, but Jean said she was only sad because she'd have to start all over warning a new batch of girls not to mess with Nug. Neither L.C. nor the Cap'n was anywhere in sight, but I didn't mind. I just wanted to make tracks.

When we pulled up in front of our house on Gibb Street, I was surprised to see how much Mama had aged, and how unkempt she looked. There were a couple of brown spots on the front of her once-spotless smock—snuff juice, I imagined—and she was wearing two dresses, with the bottom one hanging longer than the top. But her face broke into a big smile, and for the third time in my life I heard her cry. Dossie Ree and Miss Susie brought plates of food covered with white cloths, and May Liza and Pearlie brought me some of their old maternity clothes. Some of the church folks came and prayed and sang.

I was so happy to be home, I nearly forgot that Ike wasn't there until Mama took me in the house and began to "listen" to my stomach. She cupped her beautiful hands around my belly to measure it, then she rubbed me down with tallow while she talked to the baby in my stomach. Jean came inside and the three of us held each other and cried.

Jean kept saying over and over again, "I look out for li'l Cat, Mama."

"She sho' did, Mama!" I said.

"My gals done come home," Mama said. "Thank you, Lawd Jesus Christ!"

We hugged until Eddie unwound Jean's arms and ushered her to his car. I curled up beside Mama in her big iron bed and slept like I hadn't slept in over two months. Later that night, Bud staggered in drunk, kissed my forehead, and promptly passed out.

Eleven

AT 7:45 IN THE MORNING ON JULY 10, 1961, MY WATER BROKE AND I WENT INTO LABOR.

I had often heard Mama and her ladies talk about "birthin' pain," but nothing really prepared me for experiencing it. It felt like a knife that entered at my ankle, cut upward to my right calf, then commenced to twist.

"Ooooweeee!" I cried and tried to get up from my bed.

Mama hobbled into the room from the kitchen, still bleary-eyed. "What be de matter wit' you?"

"Leg hurtin', Mama!"

Mama grunted, "Well, you jest *thank* you hurtin'. Wait 'til yo' belly start gripin'—*den* you knows 'bout hurtin'!" She started to go back to the kitchen.

"Wait, Mama," I said. "My stomach be hurtin' a little bit. Looky here—dis bed be soakin' wet."

"You done piss de bed 'afore, Ida Mae—"

"Not like dis, Mama—"

She came over, crouched down, took a look and a smell. Her disdainful expression softened.

"Oww! Oooo." I stiffened on the bed. "De pain come back now, Mama. Cuttin' me rat up de leg!"

"All right—git up, gal," Mama said. "Lemme change de bed. I gwine put dis here newspaper underneath you—you be havin' de baby."

Having the baby had been the last thing on my mind. Lately I'd been much more interested in how good a step I could cut on the dance floor. I had a certain status because I was carrying Ike's child, and none of the boys or men got out of line with me. In fact, one of the only times that a married woman was allowed to go out dancing unescorted was when she was expecting, and there had been several of us pregnant women flashing and twirling across the dance floor. But none of them could out bebop me.

The night before, I'd danced at Sam Ciroe's until they put out the lights, even though my back was killing me. I was hoping to get a glimpse of Ike, who was rumored to be dating a girl named Poochie and an older woman, Ba-Ba. May Liza had seen Poochie riding in Ike's car, and Pearlie had spotted Ike dancing with Ba-Ba in Booker's Cafe. I'd cried and low-rated myself for being so gullible and Ike for getting me in this situation. I would've given anything to turn back the clock to nine months ago. Now, I'd give anything to roll back the clock even for a few hours.

"No I'm not, Mama. I—*eeeeoowwww!!*" An electric charge ran through me and I arched high on my shoulders and heels, then fell back to the bed.

"Lawd a'mercy, I hope you wasn't hollerin' like dat when de baby got put in dere!" Mama's practiced hands felt their way across my abdomen.

"I can't have dis baby now, Mama—not now," I said, panting.

Outside, Gee Pee was getting up and going to work and my shrieks and hollers served notice that Li'l Cat was finally "gettin' down" at 119 East Gibb. Some of the women came to wish me luck and pat my stomach on their way to work. May Liza came to help, bringing her coffee can spittoon. A few men stopped by to chat with Bud in low tones at the back door. Bud tried to act all calm and brave, but there was a tremble in his voice. I could hear him cussing Ike—"He oughta be here, oughta be here"—over and over.

Miss Nollie B., who had the only telephone on our block, ran down to see about me, then went home to call long-distance to the plantation where Jean and her husband lived. She reported back to Mama that she'd left word with the bossman that Jean was needed in Greenwood.

"Oh, Lawdy—help me!" I shrieked.

"You oughtsta call out de name o' dat rascal what done dis to you instead," Mama said. I knew she was trying to make me mad, to give me a way to master my fear.

"Ain't gonna do dat no mo', Mama!" I promised, and I meant it. "Oh, Sweet Jesus, he'p me, he'p me now! *Oooowwww*—" Dimly, I sensed May Liza stuffing a clean newspaper under me, then Mama standing me up and helping me into an open-backed hospital gown.

"You gwine be all right, Kitty Cat," May Liza said calmly as she wiped my nose.

"Liza, Liza, Liza!" I grunted. "Jean, Jean, Jean!" I wailed.

There was a loud guffaw from the back stoop, where the neighborhood men had continued to gather with Bud like helpless puppies.

"Huumph. Wit' alla dat racket, how does dem mens 'spect us'n t' git some kinda peace?" Mama asked the ceiling. But I could see that she was secretly pleased at the crowd. It was a show of respect to have people waiting outside your door to spread the news of a birth far and wide. Today, I was Somebody.

"Let me 'xamine yo' belly 'fore you gits back in de bed," Mama said. She cupped my lower belly with her hands. "De chile done dropped. It won't be long now."

The pain bent me over like a hairpin and Mama eased me onto the newspapers. Until now, it hadn't really sunk in that something —someone—was actually going to pop out of me. I'd felt kicks during the pregnancy, but nothing more substantial than you'd feel from swallowing a fishbone or having indigestion.

Now two knives cut me, high in the chest and low between my legs. That was it. That was all I was going to take. I made a break for the back door. I flashed by Mama's and May Liza's startled faces in the kitchen, then past the outstretched hands of Bud and the neighbor men.

"Stop dat crazy gal!" Mama yelled. "Ida Mae, gal, you c'mon back in dis house 'fore you hurt dat baby!"

I was halfway down Gibb Street—gown flapping, butt hanging out in the breeze—before the men recovered enough to give chase. I pounded up the steps to Miss Clara's porch. Miss Clara was the nearest white woman we knew. I'd heard the neighbor ladies say that she had given birth to stillborn twins years ago and hadn't been able to have any children after that. Instead, she collected cats, which she treated like family. "Miss Clara! Miss Clara!" I shouted. "You gots to he'p me, ma'am!"

Miss Clara came out and took me in her arms. "Now calm down, li'l Ida Mae. What's wrong? What's the matter?" It didn't take her long to size up my condition. She pulled a clean sheet off the clothes line and wrapped it around me.

"Big Ida must be worried sick 'bout you!"

"I needs to go to de horsepital!" I cried, still breathless from the running and the pain. All I could think of was Miss Mag's filth and blood and agony, and Miss Sweet Chile Brown dying in that ambulance. In the small bit of reasoning I had left, I thought that if a white woman took me to the hospital, I had a better chance of getting a bed. And right now that's all I wanted—a hospital, lots of doctors and nurses, and all kinds of medicines and machines to make the pain go away and take the baby from my body.

"All right, hush up now," Miss Clara said, holding me close and patting my back. "Evvything's gonna be jest fine."

She walked me down the steps and back along the sidewalk to

my house. The men, who had scattered to the four winds looking for me, drifted back.

"Lawd amercy!" Mama slapped her heavy cheeks when she saw us, then opened the screen door. "Brang yo'self on in an' git in dis bed rat now, Miss 'oman! Runnin' down yon'er 'turbin' Miss Clara an' all." I don't know if she was more grateful or embarrassed. It was not good advertising for the town's best granny midwife to have her own bigged-up daughter run screaming from her house during her delivery. May Liza laughed aloud. Now she would really have a story to tell Pearlie.

"She didn't do nothin', Big Ida, she jest scared," Miss Clara said, guiding me through the doorway. It was the first time I could recall her setting foot inside our house.

"Liza, git yon'er an' git Miss Clara dat chair," Mama said. Her voice wore a hard edge I never heard in it before. "Now you *stays put,* Ida Mae. You gon' hurt yo' baby 'f'n you don't lay down an' do *'xactly* like I say."

A second later I was flat on my back, knees raised high and crooked over the backs of two cane-back chairs. Miss Clara sat in a rocker near the head of the bed, holding and stroking my hand. May Liza sat at my feet in a cane-bottom chair, talking kind and soothing and spitting her snuff juice.

Now all the pain was centered in my vagina. I felt something hot and sticky squirt up my legs.

"Bear down, Ida Mae," Mama said, giving orders like a general. But I could tell she was calling on someone else to help her because her face was lifted toward the tarpaper ceiling.

"Here it come, Ida Mae!"

"Dat dere ain't no baby—its doo-doo!" May Liza said, as Mama wiped my butt and placed clean newspaper under me.

"Lawd, amercy Jesus." Mama sank back on her heels, spun and

hurried into the kitchen. We could hear her pleading with God, "Lawd, dis be my chile!" Then we heard what sounded like two tin pots bang together and a keen wailing that started old Frisgo to barking.

Miss Clara bowed her head and silently moved her lips.

Mama continued to bang the pots together as she commanded me from the kitchen. "Push. Dat's it—push. Now catch yo' breath 'fore the next pain come."

All at once I felt myself relax. I was no longer fighting the process. It hurt, but I knew it wouldn't kill me. I raised my head and saw Mama's face between my knees, nature sack around her neck. Suddenly, my hips felt crushed between two giant hands. I heard myself scream and scream again, like a voice coming from the speakers at the Walthall picture show.

"I see de head now, Ida Mae," Mama said calmly. "Push now—*push, gal, wit' all yo' might!*"

I screamed and pushed and pushed with all my might. My belly turned inside out. Mama dipped her dog finger into my blood and made a red *X* on my stomach.

"Dere now," she said, "de baby be here, thank de Lawd!"

"Thank the Lord," Miss Clara repeated.

"Amen," May Liza whispered.

Mama cut the umbilicus, like a seamstress cutting a stray thread, then held up the baby to examine it.

"You gots a fine baby boy," she announced. "An' he gots all his fangers an' toes."

A boy! A baby boy! I couldn't believe it. Then I heard him cry.

"Let me hold him, Mama—"

"Not yet, Ida Mae. Not till you pass de afderbirth. Now where'd I put dat slop jar? Here, Miss Clara," Mama said, handing the swaddled baby to her, "y'all kin hold him for a minute."

The look on Miss Clara's face told me that this was why she had stayed. It was as close to having her own baby as she was going to get in this life, and I didn't grudge her the moment.

May Liza put a pinch of her snuff under my tongue. Then Mama put some of the leaves and twigs from her nature sack under my tongue, too. I strained again and the sack that had fed my little son for nine long months flopped into the slop jar. I twisted and reached for my baby.

"He's real special, Ida Mae," Miss Clara said as her old hands gave him up.

He had a tiny round face, a head shaped like a noble African, and a happy, hungry mouth. "Dis here boy, he gone be Somebody," I heard myself say. My arms felt strong as trees. The heat from his little body radiated like rays from the morning sun. Like every other mother before or since, I knew I had just given birth to the world.

"Ike sho' 'nough gots hisself a fine ol' boy," said May Liza.

"Whatcha gwine name him?" Mama asked.

"Cedric," I said without hesitation.

"Say what—? Gal, you done lost yo' mind! What is it dat I gwine call him? 'Cause I sho' can't 'member no *say what!*"

"I spell it for you, Mama."

"You better—'cause I ain't *never* heared de likes o' dat!"

I'd picked up the name from the movies. Like all the Mercedeses and Abraham Lincoln Washingtons and Joe Louis Roosevelts that African-American children have been showered with, it was meant to be an inspiration.

Just then, a car honked outside and tires squealed. I heard a flurry of men's voices, loudest of which was Bud shouting, "We be waitin' fo' you, Ike! Cat—y'all—gots a baby!"

"Here his daddy come," May Liza announced as she peeked from behind the curtain.

I smiled in spite of myself.

Mama took a swallow of RC. "De way you carry on—you oughta not see no man. You gwine git a *ton* o' babies, you keep dat up!"

"Wait rat out dere, Ike, 'til we gits dem cleaned up!" May Liza instructed. "Y'all got a hollin' boy—it be hard but he be here."

"Naw, I ain't gonna git no mo'e babies, Mama," I said. "It hurt too bad."

Mama just looked at me a second, then put her RC down. "Here now, gi'e dat baby back t' Miss Clara a minute. I gwine 'xamine you some mo' 'fore Ike gits in here. C'mon—put yo' legs back straddle de chairs."

"Yas'm," I said. I dutifully gave up my child and assumed the position. Mama put her whole hand in my vagina. It felt like giving birth in reverse, but I kept quiet. Inside me I felt each finger stretch out. Then a pinch—a numb thumb on my womb—then a searing pain that made my labor cramps feel like I'd only stubbed my toe. It took me so much by surprise that I couldn't even scream. Instinctively I bucked and pushed Mama's hand away, but she was already out and drying herself off.

"Dere now, dat's got it," Mama said, turning away and dropping something else in the slop jar.

"What you *do,* Mama!" I cried.

"I jest be countin' de knots on yo' womb. It tell me you gwine have lottsa younguns."

"I don't *want* no mo' chilluns, Mama!"

"I know." She looked me square in the face. "Dat be how come I jest fix it. Won't no baby come no mo'."

I lay back and tried to relax. I had no idea what she'd done, and she never told me. Whatever it was, it hurt like hell—but it worked. No thanks to me or the men I'd know in later years, Cedric's was the only soul I'd bring to earth.

• • •

IN THE months following Cedric's birth, Ike was a changed man. He took his duties as a father seriously. Every Friday evening, like clockwork, he showed up with a case of Carnation milk, a dozen diapers, RC colas and snuff for Mama, and ten or twenty dollars for me. We were living the good life and everybody knew it.

"Dat Ike, he be some kinda good to y'all," May Liza said. "Afder de Lawd made Ike, He broke up de mold."

"He sho' 'nough loves dat baby—an' you, too, Cat," Pearlie put in. "But how come y'all always gitting in fights?"

"Dat's 'cause Ike be real jealous," I laughed, more than a little pleased.

Nowadays, we were looked upon as a real twosome. We would fight every weekend in the juke houses. Ike would not let me go to the toilet more than twice, because he thought it was just my excuse for winking at some man on the way. If I went a third time, he'd be waiting just outside the door to slap me when I came back. I would slap him back, and the fight would be on. We would tussle all over the place, breaking tables and glasses and anything else that got in our way. He never hit me with his fist, but I would make sure to fall down anyway—prettily, with my clothes straight. Then Big Sis and my other girlfriends would jump him and throw him to the ground.

"Ida, you better git dis big cow off me," Ike would holler from underneath Big Sis.

"Y'all leave him 'lone," I said, signaling to my friends to let him be. By the end of the night we would go to our separate houses, still "in love."

Our fights thrilled the juke house crowd, although the owners began to demand a cash deposit before they'd let us come inside. People enjoyed the show so much that they wanted to patronize the same places we did, and they often asked if we were expected before they'd go in.

When Cedric was about a year old, Ike and I decided to set up housekeeping. I suspected that part of his motivation was wanting to keep a closer watch on my whereabouts, but I wanted to know where he was, too. So we rented our own shotgun house in Dixie Lane alley, and for a whole year, we were a picture-perfect family —something I'd never had, even in a picture. Each week after Ike got his paycheck, he'd bring home something new for me to wear, and on Saturdays, we'd go out in matching outfits, just like in the magazines. He bought Cedric the latest toys, and shirts that matched ours. His mother, Miss Mary, whom we called Muh Dear, doted on Cedric, too. She and Mama tried to outdo each other in spoiling him shamelessly.

A few months after Mama delivered Cedric, she'd lost all control of her legs. She would be walking in one direction when they'd decide to go a different way, causing her to trip and fall. She could no longer pretend to be play-liking, especially after she couldn't answer the call of a plantation woman in labor. In fact, Cedric was the last baby she delivered.

"It ain't nuttin' but de dropsy," Mama said. "Suaar, she had it, too." She consoled herself with the knowledge that her mother had the affliction. "I guess I be walkin' soon, up yon'er wit' de Lawd."

I felt bad about Mama's condition, but not so bad I couldn't leave Cedric with her or Muh Dear when I wanted to go out. I was the envy of every woman in Gee Pee, especially other teen mothers whose babies' daddies weren't as dutiful. I was in high cotton for a while.

I was walking home one evening, stewing about a fight Ike and I had. Since the novelty of his little boy had worn off, Ike had been spending more time away from home. I happened to be passing Poochie's house when I noticed a very familiar green Chevy parked high on her lawn. My heart started pounding, and I looked around for a place to hide. For the next three hours, I nestled behind some trash cans and trees across the street. About ten o'clock, Ike came out on the porch, tucking in his shirttail, and kissed a woman standing in the doorway. I could barely make her out, but I knew my "perfect life" was over.

" 'Steada you out runnin' 'round followin' people," Ike bellowed when I confronted him, "you oughta be home takin' care of de baby!"

"Mama and Muh Dear take care o' him when I be gone," I said. " 'Sides, you jest changin' de subject. What you be doin' at Poochie's all night?"

"I told you, Ida—she call de company. Her gas light be out—"

"Oh, you lightin' her fire, all right!" I said. "Why didn't you call in yo' truck?"

" 'Cause I be on de way home! Otherwise, she have t'wait till mornin'. An' Poochie be a friend, baby cakes—now what I 'posed to do, huh? You tell me!"

That was a good question. I didn't even know what I was going to do—until I did it.

A few days later, I ran into Poochie in the Chinaman's store. To tell the truth, I didn't want to see her. Ike had been keeping his distance from her, as far as I knew, and I had started telling myself that maybe things would work out. Of course, that didn't stop people from talking. Even Pearlie and May Liza told me how Poochie had been bragging about her affair with Ike. And here she was, with her tight skirt, creamy complexion, and long hair, leaning over that counter like she owned the place.

"You messin' wit' my ol' man!" I said, marching up behind her.

Wang Lee, who knew my reputation, paled and began clearing the counter.

Poochie turned. "Whatchoo talkin' 'bout, Cat? If you talkin' 'bout Ike, he be a 'much right' man!"

"I be talkin' 'bout beatin' yo' tail, dat's what!" I felt my hands ball into little fists.

"You better not mess wit' me, Cat!" Poochie warned, but her eyes were all about running, not fighting. Wang Lee ducked as I gave her a hard lick upside the face that sent her grocery sack flying. She went down, nicking her head on the edge of the counter.

I spun on my heel and marched out. I had been on my way to do something, but I couldn't remember what, so I went to Sam Ciroe's instead.

The usual party with the usual crowd was under way, so I had a drink and danced as long as people kept feeding the Seeburg. Gradually, the afternoon turned into evening and news of my "victory" spread all over town. As new people came in, I saw them pointing and whispering, giving me hard stares or smiling nods, depending on whose camp they belonged to. In the main, the smiles outnumbered the frowns, and I felt vindicated. By the end of the day, I had danced with every man in the place, most of them twice.

Around suppertime, I went back to Mama's to fetch Cedric. She was out on the porch, in the wheelchair she'd been given by the welfare when her dropsy got too bad for her to stand.

"How you doin', Mama?" I asked. I could tell from her sorrowful face that news about Poochie had preceded me.

"Ida Mae, old gal," Mama began, "ain't I done de best I could wit' you?"

"Yas'm, Mama."

"Ain't I done tol' you to keep yo' eyes open? Ain't you done seed dat what be glitterin' a long way off be de fool's gold? Ain't nothin' as good as what you gots rat here an' now in dis li'l chile? Ain't you done fount out dat 'less'n you keeps yo'self high, you ain't never gwine be Somebody?"

"Yas'm, you teach me all dat."

"Well now." Mama's chest began to heave and she raised a clean diaper to her eyes. "Dossie Ree say dat you knock some 'oman down—fightin' 'bout Ike. You oughta not done dat, gal."

"Yas'm." I looked down, not knowing what to say.

"Ida Mae, you is brangin' mo' trouble on yo'owndearself. Ain't you be in de jailhouse 'fore now? An' Ike ain't lifted a fanger t' he'p. Now you done took t' fightin' 'bout him. You let yo' tail rule yo' head, gal." Mama shook her head in frustration. "Ain't you got nothin' mo' 'portant t' be doin'?"

That's when I remembered I had promised to come back early, to help Mama clean the sores that had broken out on the backs of her thighs and under her titties in the last few months.

"Oh, Lawd, Mama!" Tears sprang to my eyes and I covered my mouth. "I forgits! I didn't mean to do it, Mama! Forgive me, Mama!" I knelt by her poor old feet, crooked on the footrests. "Lawd have mercy on my soul!"

I tended her sores, and she didn't fuss at me anymore. When I was finished, I felt like I had been in church—cleansed and ab-solved for what I'd done wrong.

The next morning, after Ike had left for work and May Liza had come over to gossip and do my hair into little croakanol ringlets, we were startled by a knock on the door. In our neighborhood, friends and family just opened the door and came in, so we knew this wasn't a social call. It was a police officer, with a warrant for my arrest on charges of "simple assault and battery."

I could see a crowd gathering around the squad car. I asked if I could change my clothes, and the officer said yes. I changed out of my ratty housedress into a new polka-dot jumpsuit I'd just received from Ike. For the second time in my life, I was arrested. I was led through a gauntlet of gawking neighbors—though this time I looked sharp and Cedric was in my arms.

"Dey gwine 'rest de baby, too?" somebody shouted.

"Dey ain't gonna do no such thang!" Pearlie shouted back. "Gi'e me dat baby, Cat." She muscled through and took Cedric. "I take him to yo' mama."

Unburdened of my boy, I commenced to walk my walk: wide-legged, shoulders back, head held high. By the time I disappeared into the squad car, most of the crowd was clapping. As we turned out of Dixie Lane alley onto East Gibb, I spied Mama on her porch, catnapping or ignoring me, I couldn't tell. The picture of her in that steel chair, head off to one side, would haunt me for years.

At my trial, I sat in the front of the room, among the white people. A large crowd of black people came to watch, all in Sunday dresses, suits, and hats. They crammed in the back of the room, sweating and fanning themselves. Mama's white ladies turned out to support me, including Miss Clara and Miss Victoria. Some other white ladies were there, too; maybe they were Poochie's. Ike wasn't there, although I prayed that he would come.

Poochie came to court teary-eyed, with a bruise on her face and a conservative dress that made her look extra innocent. I was looking smug and guilty as sin, despite my borrowed white lace dress. The bailiff called "All rise" and the judge came in, frowning. The gossip and how-do's stopped instantly. Even the babies stopped crying.

After the lawyers' opening statements, the prosecutor called Wang Lee. Since he was the only witness to the fight, his version of things would be crucial.

"Big girl hit little girl," Wang Lee said nervously, boxing with his hands. "Little girl fall down. That all!"

Wang Lee's economical testimony had a big impact on the judge. After listening to some testimonials from Mama's white ladies, he said he was inclined to have mercy, even though I was now a two-time loser. Although he could have locked me away from my baby for years at Parchman Prison, he settled for thirty days in the workhouse and a fine of a hundred dollars. Twenty minutes after it started, my trial was over.

Later that afternoon, while my friends and family were taking off their finery and relaxing with a lemonade or beer and telling each other what a tragedy it all was, I was once again on my way to visit Cap'n Arterberry.

SINCE THE officers and I all knew each other now, and I had received such good testimonials from white women, I was allowed to sit without handcuffs on the drive to the workhouse. Although I had been gone less than two years, the low buildings looked dilapidated and squalid. Even the security fence was bent back and rusted in places, almost past mending.

Once again, Cap'n Arterberry met me at the gate. Without Frisk, he just didn't look himself. His shoulders were stooped and he seemed weighed down. His face had gotten more wrinkles and his salt-and-pepper hair had turned white.

"Well, little gal," he drawled, examining my paperwork, "I see you's back."

"Yassuh," I said, blinking my eyes innocently. "It be a mistake."

"Sho' it was. Jest don't you have no mistakes happenin' 'round here."

"No suh!" I said.

I trudged to the women's dormitory, where I was the only inmate. Miss Laurel cried when she saw me. She sat across the table while I ate a really good meal of biscuits, gravy, and pan-fried rabbit and we talked long into the night. I noticed from the big keyring on her belt and the badge on her blouse that she'd been promoted to chief matron. But since I'd been gone, Nug had been killed—stabbed over a twenty-five-cent gambling debt. I wiped Miss Laurel's teary eyes with her apron and told her about Cedric and *Ike,* and we commiserated on how low-down and dirty most men were.

We had a cigarette and our conversation turned to Cap'n Arterberry.

"De Cap'n, he nevermo' git over ol' Frisk," Miss Laurel said. "De other sheriffs—dey got degether and sont him a brand-new hound dog, but dat dog never do learn how t' hunt. I hears dem out dere, runnin' round late in de night, ol' dog barkin' an' de Cap'n he be cussin', but he ain't nevermo' cotch nothin'. Poor ol' cuss."

"Pore ol' dog," I said.

"You be a sweet chile, jest like my Aintee Pie," she said. "Does you know de McNeals dat live in Gritney?"

"I sho' do—we be some kin!" I lied.

"Whatchoo say? Dey be my kinfolkses, too!" Miss Laurel beamed. "I knowed it de last time y'all was here—de minute I laid my eye on you. I tole Nug you be de spittin' image of my dead suster, Jenny. We be some kin, Lawd, Lawd, I do say!"

I knew that I had struck paydirt. From that day on, Miss Laurel thought of us as cousins. She took to calling me "Cuttin' Cat," and I called her "Cuz" in return. I noticed that she talked a lot about old Frisk, but I realized it wasn't really because she mourned him. Cap'n Arterberry had told her not to mention the death of Nug—

it was bad for camp discipline—so every day she found something nice to remember about old Frisk, as a way of getting at who she really missed.

Since we didn't need much food—there were only ten prisoners in the men's dormitory at the time—I didn't have to work in the weed-choked garden. Instead, I swept the dark hallways and helped Cuz in the kitchen, shelling butterbeans and slicing salt pork and mixing up hot-water cornbread. We only saw Cap'n Arterberry when he came down in the morning and at night, when he counted heads and locked the dormitories. As soon as he left, Cuz unlocked my dorm door. We would talk and cry and giggle until early morning, when she locked the door again, just before the Cap'n arrived.

Once again, I ended up serving two months in the workhouse, but this time it seemed more like a vacation. I didn't have to tend Cedric or fuss with Ike or put up with Mama's scolding. Cuz was happy to have company, and because my crime this time was not so shameful, I had a lot of visitors on Sundays.

One of my regular visitors was my cousin T.C., whose mother was Bud's real mother. He was a few years older than me, lean and handsome, with large flat feet and a love of gossip. He read Negro newspapers from several different northern cities, and he kept me abreast of news about movie stars and blues singers. It was from him I'd first heard about the Freedom Riders—"not here in Mis-s'ippi," he'd told me, "but dey be ridin' for us!"

T.C. was also an excellent cook. We would sit on the workhouse front porch and eat his home-cooked food and store-bought snacks, drink RC colas and smoke cigarettes, and gossip. He would tell me how everyone was doing at home, who sent their hellos, what the townspeople were saying about my fight, and who Ike was dating.

Halfway through my incarceration, Ike himself came to visit. He said he hadn't been able to make it to court or to the workhouse before now because of work, and he avoided mentioning why he didn't pay my fine.

"Dey tole me 'bout you goin' out wit' Ba-Ba," I said.

"Dey jest be lyin' on me, Ida," he protested. "Ain't foolin 'round no such thang!"

"Don't look like we gon' ever marry an' raise our son degether," I said.

"We can't git marry," he said, " 'cause you be in de jailhouse alla time."

That shut me up, but deep down I knew that T.C. wasn't lying. That night, I didn't go to the kitchen for my supper. I wanted some time to think through my situation—to look at what I'd done with my life and what I could do. After a while, I went to the kitchen to help Laurel clean up.

"I wouldn'ta hit de gal," she said, squinting through the smoke of her cigarette. "I'd a knocked ol' Ike 'side de head!"

"Oh, I dunno know, Cuz," I sighed. "I sees dat gal an' a dam jest bus' inside me. When I come to myself, everythang be over. Poochie be layin' on de flo', lookin' real pitiful. I feel sorry inside. I thought 'bout runnin' over an' sayin' I'm sorry an' beggin' her pardon and all, but her eye be already swole up an' I guess I jest got scared."

"Us all make mistakes, Cuttin' Cat," she said. "Don'cha be too hard on yo'owndearself." She took a big drag of blue smoke and added, "Jest don'cha be hittin' folkses no mo'! 'F'n you do, dese white folkses gwine keep puttin' you in jail. Pretty soon, you gwine end up killin' somebody an' den you be sont to Parchman—like de S.O.B. what kilt my Nug."

"Ain't never gonna do dat," I swore.

"Bought sense be better den borrowed sense, Cuttin' Cat. You jest 'member dat next time you loses dat temper."

That night, I tossed and turned in my bunk. The harder I tried, it seemed, the harder it was to get anywhere, let alone out of the Delta. I just didn't know what to do.

TIME CAME and went. My Sunday visitors came and talked and left. Eva Mae Brown told me about the happenings at the Big 25 and Booker's, and we talked about the men friends she was juggling, Mama's dropsy was too bad for her to leave the house, and no former convict could come to visit—at least the ones Mr. Arterberry remembered—so May Liza and Pearlie brought news of Mama, Jean, and Bud, of Cedric's growth, of Ike and Ba-Ba. Some Sundays I was glad when they left.

But it was T.C.'s visits I anticipated the most. He brought me the latest news, including information about the growing civil rights movement.

"Well, I sho' 'nough doesn't wanna hear 'bout dem crazy folkses," I said. "Eversomebody tryin' to git outta here and dey be tryin' to git in! You ever seed de likes?"

IN WHAT seemed like days instead of weeks, my workhouse stay was over. I said good-bye to Laurel, and she held my hand and cried:

"I loves you, Cuttin' Cat," she said. She was almost out of the kitchen when she turned back to me and whispered, "Nug, he loves you, too!"

I picked up my grip and went out through the compound, where Buddy Boy was waiting in his lopsided cab to take me home.

"Dis be de first time I pick up a ride at de workhouse!" Buddy Boy said.

"Well, you ain't gon' be pickin' me up here no mo'," I said, hoping it was true.

Nearing town, we passed by the Big 25. "Say, Cat," said Buddy Boy, "you want me t' pull over so you kin wet yo' whistle?"

"Naw, dat be okay, Buddy Boy," I said. "Jest keep drivin'. Jest take me home." But I wasn't sure anymore just where home was. At Ike's? At Mama's? At Sam Ciroe's or Miss Lussie Bee's?

We turned down McLauren and I saw a gang of people, mostly strangers, milling around outside of Booker's Cafe.

"Now who de hell be dat?" I asked.

Buddy let out a short breath. "Dem be de Riders. Dey gwine git us all kilt, you see 'f'n dey don't!"

"De Riders?"

"Yas'm. Dat good-lookin' boy in de overhalls an' dat other'un, dey be wit' dem Freedom Riders." I'd been hearing about the Freedom Riders from T.C. for a long time, but I'd never laid eyes on one before.

"What dey doin' in Greenwood?" I asked. "I thought dey'd gone back north by now."

"Dey back," said Buddy Boy. "Dey gots an office right here in town. Dey say dey gwine make us free."

"Somebody oughta tell dem ol' boys we ain't slaves no mo'!" I said. I had to admit, the Riders—as we continued to call the civil rights workers long after the Freedom Rides were over—intrigued me.

"Somebody oughter tell dem dat dey be in Greenwood now," said Buddy Boy. "An' de white folkses here don't mess 'round wit' no foolishness!"

I asked Buddy Boy what sort of trouble they'd stirred up.

"Ol' Man Jordan and Edward Cochran done th'owed in wit' dem. He be tryin' t' git dem de Elk's Hall for a meetin', but ain't nosomebody goin'! Long as I be a cab driver, I ain't never seed de likes 'fore now. Down yon'er in Jackson de NAACP don' tole de colored folkses not t' buy nothin' outta de store. 'Round here dey got dat preacher Aaron Johnson to side wit' dem, afder dat colored boy, Meredith, wanta go t' de white folkses college—dat stunt ain't gwine work." Buddy Boy wheeled the car over the railroad tracks. "You chilluns, git outta de way!" he hollered out the window. "Say, Cat, is you gwine vote?"

"Naw!" I said. I didn't know anyone who voted, and didn't think I ever would. And then the crowd of well-wishers standing in front of 119 East Gibb to welcome me home put the strange Freedom Riders right out of my head.

About twenty people in their Sunday best were congregated around a long table covered with white lace, bearing bowls and platters of turnip greens, candied yams, potato salad, chittlins, coconut cake, pinto beans, fried chicken wings and backs, chicken foot stew, and pans of cornbread and biscuits. It was an old-time Delta feast presided over by Mama, who sat like a queen in her iron wheelchair atop the porch.

Buddy Boy helped me out of the car and the crowd waved and cheered. I made a beeline for Mama and little Cedric, who was clutching her legs and did not seem sure about who I was. Charles, Bud's little boy, who was a year older than Cedric, had come to stay with Mama, too, and I hugged him and Cedric and Mama tight.

Bro Pastor led the assembly in prayer and Dossie Ree sang a song. Miss Lizzie Bell Strong testified about the power of the Lord and Miss Crying Shame honored me with a play-like. Old Dell did her Camel Walk and Miss Susie admonished me to be good from here on out. Mercifully, she did not evoke her daughters, who did not join the party but watched from their porch.

My homecoming feast lasted until dark. People stopped by on their way home from work, attracted by the food and merriment.

All gave me a kind word, a piece of advice, or a pat on the back before they went on their way.

Only two things spoiled my party. One was a fight between Miss Neddie Ruth, a man who had become a woman, and Powder-Face Sug over Mr. Scarecrow Magee, a gent attractive to both sexes.

"Ugly as dat man be, I don't see what dey be fighin' 'bout," Mama said, salting her sliced watermelon.

"Heap sees, few knows," Miss Dossie Ree said.

The other was the fact that Ike didn't show up. I didn't really expect to see him, but that didn't stop me from hoping.

When everyone was gone and everything was cleaned up, I told Mama I'd be taking Cedric home to wait for Ike.

"How come y'all don't sleep here denight?" Mama inquired, not meeting my eye.

"How come?" I said. I looked her straight in the eye, but my stomach did a flipflop.

Mama hung her head. " 'Bout three weeks afder you be in de prison, Ike jest up an' move. He gi'e me yo' bed an' yo' closes. De house it be rented to somebody else." Her head bent even lower. "He do brang me a li'l change to eat wit'. For de life o' me, I don't see what Ike want dat Ba-Ba for—her be ol' as de hills an' part o' de swamps."

I felt a dull throbbing in my chest, but I was determined not to show my grief and fear. I spent the rest of the evening setting up a place to sleep and putting my things away in the middle room of Mama's house. Mama fell asleep in her wheelchair and Cedric, Charles, and I cuddled on my pallet by the front door. Somehow, I didn't feel so bad. I was alive and healthy and more determined than ever to get out of the Delta. I had a little boy now and I chose to regard him as a symbol of my new life—not a chain to the old one.

I lay there and searched myself. I knew that I hadn't been a good mother to Cedric, always in the juke house or the jailhouse and leaving him for Mama to look after. I could see that he was smart. I vowed to give him all my Perry Mason books and teach him how to play ball like Casey. I traced the outline of his small face as he slept. We'd be a team—me and him against the world.

I hid my face under the covers to keep the roaches off, and sleep finally came.

Twelve

A SUMMER STORM GATHERED OVER GREEN-
WOOD. ALL MORNING, THE AIR WAS THICK AND
still, and then the day got dark. Lightning flashed on the walls and
power poles, and thunder rattled our teeth. In Baptist Town and
Gritney and Gee Pee, where kids and drunks dodged traffic at all
hours of the day or night, the streets emptied.

"Thunder 'fore seven, gwine rain 'fore 'leven," Mama said,
scanning the sky. She pointed to the mirror hanging near the front
door. "Kiver dat glass up, Ida Mae." She was superstitious about
"de Lawd doin' his work."

When rain finally came, the deluge was biblical. The wind-
driven sheets found every crack in our house. Rivulets drained
from our tar-paper ceiling into buckets and bowls. The walls bled
water. Our roaches darted here and there, trying to escape a watery
grave.

"Gather up de tears o' de Lawd," Mama said, directing our
efforts to keep dry from her wheelchair, like a battlefield general
in her tank. I ran to the kitchen for another pot to put under a leak
in the front room. Cedric and Charles ran around, laughing and
clapping and stomping their feet.

"Y'all chilluns better set down an' stop makin' so much racket,"
Mama yelled. "Light'in' gwine skin all de hide off'n y'all!"

A man came running up our steps with his jacket over his head.
Mama yelled through the screen door, "Say dere, ol' Scarecrow,
you gyp—why don'cha git on home? Can't you 'cern dat de Lawd
be workin'?"

"How-do, Aint Baby," Scarecrow called. "Fine weather, ain't it? Is de li'l Cat home?"

"You git on 'way from here wit' yo' ugly self!" Mama shooed him like a fly. "Ida Mae ain't comin' out in dis weather and you ain't comin' in!" Mama viewed Scarecrow as a lowlife. Not only was he a juke house regular, but he was one of the first local men to take up with the Freedom Riders, whom most people in Gee Pee feared and mistrusted almost as much as the Klan.

Scarecrow proudly passed out leaflets to anyone who had the nerve to take them. He had started wearing overalls just like the freedom workers, and he tried to talk all proper about "our place in life." Many of the townspeople ignored him, but I enjoyed hearing him talk about the wrongs of the white man, and how we colored people were kings and queens.

Unfortunately, I knew why he was here. He had loaned me five dollars out of friendship, and now he wanted to collect.

"Let him in, Mama," I called, juggling pans in both hands. "I owes him some money."

"For what does you owe money t' dis gyp?"

"Aw, Mama, c'mon! De man be soakin' wet!"

"Dat ain't all he gwine be 'f he keep messin' wit' dem Riders! Git off'n my stoop! Close my do', man!" Mama began bumping his legs with her wheelchair—up, back, up, back—like a battering ram.

"Ow—dat hurt, Aint Baby! Okay, okay—I be goin'." He gathered his jacket over his head and called to me, "I be waitin' for you t' pay me, Cat!"

When he was gone, I felt relieved, but also a little guilty. Scarecrow had confided in me, jokingly, about his fear of being alone during rainstorms, especially when there was thunder and lightning. I'd told him I took reservations "for de scaredy cat t' come t' my house whensoever it storm." He'd laughed and handed me the five dollars. It seemed he hadn't been joking.

But the sad fact was, I'd already spent the money, and Mama's rent was coming due. Now that I was back at home, her rent was mine, and since the dropsy had dropped her in a wheelchair, she'd had to stop midwifing. What she made ironing just wasn't enough.

The storm blew through, and the next morning I was back on the street, walkin' my walk to pay the rent. Since my second release from the workhouse, I had been trying to honor my promise to get on with my life and stop waiting for Ike. But although I had been "makin' more tracks" than ever, I seemed to be standing still. I turned tricks when I could—ten dollars for white men, five dollars for colored—but it could be a risky business.

One time at Black Mary's, I'd trotted out my wares for Mr. Cain, a white landlord with lots of rentals in Gee Pee. He tried to bargain me down to six. When I held out for the price we'd agreed on, he got offended and called the police. While we were waiting, he threw a tantrum and tried to scare me by kicking over some furniture. I'd seen enough real violence to know when to get scared, and what he did only made me laugh. But he was white, and I couldn't afford another trip to the workhouse. While he was showing his temper, I pulled out my "craibabby switch"—the safety razor I carried in my bosom. It gave me a tough reputation and some confidence, but I'd never had to actually pull it on anybody before.

Mr. Cain stopped breaking things long enough to ask, "Now who you think you gonna scare with that razor, little gal?"

"You," I said calmly, and proceeded to muss my hair and give myself a few superficial cuts on the topside of my arms.

His face fell in disbelief as Mr. Big Smitty walked through the door, answering his call. I grabbed the policeman's arm and worked up some tears. "Oh, Mr. Big Smitty—thank de Lawd you be here!"

Mr. Cain babbled something about it all being a mistake. Big Smitty gave him a hard stare, to warn him to not let things go so far the next time, and told me I'd better be more careful in the future.

After that, I had trouble "dating" local white men. Mr. Cain put out the word that I was crazy, and nobody wanted hassles like that while there were cheaper, safer black women to be had. Fortunately, this had no effect on the colored men in town, and my business with them picked up. This naturally caused their wives and girlfriends to complain more loudly and more often, and some of that got back to Mama.

Funny thing was, I didn't care, and if Mama did, nowadays she took pains not to show it. She knew what a heavy financial weight I had to carry for her, Cedric, Charles, and myself. Her landlord, a white lady named Miss Hall, didn't care about Mama's good record or standing in the community. All she knew was what she was owed and when.

"I want my rent, Ida Lou!" she'd yell from her car so that all the neighbors could hear. Mama said she never got out of her car because she was scared of the neighborhood. She also never got Mama's name right.

"Yo' rent money be on de way!" Mama would yell back from the porch. "Dat 'oman over yon'er still owes me for catchin' her baby—she gwine git me somethin' dis mornin'!"

"She better, else you gotta find another house!" Miss Hall said, though she must have known Mama was lying. She was aware that Mama's condition had prevented her from catching babies for the last few years.

"Wait a minute!" Mama cocked her head and cupped one ear. "Dat sound like her boy comin' wit' de money! Hey, Ida Mae—is dat Nancy Lee's boy I hears in de alley?"

"No'm, I don't see him," I said, acting like I was looking for the boy.

"Well, I guess dat ain't him. But you wait right dere, Miss Hall. He gwine be 'round in a minute."

Miss Hall rolled up her windows for protection and waited. After a while, Mama sent me out to her car with a cold drink of water in one of our nice store-bought glasses. When Miss Hall rolled down her window and reached for the glass, Mama called, "Now Ida Mae, I hope you rinse out dat glass real good, 'cause you know how bad dem roaches be in de cupboard!"

Miss Hall declined Mama's hospitality just as Miss Shocker set loose her buck-naked two-year-old, Li'l Ug. He ran up to the pretty car and smeared the side with his molasses-covered hand. Miss Shocker barely had time to pluck him back before the big black car peeled away from the curb.

"Well, I 'spect she ain't got de time to wait," Mama chuckled, drinking the water Miss Hall had turned down. "Thankee, Shocker!" Mama waved, and Miss Shocker waved back. "Now why don't you g'won and put de glass back on de shelf, Ida Mae. We save it 'til comp'ny come 'gin." She dug out a big pinch of snuff and poked it under her lower lip. "I owes dis to my owndearself!" she said.

Not long after my run-in with Mr. Cain, I was waiting for Buddy Boy's cab to pick me up by the Walthall theater. The rent was due again and we were short by about five tricks. "Hey dere, Miss Kitty Cat!" Buddy Boy called, pulling up to the curb in his big, beat-up car. I got inside and shut the door.

"You workin' de kiddie show?" Buddy Boy's eyes teased me in the rearview mirror.

"Mind you own bidness, Buddy Boy," I snapped. "Jest drop me 'cross de tracks."

"You got it, Miss Cat. Hope you brang yo' umbrella—look like it gwine to rain some mo'."

"Hmph," I snorted. "I'm feelin' so hongry and skinny I jest walk twixt de raindrops!"

We had not quite reached the railroad tracks when I spied a nicely dressed, clean-looking black gent walking in our direction.

"Whoa up, Buddy Boy," I said. "Y'all kin jest drop me here."

"I dunno, Miss Cat. He be one o' dem Riders."

"I don't care what he be. All I knows is he be a stranger an' strangers gots money. Lemme out here."

"Money ain't ev'ythang, Cat."

"It pay de rent. 'Sides, who make you my daddy, huh? C'mon, fool, stop de car!"

I got out, slamming the door real hard so the gent would know I was behind him. He didn't look back, so I wiggled and undulated behind him all the way down McLauren Street. I didn't know if he had any money, but he did look like he was from the North, and I still had my sights set on leaving the Delta. People on the sidewalk began clapping their hands and shouting, "Go on, Cat—walk dat walk—git his 'tention!" Finally he turned, looked me up and down, smiled like an amused daddy at his little girl, then kept walking.

Now that he knew I was there, I tried a little advertising.

"I got it—come an' git it—" I sang, just loud enough for him to hear. "Come an' git you some—"

He kept walking. Now I was getting mad. The old Cat would've given up, called out, "Fool—go back to yo' mama!" and gone for a drink at Sam Ciroe's. But the new Cat kept right after him—past the intersections that led somewhere else, past easier marks. I had a bull by the horns, and this time, I was not about to be thrown.

Our long walk ended at a modest brick building surrounded by shacks. The front door, shaded by a brick arch, bore a sign showing two clasped hands, one white, one black, and the words "Student Nonviolent Coordinating Committee." Most of the townspeople crossed the street when they passed the office and averted their heads. Mama had heard that inside there was a picture of a white man and a colored man hugging one another.

"*Humpph!*" she said. "I ain't nevermo' seed no sich thang. Don't 'spect t' see it in dis here lifetime neither." And she warned me repeatedly, "Don'cha mess 'round wit' dem Riders, Ida Mae!"

"No'm, I ain't!" I said.

But outside the SNCC building, a small group of colored people was milling around, and I could see as the stranger went in that it was crowded inside. I caught a glimpse of a colored woman sitting at a desk typing real fast and not even looking down at the keyboard.

"What be happenin', Miss Nonnie?" I asked a woman I recognized in line.

"Dey be writin' down ou' name 'cause us'n ain't got no some-teet," she answered loudly.

At that time, there were very few welfare programs in existence. People who did receive government aid were ashamed to speak of it, and their neighbors knew better than to ask. One of the few assistance programs people were not ashamed to speak of, however, was the Surplus Food Program. Most of the poor people living in the outlying districts and in Greenwood—both black and white— were dependent on the federal government for commodities like cheese, flour, milk, rice, beans, and sometimes canned chopped meat to make it between harvests.

Mama would awaken me early in the morning to go down to the commodity house in the old compress near the railroad track to pick up her supplies. Once inside, we had to form a single line and holler out our names, saying whether we knew how to sign them. The white county worker sitting behind her neat desk enjoyed causing us as much misery and shame as possible.

"Now boy," she'd say to old Mr. Brace, who was nearly eighty, "you and this gal"—referring to his wife, Miss Beulah—"y'all git up to the white line and don't move 'til I call yo' name." Then she would call on several people and fuss at them because they could only sign their name with an X. Hours later, she would remember the old couple, who were still standing near the white line. They would be tired, hot, and in need of a bathroom, but they hadn't dared leave the spot for fear of having their food withheld.

The surplus food came from the federal government, but the program had always been administered by Leflore County officials. That summer, under pressure from the Ku Klux Klan and its upscale auxiliary, the White Citizens Council, they had stopped distribution and locked up the commodities. I hadn't minded the interruption, and I hadn't thought about what had caused it. I hated the trip to the commodity house and back and the humiliation of the process. And since Ike sent money and sacks of grocery for Cedric, we were able to get by. But now I was curious about what had given the county the right to withhold goods that weren't theirs in the first place.

"It be dese Riders," Miss Nonnie said, "tryin' t' reddish us'n t' vote. Mayor Sampson an' Chief Lary be all shook up! Dey ain't gwine gi'e us'n no some-teet 'til de Riders leave dis town." She rolled her eyes heavenward. "So de Riders tell us'n t' c'mere an' git de grocies sont by folkses up nawth! Jest 'fore you gits here, a carload o' dem white mens drive by. Dey be talkin' underneath our closes an' call us'n 'Moses niggers' an' 'block coons' an' 'peacock skunks,' an' dey says for us'n t' git on home where us'n b'long! But you knows us'n needs de grocies. What else us'n gwine do?"

That was a good question. Though I had lived in Greenwood all my life, I had never seen people scratching for food the way my friends and neighbors were doing now.

"Who you gwine b'lieve," Miss Nonnie asked no one in particular, "dese white folkses who done been feedin' you for a long time, or de Riders? Dey be like a birds who be flyin' 'cross de sky—dey soon be gone."

The handsome stranger I had followed stood in the doorway. "We need help to get all these people signed up. Who can read and write and is willing to help us with this task?" His voice was cool and deep—like Ike's without the jazz, but dressed up with education. He was looking directly at me.

"G'won, Cat." Miss Nonnie pushed me forward. "Dis 'un kin read an' write real good—her make out all my chilluns' birth 'tificates!"

Nobody else stepped forward, but if life had taught me nothing else, it had taught me to recognize a cue to get onstage. I followed the stranger inside.

Rows of fluorescent lights glowed overhead, and notices, letters, cards, and clippings were tacked and taped all over the walls. On the far wall was a map of the entire Delta, covered with pushpins. Desks and tabletops sported all kinds of magazines and newspapers I had never seen. Some even had black faces on their covers: *Negro Digest, Our World, Ebony,* and *Jet.*

A couple of teenagers I knew from Baptist Town said "How do" as I passed and nodded nervously at me, which made me nervous, too. A bunch of colored folks I didn't know sat in knots about the room, in chairs and on the edge of desks, slouching or standing, and talking with animation and wit. Some just had their heads down, writing busily in notebooks or files as they interviewed pairs of people I knew—the poor people who had come for food. Mixed among them were a handful of white folks, but nobody seemed to be paying attention to them except the black people they were talking to.

I made a beeline to look over the shoulder of the young colored woman who'd been typing. I expected to see a lot of *P*s and *Q*s on the paper, but she hadn't missed a word.

Someone called out "Bob," and the stranger I had followed turned his calm eyes to mine.

The Student Nonviolent Coordinating Committee—SNCC, pronounced "snick" by movement regulars—had been formed a few years earlier in North Carolina after black students there had staged a sit-in at the lunch counter of a local five-and-dime. They thought our older self-help organizations like the NAACP and CORE, the Congress of Racial Equality, had grown too fat and lazy in their old age. SNCC provided younger blood and new energy to fight a war the Kennedy administration said was just beginning: to wipe out Jim Crow, starting at the ballot box and courthouse. To bring together all the various black groups that had a finger in this pie into one powerful fist, the leaders of SNCC, the SCLC, the NAACP, and CORE founded the Council of Federated Organizations (COFO), a kind of United Nations of black America. And white America, at least in the South, didn't like that one bit.

Twenty-seven-year-old Bob Moses was director of COFO's voter registration drive, which brought him—and a whole lot of trouble —to Mississippi. He'd begun in McComb the previous year, and this summer had targeted Greenwood and the Yazoo River region, where only 2 percent of the black people (compared to 95 percent of the whites) were registered to vote. We were to be a make-or-break showcase project, but at this point, with only a handful of new voters to show for a whole summer's worth of work, we seemed to be breaking.

At first glance, Moses didn't look like the inspirational leader some already knew him to be, and the rest of us would soon discover. He was not tall or powerfully built. He had freckles and wore glasses and spoke softly. Yet, as I would soon learn, no packhorse could teach him anything about stamina; no history book patriot or bloodied war hero could show him how to stand firm against his enemies. When the going was toughest, his very presence calmed people better than a shot of whiskey. With quiet, soulful eyes, this math teacher from the Harlem projects shared his creed before each battle: "Each and every one of us can strike a blow for freedom."

Bob had been preceded in Greenwood by Mississippi natives Sam Block and Willie Peacock. Willie was as handsome as his name: tall, raw-boned, with fine African features—oval head, long jaw, broad, thoughtful forehead. Like Bob Moses, he was a college graduate and one of SNCC's first field secretaries. When he and Sam first came to Greenwood, neither had a car, so they rode a borrowed mule around town and into the country to register their voters.

Sam Block was a twenty-three-year-old music student from Mississippi Vocational College in nearby Itta Bena. He was not a handsome man, but he had enormous courage. At the beginning of the summer, a Negro man was arrested for "peeping on a white woman." The man was bull-whipped in jail and might have died if Sam hadn't made a complaint to the FBI. Nothing happened to his assailants, of course—the FBI was years away from taking a hard stand against any southern police force—but his action made Sam a folk hero to Greenwood's blacks.

At SNCC's first voter registration drive, Leflore County sheriff John Ed Cothron came up to Sam and asked, "Nigger, where you from?" Sam answered, "Well, I'm a native Mississippian." The sheriff said he knew "every nigger and his mammy" in Greenwood, and he didn't know Sam. Sam replied, "Well, you know all the niggers, do you know any colored people?"

Sheriff Cothron spat in Sam's face and told him, "I don't want to see you in town anymore. The thing you better do is pack your clothes and get out and don't never come back no more."

Sam replied, calm as he could be, "Well, Sheriff, if you don't want to see me here, I think the thing for you to do is pack your clothes and get out of town, 'cause I'm here to stay. I came here to do a job and I'm going to do it."

Bob Moses arrived in Mississippi with a group of SNCC workers. They were referred to jokingly as "Moses and his Twelve Disciples." A few local people came forward to help: in addition to the Reverend Aaron Johnson and B. T. McSwine, there were Mr. Robert Burns, the picture taker, the old agitator Mr. Cleveland Jordan, former local NAACP president Edward "Deadeye" Cochran, and Dewey Greene, a classmate of Block's, among others. Soon the SNCC workers had to flee by the windows of their office to escape a gang of angry white thugs.

That was just the beginning of the backlash, which escalated to firebombs, shotgun blasts, and beatings. Strangely enough, the KKK wasn't as active in Leflore County as elsewhere in the Delta. It didn't have to be: before the Movement came, everybody knew their place and stayed in it. But when the local klaverns did strike, they did so with terrible effect, leaving behind wooden crosses wrapped with flaming cloth, dynamite-filled shoeboxes, or whiskey jugs filled with white gas, lighted rags jammed in their mouths. Black people were afraid, and began to denounce the movement and the workers before whites.

"My boss lady axed me 'f'n I be don' th'ow in wit' de votin' folkses," Mama's friend Miss Loddie whispered to her. "I tol' her dat dem folkses ain't no earthly good."

"You be right, Loddie," Mama whispered back. Greenwood's Negroes seemed to have lost their ability to speak above a whisper.

But SNCC wasn't leaving Greenwood; in fact, the troops continued to grow. Lawrence Guyot, a heavyset Tougaloo student, came on board. At eighteen, Luvaghn Brown from Jackson was for a time the youngest SNCC staffer. The white male workers, like Dick Frey, all looked a little older, especially with the tidy mustaches and horn-rimmed glasses some of them sported. Their uniform was the same sweat-stained, open-collared sports shirts many of the black men wore.

The few white women, like Toni Lang and Karen Trusty, looked like no kind of woman I'd seen, with long, wavy hair pulled up in ponytails or pigtails against the heat, thin unpainted lips, earnest eyes, and big hoop earrings that made them look like Gypsies. I stared and stared at them, fascinated and confused.

Bob Moses led me to a desk with two chairs—one empty, the other occupied by the typist who hadn't missed a word. "Ida— that's your name?" he asked politely.

"Yassuh," I said. "Ida Mae Holland. But people jest calls me Cat."

"Well, Ida, this is Emma Bell—Emma, Ida Mae Holland," he said, introducing me to the fast-typing gal. She looked up and grinned and crinkled her eyes in a friendly welcome without missing a stroke. "This is your desk," he said, pulling out the chair for me, like a gentleman on a date.

I sat down softly, feeling as if everyone in the place was looking at me. Of course, they weren't. They were all busy looking at maps and papers and lists and talking about things like "voter registration forms" and "the food program" and "mass meetings" and such. It was like school—but a school where the students were teachers.

"Don't worry, Ida," Emma said. "You'll get used to this mad-house."

I watched Emma type for a minute—fingers flying across the keyboard, eyes dancing from line to line on the scrawly notebook beside her—until another man appeared, this one with a type-writer in his arms.

"How you doin', sister?" he asked.

"I be doin' fine, how you doin'?" I replied.

"Glad you're here," he said, shifting the typewriter in his arms. "We need you bad. Mind if I set this on your desk?"

On *my* desk! A typewriter on my very own desk? "Sho' thang," I said, pushing books, binders, and papers out of the way to make room.

"Okay, now that you've got your typewriter," Emma said, "here's what we've got to do."

What *we've* got to do? Somehow, just by walking in and being who I was, I'd made the grade. I was on the team, and now I had responsibilities like everyone else.

A pair of sharecroppers came in—my first customers. Emma and I took their names and addresses and whatever else the form said. Emma typed while I printed neatly on the long yellow-lined pad. I was afraid of the typewriter, but I had them sign their names or leave their mark, then pointed them back to the place where they could pick up some emergency rations. "There," Emma said, grinning, "you just signed up your first pledge—that fella says he'll go down to the courthouse with us and register to vote!" Emma typed the information onto another form as fast as she could, then signaled for the next applicants.

As the afternoon wore on, I began to see my own pride and relief reflected in the faces of our "clients." Each man or woman was treated with courtesy and respect—no hollering or ignoring or bullying as usually happened at city hall, the county courthouse, the commodity house, or any other place where colored people went to take care of even the most routine business. And although we didn't know it then, each person we signed up would bring back five, ten, fifteen, even twenty others over the next two years. As one White Citizens Council member said years later, "When we cut out the food giveaway program, that was our biggest mistake—'cause that's when our nigras embraced the civil rights crusade!"

Someone—I think it was Willie Peacock—started singing. "One man's hands can't change the status quo. Two men's hands can't change the status quo. But if one and one and fifty make a million, we'll see that day come 'round—we'll see that day come 'round!" Everyone else in the office picked up the tune, and before the song was over I had learned it, too.

By the time we had processed and provisioned the last hungry person, it was dark.

"You did a great job, Ida. Thanks," Emma said, pulling the plastic cover over her typewriter. "Tomorrow I will show you how to type." Then she added, "I'm hungry, let's go eat."

As I tidied up my desk and got my things together, I realized I had taken to these newcomers like a duck to water. Being treated with respect was something wholly new for me. I was impressed that none of the men in the Freedom Office showed even the slightest interest in wanting to have sex with me. It struck me that the people I was working with—men and women, black and white—were interested in one thing and one thing only: freedom.

I left the Freedom Office feeling ten feet tall, but by the time I had run the gauntlet of cold stares, evasive glances, and unreturned greetings on the way home, I had been whittled down to inches. The news that "Cat be up yon'er wit' dem Riders" had spread before me like an unwelcome mat in my neighborhood.

Mama shouted my name as soon as I turned off Walthall onto East Gibb. By the time I climbed the steps to the porch, I could see she was spitting mad.

"You c'mere, gal, an' tell me where you be at all day!"

"I be writin', Mama—signin' up de folkses to go to de courthouse to vote." I hoped the worship word *writing* would calm her down.

"Vote! Vote! You be messin' 'round wit' dem Riders—ol' 'omanish gal, who ain't got no sense, who be crazier den a betsy bug!"

"I tol' you, Mama. I be teachin' de folkses to write dey name—"

"Gal, I ain't axe you *what* you be doin', I axe you *where* you be doin' it! Who you be wit'?"

"Be at de Freedom Office," I said in a small voice.

"De Freedom Office!" She jerked in her wheelchair as if she'd been shot, and her eyes fluttered heavenward. "Lawd, have mercy on yo' servant!"

Suddenly I was more angry than scared. "Dey be a different kind o' colored folkses, Mama," I said firmly. "Dey be real good people. Dis here one lady—she don't be talkin' to me, but I hear her say it—say we gonna git our freedom—"

"Git our freedom! Git our freedom! Ida Mae, gal, us'n be *already* free. Dat dere 'oman don't know what she talkin' 'bout!"

"You oughta hear dem, Mama. Dey talk real pretty and proper-like. Dey don't break no verbs, neither." Mama loved proper talk.

"Don't wanna hear dem," she said, covering both ears with her hands. "Ain't got no time t' fool 'round wit' dat mess. Git our freedom! You best lissen t' me, gal. Don'cha git in wit' dem fools. All dey gwine do is git a lotta folkses kilt. Den dey gwine go back home up nawth—"

"Dey ain't jest from de nawth, Mama," I said. "Dey be from de Delta, too—an' from Jackson, 'lanta, Memphis—uh, lessee, an' from Chicago, too!" I tried to think of the places Mama respected.

"Dey c'mere from Hell—stirrin' up trouble twix de white folkses an' us coloreds." Mama rolled her chair away and wouldn't look at me. "Yo' mama ain't jest fall off'n de dray wagon, Ida Mae. Us'n knowed a long time now dat dese folkses be comin' here, makin' us 'fraid for our life. Dem Freedom Riders done slip in dis town like a thief an' robber in de night! Dey gwine git us all kilt wit' dey talk 'bout reddishin' t' vote an' bein' good as de white folkses. Lawdy, Lawd"—she looked to the sky again—"us'n poor ol' colored folkses needs you now!"

"Mama, dey jest want me to he'p dem write down de folkses' name an' show dem how to write."

"Lawd amercy—you tol' dem outsiders dat you gots a education?" Now she did look at me, with panic in her eyes.

"Didn't open my mouth 'cept to say yes, Mama. I swears it." I crossed my heart and hoped to die.

Mama looked at me suspiciously. "Now, I knows you be real 'omanish—"

"Miss Nonnie did it, Mama. She jest 'bout push me through de door! *She* tol' de Civil Righters—dat's what dey is—dat I be de one who fill out de birth 'tificates for her chilluns."

"Dat crack-brain ol' 'oman! She oughta mind her own dear bidness. Den she oughta *pay* me for catchin' dat water-head boy o' hers!"

I'd succeeded in getting Mama off on a tangent, the opportunity I'd been looking for. I walked off to tend the mound of dirty laundry that was waiting for me and to kiss sleeping Cedric and Charles.

"But you promise me one thang, Ida Mae," Mama shouted after me. "Even though you ain't never once done a thang I axe you—"

"What dat, Mama?"

"Promise yo' ol' Mama on a stack o' Bibles dat you ain't gwine git mix up wit' dem Righters. C'mon now, gal. Say it."

I sighed. "Okay, Mama—ain't never gonna mess 'round wit' dem Righters." I crossed my heart again, but in the reverse direction from before. If God was watching as close as Mama, He knew what I meant.

Thirteen

DESPITE MY PROMISE TO MAMA, I WENT BACK TO THE FREEDOM OFFICE THE NEXT DAY. IT TURNED out that learning to type wasn't as easy for me as Emma imagined. But I got pretty good with two fingers (the way I type to this very day), and I learned my way around an office—filing, answering phones, filling out forms, greeting people, handling problems, even creating problems if that's what was needed to get things done.

I began working with Judy Richardson and Sally Belfrage, two white girls from the North, in the Freedom Library, which suited me since I liked to read. The Freedom Library supplied books and materials to COFO's "Freedom Schools," little one-room, one-teacher "campuses" where black adults and kids could learn something about their own history and legal rights, and brush up on their basic skills.

In the mornings I filled out forms and taught people how to read and write. When I got to the office each day, there was a crowd waiting to be taught their ABC's and to print their names in big, awkward letters. I was surprised to discover how many of my neighbors were illiterate. In the afternoons, I would go out into the neigborhoods to canvass for voters with the other SNCC workers, feeling smart and enviable. Sometimes we were chased away from people's doors at gunpoint. Other times, we were invited in for a meager meal.

But however well the Freedom Schools and libraries and food-giveaway program were working, the voter registration plan was failing. At this early stage we gauged our progress by the number

214

willing to go and try to register to vote. Most often they were
foiled by technicalities, in the person of Miss Martha Lamb, the
country registrar:

"You see there, Cleve, you didn't pass the test. See here—you
didn't write nothing in that section. You didn't pass!" Miss Martha
said sympathetically to Mr. Cleveland Jordan, the old agitator.

"Can't nobody pass that test," Mr. Jordan complained bitterly.
"My son can't pass the test." Mr. Jordan's son was a college graduate and president of the local chapter of the NAACP. He reared
back and hooked his thumbs under his suspenders. "I bet you Miss
Martha Lamb can't 'terpret the Con'tution to my sat'faction."

In an effort to get the voter registration plan rolling, Greenwood's SNCC leadership decided to trade their clipboards for the
pulpit of Reverend Johnson's Christian Church. I knew right away
that would mean another run-in with Mama.

News of the rally spread all over town, faster than the gusty
wind that blew our leaflets across the sidewalks and gutters. The
colored people tossed them away as soon as they got them because
they were afraid, the whites because they were angry. On the day
of the rally, shades drew down behind plate-glass windows and
door locks snapped. Colored maids all over town were sent home
early, even before the chores were done and the evening meal was
fixed. Stores in both communities closed early; Miss Ellen and Mr.
Pete shuttered and bolted their grocery and left in their truck for
a "short vacation."

"I won'er what de matter be?" Mama asked Dossie Ree. "Dis
de first time in twenty years dat 'oman pass up a chance to holler
at me on de way home!"

"Miss Ellen pass you up like Jesus pass up Cicero!" Dossie Ree
explained, showing off her confused knowledge of the Bible.

"Dere be a dead cat on de line somewheres," Mama said, shaking
her head.

" 'Xactly! So you better git ready t' go t' dat mass meetin' an' find out where!"

Mama rolled her chair around the room, pulling down the shades. "I ain't gwine nowheres. Gwine shut my do', turn out de lights, an' set here wit' de Lawd an' pray for dem foolish folk in de church house."

Dossie Ree laughed. "Den leave yo' do' open, 'cause you gwine have lots o' comp'ny! Dis house gwine be de place t' be!"

"I ain't jokin', Dossie Ree. Dem white folk gwine put dem Righters an' anysomebody wit' dem in de river. How fast you think I kin run in dis ol' wheelchair?"

"You jest gits t' *ride* t' de river, Mama," I teased her. I walked to the front door, putting the finishing touches on my hair.

"An' where de devil *you* be goin', chile?" Mama asked, as if she couldn't guess. "You ain't gwine to de church house. You go out de back an' see dat ol Frisgo be tied up—don't want him t' git kilt denight. Dere gwine be a lotta trouble."

"Yas'm, Mama," I said. I marched out the kitchen door to check Frisgo's chain. From the backyard, I could see people streaming toward the church. Some walked timidly, looking over their shoulders, others marched boldly. When Frisgo's chain was secure, I slipped away to join the parade.

By the time I got to the chapel, it was standing room only, so I squeezed along the wall with the other latecomers. In addition to our Gee Pee neighbors and people I recognized from Gritney, I saw lots of people from Baptist Town and many of the plantation workers we had signed up at the office. The area around the pulpit was filled with church officials—ordained and jackleg preachers, deacons, and Mothers of the Church. Reverend Johnson led us in the Lord's Prayer. Bro Pastor read from the Twenty-third Psalm and called on God to appear.

Bro Pastor was wearing the blue-black gabardine frock coat with the satin lapels he donned only on high occasions sanctioned by God. He'd worn it to the Walthall picture show to see *Samson and Delilah* and *The Ten Commandments,* so that the congregation could rest assured that the theater wouldn't come tumbling down on their heads if they paid twenty-five cents to see the lascivious Samaritan and Moses parting the Red Sea. When he wore it to funerals, it was a clear indication that the dearly departed was earmarked for heaven. (I suspect he'd have come to mine in his shirtsleeves.) Its appearance tonight was the clearest sign yet that God was on the movement's side.

A couple of deacons took up offerings for the freedom workers and for the church's building fund, and some of the SNCC workers led us in a song. I had seen the words typed out in the Freedom Office, but hadn't heard the tune until now—an old spiritual that everybody knew, so we could all sing along:

Paul and Silas were bound in jail,
Had no money to go their bail.
Keep your eyes on the prize
And hold on.

Sam Block spoke first. He talked about our right to vote, as citizens of this country, and about our fears—which were real, but not enough, he said, to keep us from the franchise. When he finished, there was not one dry eye in the church. People applauded with a frenzy, shouting "Amen!" and "Yes, Lawd!" Then Willie Peacock and two other SNCC workers rocked the church with more civil rights songs they'd set to the tune of old-time spirituals like "This Little Light of Mine" and "Wade in the Water."

Meetings like these encouraged people to join the movement and to stay in it. It was hard to turn back once you had heard such soul-wrenching speeches and joined in such fervent singing.

So far, most of SNCC's local support had come from the young and the uneducated. Some young people joined because they were really interested in freedom, some as a way of challenging their parents or getting kicked out of school. Country people who were tired of making crops for white plantation owners and "trash" in Gee Pee, Gritney, and Baptist Town—in other words, people who thought they had nothing to lose—were quick to join, too.

But most people with education or a good job were reluctant to rock the boat that had carried them down the rapids where so many others had drowned. Once you got tagged as a "Righter," neighbors who used to smile and wave and call "How do" crossed the street rather than be seen talking to a troublemaker.

The principal of Broad Street High School suspended or expelled any kid who participated in a demonstration. No mention of the work done by the Freedom Fighters was made in school, so pervasive was the fear on the part of the teachers, many of whom worked in secret with the Movement. Years later, a woman named Jeanette Cunningham recalled to me how her teacher at Stone Street School had told the class, "Get up and look out the window and watch while history is being made!" as we marched past on our way to the courthouse.

People who did get involved in the Movement kept their involvement to themselves—no mean feat in a small community where everyone knew everyone else's business. Brothers lied to brothers, and daughters lied to mothers. Friends and relatives who betrayed them thought of themselves as protecting their families. Some local blacks even curried favor with the police by tipping them off about SNCC's movements and plans, often for a "reward" of several dollars.

My reasons for joining were simple: It got the white man's goat —and it also gave me a reason to flaunt my borrowed clothes.

Within the little town of Greenwood, I lived in my own country. I was an outsider on the inside, a bit like the freedom workers. Perhaps this was what growing up really meant, I thought: to take that small space hidden within you and to pull it out, then stretch it until you could fit within it. Being around the SNCC people had turned my narrow space into a country bigger than I'd ever imagined. Still, every country has its borders, and there were always those who lurked outside, trying to beat my borders back, to make me small again. I swore I would not let that happen again.

Yet day by day, the staff was growing with people I knew—Miss Susie and her daughters, Old Man "Freedom" Smith (a name the workers gave him because of his boldness), Willie Shaw, John Handy, Rosemary Freeman, Willie James Earl—and I was beginning to make new friends. Greenwood teenager June Johnson's mother forbade her to get involved with the Freedom Movement. Her mother, Miss Lula Bell Johnson, was a powerful force in the lives of her twelve children and us other young people. But June was just as strong-willed, and she kept sneaking off to the Freedom Office. After a while Miss Lula Bell followed her, expecting to find her doing something bad. But when Miss Lula Bell walked into the SNCC office and listened to what the workers were truly about, she became a convert on the spot. She went on to become a crucial force in the Movement, and so did June.

Even the violent white backlash began to backfire, creating the very sense of solidarity it was trying to defeat.

In December 1962, two white civil rights workers from Michigan State University were arrested while trying to bring food and clothing into Greenwood during the Leflore County supervisors' "strike" against federal assistance to poor people. Now that out-of-state white folks were on the receiving end of the racists' wrath, the national news media got interested. Black entertainer Harry

Belafonte gave a relief appeal concert at Carnegie Hall, and black comedian Dick Gregory was said to be chartering a plane to deliver emergency rations personally to Greenwood.

This news was too big to escape Mama's notice for long.

"You think 'cause you don't tell me nothin' 'bout where you be or where you goin', dat I don't know—but Dossie Ree say de Righters gwine brang a great big plane in here loaded down wit' some-teet an' closes for folkses t' put on!"

"Yas'm, Mama," I said. "Dey say a famous man—a *movie star*, Mama!—name Dick Gregory gonna gi'e us a airplane full o' food!"

Mama wriggled in her chair, pessimism wrestling with excitement. "Well, I hopes you be Somebody wit' dem folkses so you kin git us some-teet. An' when you go through dem closes, be sho' t' git me a new smock. Ain't had me a new frock since I stop waitin' babies, an' dis un 'bout t' give out."

With Gregory's relief flight in the works, we SNCC workers felt a new surge of optimism—and that translated into longer days, more hours, and bigger risks.

In early 1963, a black cab driver named Milton Hancock, who had been hauling the freedom workers for free, was stopped by a deputy on a trumped-up traffic violation and warned, "Git yo' black ass out of town—you know what happen' to Emmett Till!" Anybody with facial hair was subject to arrest. A goateed black worker and a bearded white worker were hauled in on identification charges (supposedly they looked like escaped prisoners from Parchman), beaten severely, and had their "beatnik" goatee and beard pulled out by the handful. Booker Wright, who had worked for years in a white-owned cafe, went to the courthouse to register to vote one morning, only to find his job gone that afternoon. David Vasser, a local black man who canvassed for the movement, was shot at by a group of white men in a truck.

The strange thing was, the KKK and the WCC served much the

same emotional function for our enemies as SNCC and the NAACP did for us. They bestowed on their members what those people most lacked in life: a sense of worth, self-respect, common purpose, and power. What motivated us to march on, despite axe handles, police dogs, cattle prods, shotguns, and firebombs, was not that much different from what motivated the angry white fists wielding them: pride and the wish to control one's own future.

One day, overhearing some of the SNCC workers talking, it struck me that they had no regular place to sleep. Although they could eat at Bullins' Cafe for free—some SNCC patrons up North were picking up the check—Blood, the owner, did not provide accommodations.

Besides, as a freedom worker in Greenwood in early 1963, where you slept was a lot more than a question of convenience. I listened as one of the field secretaries reminded everyone of the standing rules for safety: "When you're away from the Freedom Office, check in by phone every two hours. If you get arrested, we will bombard the jailhouse with queries about you, around the clock. Above all, don't attract attention. Don't sleep in the same place for more than two nights, and always sleep with your clothes on."

I was thinking how Mama always encouraged me to bring home lodgers when she had a spare room to rent. But the urge to repay the kindness I'd been shown with an invitation to my house stuck in my throat. Most of Mama's life had been spent avoiding or getting out of trouble, and this was just the kind of aggravation she didn't need.

On February 20, 1963, we gave away four tons of food in one day—a new record. People who'd been afraid of white retaliation began to think of us as a source of help. Those who'd shunned us on the street now smiled and said "How do." This breakthrough in community relations, however, didn't last long.

The day after our record giveaway, four black-owned businesses in Greenwood got firebombed. Bob Moses led us through the smoldering ruins—most of it left to burn itself out. Sam Block gave a press conference on the spot. He said the firebombings were a retaliation for our relief work and complained about the police dragging their heels in the "investigation"—which mostly took the form of lawmen photographing those of us who came to inspect the ruins and console the victims. Shortly after his speech, Sam was arrested and charged with "inciting a riot." A crisis was suddenly upon us.

On February 25, a hundred of us workers and neighborhood supporters marched on Greenwood City Hall to protest Sam's imprisonment, chanting "One man, one vote!" The seasoned SNCC workers tried to dissuade us, because Bob Moses was out of town and we didn't have much of a plan, but a group of us got together and decided that now was the time.

SNCC had strict rules for people participating in protest marches and sit-ins, and our leaders made sure we understood them. We weren't allowed to answer back if we got cursed or fight back if we got whupped. Although I was raised in a Christian home, "turning the other cheek" was a talent I had not cultivated. Fortunately, most of my abusers were white, and it was a lot easier to think twice about raising my voice or my fist to one of them— one of the many side effects of Jim Crow culture that came to boomerang on the oppressors.

We weren't allowed to chitchat with bystanders or workers, but we were encouraged to be courteous and friendly. Like soldiers, we were expected to hold ourselves erect, face forward, and keep our ranks until we were told it was okay to leave. Above all, we were supposed to remember to love one another and, in Bob Moses's words, "live, breathe, eat, and think" nonviolence.

If worse came to worst (and before things were over, it would), we were given tips on how to protect ourselves "nonviolently." If we were wearing jackets, we were supposed to pull them up over our heads to soften the billy club's blows. We all took a turn at falling down, curling into a tight ball, and covering our heads with our arms. If we were attacked by a police dog, we could stun it by hitting its nose—provided our hands made it past those flashing teeth—or disorient it by throwing cayenne pepper in its face.

Between demonstrations, we were encouraged to avoid lighted windows, which could make us easy targets for bullets. We were urged to know the escape route from any building or part of town in which we might find ourselves, and we were discouraged from traveling alone. For workers from the North, these rules were eye-opening and unsettling. For those of us raised in the Delta, they were pretty much identical to the commandments we'd grown up with.

The boldness of our first demonstration stunned the white and black communities alike. James Jones and Willie Peacock joined our short column of workers walking two abreast as we headed for Greenwood's business district. I was so scared, I could feel my left leg twitching. On McLauren Street, we picked up two drunken men from Baptist Town in front of Miss Georgia's juke house.

People were peeping from behind their curtains when we topped the railroad tracks that separate Gritney from Gee Pee. Bystanders started chanting, and I heard Mr. Clifton Lott say, "Go for it, Cat! Walk that walk, gal! Wait till I tell Nellie 'bout this." Carloads of people drove past, gawking and honking.

We stepped around the corner of Walthall and East Gibb. We'd been singing freedom songs since we started marching, and by now we'd managed to get the fear out of our voices. "Ain't scared of your jail, 'cause I want my freedom," we sang. I wanted to shock

Mama, and I wanted her to be proud of me. So I lifted my voice, threw my shoulders back, and marched at the head of the column as we marched around the corners of Gibb and Main:

"Lawd, Lawd, Lawdy!" Mama exclaimed when she saw our ragtail band of paraders. "Ain't dat Ida Mae? Dossie Ree! Uh, Dossie Ree!" She rolled to the side of the porch.

Dossie Ree rushed to her front door. "What in de world be de matter, Aint Baby?"

Mama pointed her fly swatter in our direction.

Dossie Ree took one look and fell to her knees, making the sign of the Cross. "Lawd he'p 'em, 'cause dey don't know no better, sweet Jesus!"

"Eversomebody knows dat my gal done gone 'ginst de white folkses, talkin' 'bout 'freedom,' " Mama said. "Lawd, Lawd, Lawdy!"

Our march was not rowdy, so other than drawing astounded and disapproving looks from both blacks and whites, nothing much happened. The police weren't prepared for us, and our discipline surprised them. The police chief was out of town, and the deputy chief didn't quite know what to do. We didn't know what to do either, so James Jones and Willie Peacock told us to disperse and meet back at the office. I was secretly glad that we hadn't had to use our nonviolence training.

That night, we held another mass meeting. The next day, we headed for the Leflore County courthouse, with two hundred prospective black voters ready and willing to be registered. Those who made it inside before the doors were locked got turned away by the red tape. Those waiting outside were told to disperse or be cited for blocking a public thoroughfare. We dispersed, but I broke rank last, anxious to live up to the reputation for bravery I'd established on the previous march. In all my eighteen years, I had never experienced anything so rewarding.

With Mama no longer able to catch babies and all my time spent volunteering at the Freedom Office, I was struggling to make ends meet. Ike still helped out sometimes, putting the money that used to go toward matching outfits for me, him, and Cedric toward rent and food. It was odd how those matching outfits made us look like we belonged to each other, when it was becoming clear just how mismatched we were. Ike's disdain for the movement was well known; his bossman had threatened to fire him and José, the Mexican-American man who worked alongside him, if they ever got involved in the movement.

I admit I still needed to turn an occasional trick or two when things got really tight, but that was rare. A number of my past tricks gave me money, not for services rendered, but out of friendship and respect for my work in the movement. Sometimes, northern friends of SNCC would send small donations of cash earmarked for us volunteers. Eventually I was promoted to field secretary, which paid the modest salary of $10.00 a week—when we got paid, which wasn't often. After taxes, I had $9.64. The ends never quite met, but they were real close.

Sometimes, when I was teaching somebody his ABC's in the Freedom School, my mind would wander off in search of its "someday space." But I'd come back to where I was quickly when someone asked me a question about direct action or a group of small children greeted me as a "freedom fighter." At times like those, I swore I would never leave Mama and Cedric and the Delta. I didn't have to anymore, and I didn't want to.

ON THE last day of the month, after a meeting at the Greenwood SNCC office, a SNCC worker named Jimmy Travis left in a car with Bob Moses and a COFO worker, Randolph Blackwell.

They were tailed by another car bearing several unidentified whites. When the highway traffic thinned, the second car drew up alongside them and sprayed their car with bullets. Jimmy got hit in the neck, screamed, and fell back. Bob grabbed the wheel and managed to stop the car as the assailants drove off at full speed.

Jimmy was alive, but Bob knew he wouldn't stay that way if they returned to Greenwood for treatment. Instead, they drove eighty-odd miles to Jackson—carefully observing the speed limit —where a surgeon saved Jimmy's life.

Everybody was shaken, but you'd never have known it from Bob. In his unique, low-key way, he called the staff and volunteers together and announced an all-out, month-long "saturation campaign" to register black voters in Leflore County. We sent out letters and cables to political and media figures everywhere, including telegrams to President Kennedy, his brother Bobby, and Mississippi governor Ross Barnett. As our launch date neared, newsmen gathered and political staffers showed up to nose around on behalf of their bosses. I led a group of volunteers who fanned out into the neighborhoods and countryside to canvass. Once again, some people were receptive, while others were downright hostile.

"Git on 'way from here wit' dat vote mess," one man told us from behind his door. "Y'all stir up misery twixt de race—gwone, git 'way from my house."

And once again, the best measure of our success was the pain we endured because of it. On March 6, 1963, a car parked in front of the SNCC office had its windows blown out by a shotgun. On March 24, the Freedom Office itself was set on fire, though we managed to save most of our records. Days later, more night riders fired shots into the home of a local black volunteer, Dewey Greene, whose son, Dewey Jr., had announced he was going to follow in James Meredith's footsteps and enroll at Ole Miss. Nobody got hurt, but talk on the street was that it was now open season on anybody connected with the Movement.

Stung by national news reports about his lax and ineffective efforts to hunt down the vigilantes behind these attacks, the mayor gave a speech. He suggested that these incidents had been staged by COFO to win sympathy, make its opponents look bad, and shore up support among Greenwood's blacks who were still hesitant about embracing SNCC's actions.

In response, Bob Moses organized a new march on City Hall, calling in James Forman, SNCC's executive secretary in Atlanta, to help. We got as far as the Leflore Theater, through a gauntlet of jeering white onlookers, before Police Chief Lary's dog handler, backed up by most of the force in riot gear, told us to "break it up or we'll turn him loose!" At that time, the Greenwood Police Department had only one dog, a German shepherd, but it was a terror.

Now, most of us in the Delta had been raised around dogs, but not Bob Moses. Growing up in Harlem, he felt goosey just passing one leashed in the street, let alone a snarling attack dog whipped up to a fevered frenzy. But instead of running or melting back into the group, Bob swallowed hard and kept walking.

He didn't get ten paces when the shepherd leaped forward, dragging its handler behind. It tore off a hunk from Bob's pants and went on like a bullet into our ranks, knocking us down like bowling pins. A big cheer went up from the white onlookers.

Still, Bob kept on marching, torn pants flapping like a tattered flag. At the end of the block, the line of police waited, nightsticks pounding their palms, blood lust in their eyes. Before the rest of us could catch up, they had surrounded Bob and James Forman and hauled them off to jail. Willie Peacock told us all to break up the demonstration and, two by two, move onto the sidewalk to avoid arrest. Then the police grabbed him, Lawrence Guyot, and four others, charging them with "disorderly conduct."

We never knew how many people were injured by the dog, who rampaged like Hannibal's elephant after Bob Moses passed. Charlie Cobb and Matthew Little and Reverend Tucker got chewed up, along with an elderly black lady who'd sought refuge in a nearby store only to be thrown out by the white proprietor.

Reverend Tucker cried out from the ground, "Help me, Jesus!"

"He ain't gonna help you, boy—you better call the NAACP!" said a policeman, kicking at Reverend Tucker's bleeding leg.

"Don'cha kick him!" I said, grabbing the policeman.

The policeman drew back to hit me with his billy club, then restrained himself. "You under arrest, gal!" he said. "Here, take this nigger to jail," he called. He and another policeman pulled me to the backseat of a squad car. That was the first time I was arrested for the Movement. I wasn't afraid of getting arrested, but I was afraid of getting arrested for freedom.

When we reached the jail, several white men came and peered into the back of the car, then left me sitting there for about two hours. I said my prayers and cursed my "disorderly conduct." I knew better than to grab a policeman, but Reverend Tucker had looked so lost and scared and in pain—and anyway, Mama would be proud that I stuck up for her favorite pastor. Still, once again Cedric wouldn't have a mother.

Finally, Chief Lary unlocked the car and told me to go on home, cautioning me to stop working with the "outside agitators."

"Yassuh," I nodded, glad to be free.

I went straight to the Freedom Office, where I was welcomed like a conquering hero. Some people, like me, had been held for a while and released; a few had been taken to the station but never booked. This leniency was intended to show white folks' loving nature, but no one was fooled. Bob Moses and six other SNCC workers were arrested. Lots of reporters got roughed up, including ones from *Newsweek* and *The New York Times,* which was not good PR for the segregationists' cause. A CBS cameraman who had photographed the whole scene was arrested and had his film confiscated.

From jail, Bob managed to escalate the war. He refused the bail SNCC was ready to pay, in an effort to get the U.S. Department of Justice directly involved. As in one of my Perry Mason stories, he wanted Bobby Kennedy to file a suit of *habeas corpus* to get the seven SNCC prisoners released.

Bobby Kennedy didn't ride into Greenwood on a white horse to emancipate our friends, but he did finally file a restraining order in federal court, forcing the city to release the protestors and to promise to stop interfering with our peaceful voter registration drive. Bob got out of jail and got a new pair of pants, but for the rest of us, the real excitement had yet to begin.

Fourteen

On April 1, 1963, Dick Gregory and his
entourage—including an army of newspaper,
TV, and radio reporters—swept into Greenwood. Many of us
became instant celebrities simply for having been born and raised
in the Delta. A documentary filmmaker followed me all over town
in order to get some "direct action" footage. We were asked what
it felt like to be in a demonstration, to face armed police and angry
white mobs, to be attacked by dogs and shot at in our homes. The
reporters also wanted to know what we ate for supper, what we'd
been taught in school about the Civil War, and what we thought of
the Kennedys.

In short, America had discovered the Civil Rights Movement
and the southern Negro, and we were some of its spokespeople.
But what we said was always less important than what people
saw on their TVs, and that's what Dick Gregory's visit was all
about.

Gregory arrived at Wesley Chapel amid hundreds of local people
and a fanfare of applause, flashbulbs, and glaring TV lights. He was
a tall, handsome, well-dressed man sporting a pack of cigarettes, a
trim mustache and goatee, flashy cufflinks, and wraparound Foster
Grants that covered a pair of heavy-lidded eyes. Although most of
us had never heard his act, he was at the peak of his career as a
popular comedian, loved by white audiences as well as black.

I had been working upstairs in the church, sorting new donations
of food and clothing, when he arrived. I decided to sneak a peak at
our celebrity guest as he gave a press conference down below. I

wanted to remember what he said and how he said it, so that I could repeat it without embarrassing the Movement in case I got asked. I had aspirations to learn more about the ideals I was helping to support.

Gregory immediately showed why he was both a good performer and a valuable ally. He talked about his own black heritage—he was raised in the St. Louis ghetto—with humor and without embarrassment. He talked openly about things that got the rest of us beat upside the head or put in jail. "There's your story," he would tell reporters the next day in front of the courthouse, pointing to the police who followed him everywhere. "Guns and nightsticks for old women who want to register!"

That night, he came to a mass meeting at Turner's Chapel AME Church, where Reverend Tucker pastored. While we were waiting for the meeting to start, I fell into a long conversation with a friendly, knowledgeable man who turned out to be Dick Gregory's manager. He pulled me over to where Gregory and Willie Peacock were talking.

"Dick, this is Ida," Peacock said. "She's one of our key local people."

I shook Dick Gregory's hand and thought about how somebody who was aiming to be Somebody ought to talk to a national celebrity. "Glad to meet you, I'm sho'!" I said.

To be honest, I can't remember a thing he said back, but I do know that I talked some more to his manager and got so excited that I had trouble getting to sleep that night—not just because I'd met Dick Gregory but because Willie Peacock had called me a "key person."

The next morning, we scheduled a march to the courthouse. Our visitor was just the thing we needed to draw a crowd, and our turnout was bigger than ever. Even people who usually came for a sack of groceries and then hightailed it stayed and took part in the demonstration. I marched at the head of the procession, right next to Peacock and Gregory.

A block down the street we joined hands and began singing "Ain't Gonna Let Nobody Turn Me Around." Along the route, black people joined in or followed our path along the sidewalk. By the time we reached Main Street, even our record number of marchers had doubled. White people who usually stood in loose groups to cuss and jeer at us now melted into the side streets and alleys, uneasy at seeing such a large group of colored people moving with such determination.

Until now, Greenwood's white establishment had decided to leave Gregory alone—to deny him the publicity of an arrest or even a serious confrontation. Now, faced with the biggest demonstration in its history and Gregory's increasingly inflammatory rhetoric, Chief Lary changed his strategy. Greenwood's men in blue moved in. We were under arrest, Chief Lary said through his bullhorn, for "parading without a permit."

Automatically, James Moore and I and others in the immediate vicinity of Gregory locked arms around him. The police piled us all into a squad car and took off toward the courthouse. I knew the policeman driving the car, Mr. Slim Henderson. He owned a small grocery store on Avenue I in Gritney, and although he was no particular friend to the black community, he was respectful of the celebrity in his car. He began to explain that there was probably some confusion—that we wouldn't be held long once they realized down at the courthouse who Dick Gregory actually was.

Now, oddly enough, the roles in the backseat got reversed. Heading toward jail—an environment I knew well—I became more comfortable and self-assured, even cocky, while Dick Gregory got more introspective, edgy, and quiet. He dug out a cigarette and began smoking, blowing smoke rings. I guess he'd heard stories about what happens to people in southern jails.

I was contemplating different stories, the ones I'd been hearing about how black people in Alabama had refused to ride the buses as long as they were forced to sit in the back. Without its primary customers, the bus line was out of business. Greenwood didn't have a bus line, but it did have Slim Henderson's grocery store.

"You know what we gonna do now, Mr. Slim?" I asked our driver in a teasing voice.

"No, what you gonna do, Ida Mae?" the patrolman said, grinning at us in the rearview mirror.

"We gonna organize a boycott of yo' store—all us Negroes— not gonna buy a thing from you until we get to vote! We gonna let yo' meat rot!"

Slim Henderson's face fell and I felt Dick's body shift and relax beside me. He took a deep drag on his cigarette and gave me a big smile. Boycott! I didn't even know I knew the word until it left my lips—but I'd said it. It had finally struck me that all this time, we black folks had been thinking that our lives depended entirely upon the white man. We thought we were at his mercy for food, shelter, clothing—all the necessities of life. But all this time, we'd been wrong; the white man needed us more than we needed him. Southern white wealth had been built upon the backs of its blacks, through the unwilling, unwitting participation of a cheap black workforce.

Slim no longer talked to us or turned his head around to look at us. I snuggled into the cushions of the backseat. I was enjoying this. The rest of the way to the courthouse, we sang:

Ain't scared of your jail
'Cause I want my freedom
Want my freedom
Want my freedom
Now.

At the city jail, we all got booked, and Dick Gregory immediately received a person-to-person phone call from Chicago. The atmosphere was the exact opposite of the previous times I'd been arrested. Instead of the prisoners being worried, the Greenwood policemen all ran around with long faces and nervous glances, jumping whenever the phone rang. After his phone call, Dick Gregory laughed and laughed, confusing the police even more. It turned out that he'd given instructions before leaving on his trip that if anybody wanted to contact him, he could be reached at the Greenwood city jail.

About as quickly as we'd been arrested, we were released. Some people said it was because Chief Lary decided he didn't want to deal with the problems of jailing a celebrity. Others said it was because of a behind-the-scenes deal between Mayor Sampson and the Justice Department. Either way, Dick Gregory finished his visit in high style—walking the streets of Greenwood, visiting stores in a big white Stetson hat, poking fun at the "illiterate white police who couldn't even pass their own voting test."

Bob Moses and the others followed us to freedom on April 4. John Doar from the Justice Department—a new figure in Greenwood, but a man we'd see a lot more of in the future—had negotiated a compromise with the city. The temporary restraining order was dropped in exchange for the release of SNCC's leaders, but Doar promised to continue monitoring the situation and to seek a permanent injunction against the police.

You'd think all this would have made Bob happy, but he returned to the office depressed. He had staked just about everything on getting the Kennedy administration involved in the conflict—to send in federal marshals to protect us workers and the people we were trying to register—but he now saw that wasn't in the cards.

By election day in September, despite all our efforts and all the publicity, only fifty new black voters had been registered in Leflore County, thanks to the registrar's obstruction. But that didn't stop us. We continued the mass meetings and protest marches, and the police continued to counter with arrests and speedy releases, which were fast becoming their tactics for ending demonstrations swiftly. Over the next two years I saw beatings, burnings, and shootings as we kept canvassing and singing freedom songs and going to the courthouse. We sang often:

I shall not, I shall not be moved—
Just like a tree that's planted by the water,
I shall not be moved!

And despite Bob Moses's disappointment, our slow progress at turning goodwill into votes, and the federal government's unwillingness to dirty its hands too much in our mess, the summer and fall of 1963 would see landmark—and tragic—events in the Movement and beyond.

SNCC had uncovered a little-known clause in the Mississippi constitution that allowed for "early balloting" in special situations. Since it was unlikely that we would have enough new black voters to sway the regular election, the organization conceived a special "protest" or "freedom" vote, as it was later called, to give black voters a chance to test their voices in unison. This target now gave us something real to shoot for. We went to work with a vengeance. So did the opposition.

"Dese here Riders done got up some kinda mess," Mama fumed one morning after police dogs had barked all night in our neighborhood, getting Frisgo all riled. "I hope dese white folkses knows dat I ain't got nothin' t' do wit' de mess!"

"They don't scare me none," I yelled from the middle room.

"Dat 'cause you ain't got no kinda sense!"

I came out of the middle room with another kind of a shock for Mama.

"What de devil you done wit' yo' hair, gal?" Mama said. "Why you be runnin' 'round here wit' yo' head all nappy?"

"It called a *natural,* Mama," I said. I'd seen pictures of African queens wearing their hair all bushy and regal-looking, and some of the black women at the Freedom Office had started wearing their hair that way, too. I'd started dressing like the other women workers, too.

"Den 'fore you leave dis house, Ida Mae," Mama snapped, sensing she'd already lost the fight about my hair, "you pull dem overhalls off an' put you on a dress!"

"Can't, Mama. I may hafta go limp in the march and people could look underneath my dress."

"Den you wears some clean bloomers, gal. 'Cause when you gits shot an' dey takes you t' de horsepital, yo' bloomers oughta be clean."

With those encouraging words, I skipped down the steps and walked briskly to the SNCC office, where the marchers were forming ranks. Over the last few months, our demonstrations had gotten ever larger. This was partly due to the extra voters we'd signed up and the newcomers who arrived from out of town on an almost daily basis. But mostly it was the result of our mass meetings and the growing sense of pride our community felt in itself—a desire to defend our workers and volunteers and spokespeople against the increasingly violent white reaction. Where once we'd been quick to disperse, now our anger and determination allowed us to press on. Arresting us was becoming a burden to the police.

We lined up by twos, because the Greenwood City Council had decreed that three or more of us in a row constituted an "unlawful assembly" of people "parading without a permit." The citizens who joined us usually wore their Sunday best—short-sleeved dresses, pearls, and big earrings for women; suits, ties, vests, and fedoras for men—despite the physical risk. Part of this was pure habit: If you went downtown or out to a public event, you dressed up. But increasingly our appearance had become a matter of pride. We wanted white citizens—and the world, via the media—to see that we were decent folks.

As the tenor of our marches had changed, so did the response to them. In our earliest encounters, Greenwood's finest tried to preserve as best they could an appearance of normalcy. They wore their usual service uniforms and tried not to look like an occupying army. Now their numbers included policemen and sheriff's deputies from all over Leflore County. They were outfitted not only with construction-style helmets, but with face guards, heavy boots, long truncheons, and even, concealed in the farthest ranks, cattle prods. Some local black prisoners had even been deputized so that they could do the dirty work of loading protesters who had "gone limp" into the backs of police vans and buses. In the front ranks, Greenwood's lone police dog had now become a wolf pack. In the last ranks, red-helmeted city firefighters manned their hoses and parked their long hook-and-ladder trucks across our avenues of advance—or retreat.

"You people must disperse and leave this area," Chief Lary commanded through the bullhorn.

This time, it was my turn to answer. "We're going to the courthouse to register to vote! We're peaceable people! We're nonviolent! Our rights are guaranteed by the U.S. Constitution!" My words sounded braver than I felt. I still found it hard to look Chief Lary in the eye and defy him. But I did.

"Y'all will not be allowed to go farther," he announced. "Disperse at once!" But indecision was written all over his face, a look I had never seen on him before. It made me feel good.

Behind me, a SNCC staffer gave the signal and we all knelt on the hot pavement to pray. On the sidewalk, flashbulbs popped and TV cameras whirred. We were gambling that Chief Lary and Mayor Sampson would not want pictures of their attack dogs, fire hoses, and club-wielding bullies let loose on a crowd of harmless men and women—kneeling to pray in their Sunday best—flashed all over the country.

We were wrong.

The black-jacketed firemen worked their way to the front of the police barricade with their heavy hoses. The force of the first blast of water literally kicked me off the pavement and hurled me against a dumpster. Big men like Hancock and Vasser were tossed around like babies. Then, dragging their handlers behind, the dogs tore into us—snarling and barking, grabbing arms, legs, feet, coattails, skirts, anything we offered to protect our faces and vitals. Some of the women, including the Mothers of the Church, had bags of powdered red chili pepper to throw in the dogs' faces. But amid the confusion, the pepper had little effect.

More than two hundred of us were rounded up and manhandled by the black "deputies" into a waiting bus. I was the first one booked, but the sheer number of arrests overwhelmed Greenwood's jails. One night in the overcrowded cells turned into two, then three. Then we were moved to a larger holding tank. Finally, we were transferred to the workhouse, even though some people still hadn't appeared before a judge.

Cap'n Arterberry met the women with his usual welcoming speech, while the men waited on the bus. "If you gals git outta line, you gonna git some o' this!" He growled, cracking his riding crop against his high boots. He stared at me and said, "I know this li'l gal here. You others better git her to tell y'all that I'm not gonna have no sanging or no back talk!"

I imagined that to those who were seeing him for the first time, he must have looked real fierce. I thought he just looked older and more worn out. Despite his bluster, our numbers bewildered him, and it showed on his face.

In the women's dorm, I claimed my old spot near the bathroom and began getting things organized. I had become both cheerleader and first sergeant to a diverse group of cellmates: proper-talking ladies from Chicago and New York bunked next to streetwalkers and thieves from Gritney, Baptist Town, Gee Pee, and the countryside.

Laurel was impatient with the newcomers, some of whom seemed to be under the impression that we were in a hotel or a college dormitory. "Us ain't got no clean sheets, honey," she told one of them in a singsongy voice, then snapped, "Us ain't got no sheets, period!" She took an instant dislike to the white girls from the North. "Dey talk like dey got a mouthful o' mess!" she shook her head. "I can't understan' nary a word dat dey say!"

When one of them asked for toilet paper, she exploded. "Us'n ain't got no paper t' wipe y'all tails wit'! I know dey gots bed kivers an' rolls o' soft toilet paper where y'all come from. 'F'n you wanna keep yo' tails clean, y'all oughta keep yo' hind end up Nawth yon'er an' not come messin' up thangs for us poor colored folkses! An' Cat—I be *shame* o' you! You knowed better den t' git in wit' dese outside agitators—dese Freedom Riders."

After letting off steam, Laurel managed to come up with a handful of coarse cotton bolls, but she made it clear that this stay would be different. She no longer called me "cousin," and she wouldn't look me in the eye. She didn't mingle in the prisoners' area as she used to, but passed everything through the bars, strictly by the book. "Sho' as you born, Cat," she said, "thangs done change 'round here now. Lawd, Lawd—thangs done change."

Yet things quickly settled into the old routine—chore time, mealtime, head-count time, lights-out time—each accompanied by its rules along with the numb feeling of confinement that soon settles over you like a heavy cloak you can't shake off, even in the shower. What was different for me this time was my responsibility to the Movement and to the other girls. Some of them cried and cried and swore they would never be imprisoned again, even for freedom. Others, like Tougaloo students Joyce and Dorie Ladner —sisters in blood as well as in battle—spoke with quiet eloquence about their determination to stick with the Movement, bearing the pain of its birth like stoic mothers. That much I understood. They then went on to talk about "enfranchisement," the "status quo" in Mississippi, "Negro liberation" and of our "special relationship" to Africa, and they lost me. My kin didn't include any black Africans that I knew of, and we'd always been taught to look down our noses at "dose savages" depicted by Hollywood actors in Tarzan movies. I pretended to understand and kept quiet till the topic came back to something I knew, like "direct action."

Mary Lane, a tiny local volunteer known for her boldness, made an example of me, recounting my bravery before the police.

"Cat ain't so brave," one Gritney girl whined. "She sell herself t' de mens. An' she steal stuff—ain't dat right? She know 'bout dis workhouse 'cause she jest a ho' an' a li'l ol' rogue! How come she git t' march up front?"

Her friends murmured their agreement, but Frog Vasser stuck up for me. "Now c'mon," she said, "we all done sold our ownselves at some time, in one way or 'nother. That be how the system work. Now don't tell me you never stole a biscuit! I say anybody who got the nerve to do it can march up front. You wanna be at the head o' the parade? Go 'head—be my guest. Just remember, the front line meets the dog an' cattle prod an' billy club first. Cat would love the comp'ny!"

We had meetings like that off and on throughout our incarceration. Somehow, just talking things over made us feel closer and kept us focused on why we were there. I tried to find other things we could do in the workhouse that would give us the same feeling —keep us together inside so that we could go on with our work as a team when we got out.

One day, under a big tarp in one corner of our dormitory, I found several big cans of paint. I got the idea we could fix up our quarters for the next time we got arrested, which probably wouldn't be long. With Laurel's approval, we cleaned the toilets, laundered our rough blankets, and painted everything that didn't move. Unfortunately, for most of us, painting was as new an activity as street marching, and we got as much of it on ourselves as on the walls. Nor did we know that Edward "Dead Eye" Cochran (called Bro Moderator in some circles for his ability to resolve disputes fairly) had already been allowed to post bail to get us out and had arranged for Solomon Henderson's bus to come pick us up. As a result, most of us showed up for the unexpected bus ride home with speckled skin, white-streaked hair, and spotted clothes. Dead Eye only laughed. It was not the first time he had helped us out of a tight situation, and it wouldn't be the last.

SNCC held a mass meeting to celebrate our release. The turnout was huge, with lots of relatives and people who had never before been involved showing up. We sang up a storm—freedom songs mixed with church hymns. Then people old and young took the podium to vent their fears and anger. After a long prayer by a deacon, Reverend Tucker hobbled up to the pulpit, still nursing his damaged leg. He was applauded and cheered like the hero he was and, after prompting from Sam Block, displayed his nasty dog bite like a veteran showing off his wounds. Then Matthew Little displayed his wounds, to rousing applause, while Curtis Hayes and Hollis Watkins sang. This started an impromptu parade of other bandaged protesters and acknowledgment of another unsung hero, Dr. Aaron G. Jackson, Greenwood's handsome black physician,

who'd had his hands full washing, stitching, and dressing the casualties from our battle.

When Dr. Jackson came from Jackson, Mississippi, to Greenwood to set up his medical practice, many women between the
ages of seventeen and seventy-five suddenly took sick with a new
ailment or an old malady, among them May Liza, who sent for him
to get rid of a hex that her new boyfriend's ex-girlfriend had put
on her. But where Dr. Jackson turned out to be invaluable was
with the civil rights workers who went to him with everything
from colds to nerves to bullet wounds and burns. He was warned
not to take care of the freedom workers, but time after time he
ignored the warning and showed up, doctor's bag in hand, at a
worker's home or the SNCC office, even when the Movement
couldn't afford to pay his fee. Eventually, he himself was slightly
wounded when someone shot into his office, but even that didn't
deter him.

After the meeting, many people were afraid to walk home
alone, so the workers organized car pools to make sure everyone
got back safely. Since Mama and I lived so close by, I just ran
to our house, keeping well on the street and in the light. When
I got inside, I found out that she had watched just about the
whole meeting from the window. She seemed to have reached a
turning point herself.

"I ain't sayin' it be right dat y'all be marchin' and carryin' on,
but I knows it ain't right dat dey sic de dogs on y'all like dat." She
shook her head somberly. "I jest didn't think Chief Lary would do
dat. He knowed you since you be a li'l gal. I use t' iron his closes
—didn't leave no cat-faces or nothin'! Den he turn dem dogs loose
on Reverend Tucker—de Lawd's disciple! It ain't right, Ida Mae.
It jest ain't right. Dey do dat t' Reverend Tucker," she concluded,
"what you think dey gwine do when Luther Kang git here?"

"Who, Mama?"

"Gal, you think you knows ev'ythang but you don't know nothin'. Dat man, Luther Kang—de preacher what live in 'lanta, de one dat done stirred up dis mess in de first place."

"You mean Reverend Martin Luther King?" I said.

"Name him what you will," Mama said, "he oughta not come mere. Dis ain't Georgia. Dis be Miss'ippi!"

Mama was right about two things. First, the worst-kept secret around the office was that Dr. King was planning a trip to Greenwood, although the date had not been set. As far as the Movement was concerned, Greenwood was our Gettysburg, our Battle of the Bulge, and our Iwo Jima all wrapped up in one. Second, no place in the South was less susceptible to outside pressure or to good sense rising from within than Mississippi.

I WAS at the office when we got the news that a group of freedom workers—Miss Fannie Lou Hamer, June Johnson, Annell Ponder, Euvester Simpson, Rosemary Freeman, Lawrence Guyot, and others—had been arrested and beaten for trying to integrate the white waiting room of the Winona, Mississippi, bus station on their way home from a training session in Charleston, South Carolina. We were particularly concerned about the arrest of Miss Hamer, whom many of us considered our "mother" in the Civil Rights Movement. An intense, heavyset woman with a whole choir in her voice, she actually reminded me of Mama.

When Bob Moses asked for volunteers to go to Winona, I stepped forward with a couple of others.

"You didn't come over here to start any damn trouble, did you?" a policeman asked me at the gloomy jail in Winona.

"I don't understand what you mean," I said.

"The same damn thing the others did," he replied.

"No sir, not yet!" I said.

After conferring with some of the other officers, he allowed me to go to the cells.

The first person I saw was Annell Ponder. Her face was swollen and she had a black eye. She could hardly talk, but when she saw me, she whispered, "Freedom."

As I saw the others, I got more and more upset. Euvester and Rosemary had fared better than the other women, but June's face was so smashed and bloody I didn't recognize her. When I saw Miss Hamer, she took my hand and ran it over her lumpy, bruised flesh.

"Why y'all beat 'em like this?" I asked the policeman, who stood by leering.

"We kin give you some of the same thing," he said.

"Don't say nothing, Ida," Miss Hamer said. "You go back an' tell the others."

I left the Winona jail in tears, feeling hopeless. When we got back to the Freedom Office, I was urged to write down everything I had seen. I was afraid to tell Mama what had happened, but she could tell it was serious from the look on my face.

We went to bed but I couldn't sleep. Even counting roaches didn't help. When I finally dozed, I had my dream again—Mama rolling in flames—and woke up bathed in a sweat and pee. Outside, dawn was breaking to the sound of blowing auto horns and a banging on our screen door.

Fifteen

"GIT UP, IDA MAE, AND SEE WHO MAKIN' DAT RACKET!" MAMA CALLED FROM THE OTHER ROOM where she'd been sleeping with Cedric. "I hope dey don't wake up yo' hollerin' boy."

"Miss Ida! Cat!" a voice outside called. "Git up, gal! It's Pearlie!"

I rolled off my stinking wet mattress feeling sick. My nightmare always upset me anyway, and now the frantic knocking and shouting had my stomach in a knot.

"What is it, Pearlie?" I said through the screen, blinking and scratching my hip. "What's de matter?"

Mama was in her wheelchair now, rolling up behind me. "I smell pish, Ida Mae," she said loudly, not caring if Pearlie heard. She reached around me with her cane and pushed the door open. "Lawd, 'oman, how come you be carryin' on like dis?"

"Dey done kilt Medgar Evers!"

"Who dat?" Mama asked, suddenly guarded.

"Medgar, he live in Jackson, Mama," I said. "He run de NAACP in Mississippi." I stood back as Pearlie came in. "What you mean dey kilt him?"

"Dey shot him down to de ground like a dog!" Pearlie wiped her nose with her hand. "Now dem old redneck hillbillies from Carrol County be drivin' 'round town raisin' a ruckus."

We tiptoed to the window and looked out. Sure enough, cars loaded with white men zipped through the intersections, sounding off horns like it was New Year's Eve.

"Dat be what gwine happen t' y'all," Mama grumbled. "Dese white folkses be mad. Pull my shade down, Pearlie. I don't want dem folkses t' think I tend t' dey bidness."

"They know *you* ain't in de Movement, Mama," I said.

Mama looked up, stung. "Ol' pishy-tail gal—ol' pee-de-bed 'oman!" She pivoted her chair in disgust and wheeled away. "Don't git too big fo' yo' britches. You don't know what I seed in dis Delta—de mens dey put in de river, de way dey done t' us 'omans. I seed dem burn up a young colored boy—jest on 'count o' a white 'oman don't like him an' lie 'bout him. I knows better'n you does, young gal, how far us'n gots t' go 'fore us'n be free!"

Mama took a big dip of snuff and put her tittie pillow on her lap. "So now dem white folkses done kilt dis poor colored man in Jackson—took him 'way from his family," she went on. "Well, I tell you, gals—I knows 'bout dis here freedom. One time, I sassed out a white 'oman. Coulda got kilt my owndearself 'f'n she tol' anysomebody 'bout it. I be tired o' de way dey treats us. De man, 'fessor McSwine, he try t' git me in de NAACP."

"Don't tell me dat 'fessor McSwine b'long to de NAACP!" Pearlie exclaimed. "He be de last somebody you think of."

"Lotta folkses 'round here b'long," Mama said, "mo' den ten years now—Mr. Buckhannon, Sister Brown, Cryin' Shame, Big Red Parker, Dossie Ree—"

"Dossie Ree?" I was flabbergasted.

"Sho' do," Mama said. "An' she gots de hardest row to hoe. De Lawd say: He ain't gwine gi'e you mo' den you kin bear. She done went wit' a White Council man 'cause he talk in his sleep. She find out all de colored mens dey plot t' kill. Yas'm, lotta colored men still on de face o' dis earth 'cause o' dat Dossie Ree! She be some kinda 'oman."

I couldn't believe what I was hearing. I'd always thought the black people in Greenwood were so passive and afraid that they never even thought of being free until the Movement came along. Now I realized they'd been discussing the NAACP long before I'd ever heard of SNCC.

"Well, I do declare!" Pearlie looked as stunned as I was. "Dat Dossie Ree gots guts. Don't think I coulda laid up in bed wit' dat stanky white man, freedom or not. I gots t' beg Dossie Ree's pardon an' you, too, Cat"—she poked me—"for makin' slander 'gainst her name!"

"I'm sorry," I said to Mama. "I guess I'm just a pee-de-bed gal who don't know nothing." I laid my head on her lap and wept— for Medgar, Miss Hamer, and Dossie Ree.

"Dere, dere, now, Ida Mae, you didn't know no better—you and Pearlie go t' Dossie Ree an' tell her 'bout de man dat got kilt, an' kiss her an' make 'mirations over her." Mama stroked my back as if I were once again a baby.

IN THE days following Medgar Evers's death, feelings ran high. Unplanned demonstrations erupted everywhere, which always made SNCC leaders nervous. Students marching in Jackson were arrested and taken to the fairgrounds—the only place large enough to hold such a crowd. Meanwhile, the Klan held countermarches of their own—complete with robes and sympathetic, unmasked civilians in tow, flying the Confederate Stars and Bars.

Finally, when a few days had passed and tempers had cooled a little, Jackson's mayor Allen Thompson lifted his ban on demonstrations long enough to permit what was billed as a "silent procession" from Medgar's funeral at the Masonic Temple. More than two hundred of us left Greenwood for Jackson, joining people from all over the country who came to comfort Medgar's wife, Myrlie, his children, and his brother Charles. Martin Luther King, Jr., Roy

Wilkins, and Dr. Ralph Bunche came, along with white supporters like Allard Lowenstein. President and Mrs. Kennedy sent a message to be read at the funeral. Over Medgar's flag-draped coffin we sang:

> *Before I'll be a slave*
> *I'll be buried in my grave*
> *And go home to my Lord and be free.*
> *No more killin' here,*
> *No more killin' here.*

Like a thousand others, I had to listen to the service on loud-speakers outside the hall—the crowd was just too big to fit every-one in. The longer we waited, the sadder we got, until Dave Dennis spoke about the "southern political system" having squeezed the assassin's trigger (no suspect had been arrested). Then we got mad. Dorie Ladner, Louis McCaskill, and I rallied a few hundred students and headed off toward Lynch Street, where SNCC headquarters and the Tougaloo campus were located.

As we walked, I was aware of a humming I always heard at rallies and marches—like the sound of a thousand bees buzzing near my ear. As it grew louder, my heart seemed to beat faster, to its rhythm. I had the feeling I was going to have some sort of premonition or visitation when we reached Tougaloo—maybe because I had seen Bro Pastor among the crowd waiting to get into the funeral, and he'd been wearing his frock coat.

Despite Mayor Thompson's edict about a "silent procession," our march was anything but quiet. We had seen too many flower-draped caskets to take this last one lying down. We marched straight for the police blocking the entrance to Lynch Street. Be-hind them lay a riot squad in full gear. Near me I recognized John Doar, the tall, frizzy-haired Justice Department official with piercing eyes who had bailed Bob Moses and the others out of the

Greenwood jail. I felt a little safer with him standing by, but safety was the last thing on my mind.

"Y'all turn 'round, now, an' go back!" Deputy Police Chief Ray said through a bullhorn. "There is no march here today!"

"We goin' to Lynch Street!" I shouted, waving my fist. "You can't stop us! This be a peaceful, constitutional march!"

"Ain't gonna ask you people but one more time to disperse!" Ray bellowed. The riot police behind him snapped down their visors and aimed their shotguns.

Oddly enough, at that moment I had no fear of their guns. There were lots worse ways for a black person to die in the Delta, and lots worse reasons to die than for the Movement. My stride increased, and although a few slipped out of the crowd behind me for the safety of the sidewalk, most kept on, chanting, "We want the killer! We want the killer!" Some rocks and bottles, as well as taunts, began to fly toward the police.

At this point, John Doar walked out between the two forces, all by himself, and raised his hands like a traffic cop in a busy intersection.

"My name is John Doar—D-O-A-R," he announced, addressing us. "I'm from the Justice Department and anybody from around here knows I stand for what's right!" He said the Justice Department was looking into Medgar's murder and wouldn't rest until the killer or killers were caught. "I understand your feelings," he concluded. "But we don't want any more bloodshed!" He urged us to turn around and go back the way we came.

Most of us were unaware that the route we had chosen happened to be a main artery to Jackson's downtown business district. Deputy Chief Ray, even if he had been willing to let us march to the campus, could never have allowed us take that route—with its canyon of plate-glass windows, white-owned stores with expensive merchandise, and block after block of late-model cars parked along

the street. It was one of those little details you forget in the heat
of battle, but that can make all the difference between a successful
march and a disaster. It was one of the reasons cool heads like Bob
Moses's were so important to the Movement, and why John Doar
had earned his lifetime's pay in a single afternoon.

I was first to turn, then Dorie, then Louis McCaskill. A massacre
had been averted, but only by a thread.

I TRIED to enjoy the scenery through the window on the
bus ride back to Greenwood, but tears stung my eyes and blurred
my vision. I kept seeing fragile, noble Myrlie Evers clutching her
children, and Fannie Lou Hamer displaying her cuts and bruises. I
had felt anger before in my life—white-hot, stupid, self-destructive
anger, like when I'd fought with Poochie—but never before had I
felt cold rage. I vowed to God that I would never turn back, no
matter what Mama might say, no matter what might happen. I was
a soldier. I was in for the duration. Quietly I hummed to myself:

No! I'll never turn back
Until we've all been freed
And we'll have equality.

I sang these words over and over again in my heart until I was
elufindated—a word found only in my private lexicon, which could
be roughly translated as "illuminated."

I WAS not the only person to be so profoundly affected by
the murder of Medgar Evers. As the summer of '63 wore into fall,

many people who before wouldn't participate at all now marched with a defiance that the white community scarcely believed. Even the most extreme tactics of the segregationists—firebombings, shootings, beatings, police harassment, repossession of homes and businesses—no longer worked. Both our successes and our defeats increased our determination.

On one march, we made it all the way downtown and surrounded the courthouse with pickets. Our signs proclaimed "One Man, One Vote," "Freedom Now," and "We Demand the Ballot." This time, white agitators tried a new tactic for the ever-present news cameras: derisive street theater. They produced a monkey wearing a sign that read "Let My People Go" and inserted him into our picket line. The problem was, the monkey was so well behaved and dignified that, once the laughing on both sides stopped, he became a sympathetic figure. When he finally raised his tail and patted his behind in the direction of his handler, the white agitators jerked him away and that was that. The day ended without violence, and our mass meeting that night took on the tone of a celebration.

The gathering momentum of SNCC's first "Freedom Vote," which was rapidly coming to the test, brought in a flood of white outsiders—mostly liberal students and teachers from the North— to help with the canvassing and voter registration, and to beef up our demonstrations. This put new pressure on the local SNCC staff to find safe beds for them all. And so it was that many black families in Gee Pee suddenly found themselves running hotels out of their homes.

Often the best that could be provided was just enough space for a sleeping bag to be unrolled and spread out on the floor in a shotgun house already filled to overflowing. Still, it was clean and dry and warm. Taste buds that had never been used before were aroused at their first introduction to pickled pig's feet and collard greens with ham hocks. Eyes opened wide in sudden surprise followed by slow and greasy grins made us laugh, and hands out-stretched for second helpings always pleased the cook. In most instances, hospitality overruled the freedom workers' policy of never sleeping more than two nights in the same place, although guests would "check out" early if there was a threat of danger or reprisal.

"Dey ain't gwine stay underneath my roof!" Mama announced with finality as I swabbed the festering sores under her titties. I couldn't tend Mama now without thinking of Miss Hamer's wounds.

"But we be the onliest house in Gee Pee what don't have a white somebody!" I protested. Then I thought of an argument I knew she couldn't resist. "You know, Miss Susie gots her own white some-body comin' to stay—"

"Say what?"

"That's right. She be takin' in a white woman from New York!"

Mama just chewed her tongue a moment, then said, "Well, 'f'n Susie gwine he'p, I guess I kin, too. But jest 'cause I let dem stay here, it don't mean dat I be gwine down yon'er t' no cou'thouse t' reddish t' vote!"

" 'Course not, Mama. You ain't gotta go nowheres. Each one do what they kin—but you gotta do somethin'," I said, repeating the phrase I'd heard at a staff meeting.

I went back to the office feeling better than I had in a long time. Getting Mama to "do something," even if it was a gesture, felt like a big victory. If we had reached her, then we were reaching many others, even if they were still afraid to step forward.

I'd noticed that people were starting to treat me differently. Folks were beginning to follow my lead, without any grumbling or back talk. Now, everyone knows the Israelites didn't follow Moses just because he found himself at the front of a line. They followed him because they believed he knew where he was going and how to get there, and because he was determined to get there, no matter how long or dangerous the journey.

Even at a distance no one was about to confuse me with the biblical Moses, nor for that matter Bob Moses. What they could see, however, even at a distance, was that I knew where I was going and that I had to get there. For the first time, I had committed myself to a cause greater than myself—one that I was willing to fight, even die for—and it showed.

Where the old Cat had walked her "walk," sensuous and slow, wanting only to attract the longing gaze of hungry men, this new Cat had no time for that kind of nonsense. I raced to get where I needed to go, even arriving early, eager to get a head start on the day's work. I couldn't wait for freedom to come to me; I was poised to overtake elusive freedom in one long leap. For the first time in my life I knew who I was. I no longer needed Eva Mae Brown's clothes to feel like I was somebody. I no longer needed Ike's love to make me feel whole. I was Somebody in her own right, and that was good enough.

Neighbors who used to look down their nose at me for my whoring and fighting and stealing now looked into my eyes and said "How do." Even my jail time had become a badge of honor. Ever since that first mass arrest, when people turned to me for leader-ship at the workhouse, I had been viewed as a kind of shepherd for our "lost sheep." Drifting naturally to the front of every march, I was always one of the first to be arrested. When the others were brought in, I was there to comfort and guide them, helping them stay out of trouble while causing maximum trouble for our keepers, whose jails we clogged, food we ate, courts we tied up, and officers we kept off the street because they had to keep an eye on us. In short, my unofficial "official job" in the Movement was to be arrested, go to jail, and stay there as long as other workers needed me.

In 1963 and 1964, I was arrested thirteen times. My rap sheet included "disturbing the peace," "inciting a riot," "unlawful assembly," and "parading without a permit"—classy "crimes" that put my whoring, fighting, and shoplifting days out of people's memories. Not that we always ended up in the workhouse, or even in the Greenwood city jail. After a while, our "arrests" were just a means for the police to disrupt a demonstration. Not wanting to have to book us into their already overcrowded jails, they drove us to the city limits in police vans or buses and turned us loose. By the time we walked back, the protest would be over, but we'd have made our point.

After one mass arrest in early 1964, we were taken to the workhouse, which now seemed like a college sorority, thanks to the painting, cleaning, and maintenance of our rotating team of inmates. We were relaxing in our bunks, talking about the Movement and what we were going to do after the organization made our bail, when Laurel came in. We greeted her kindly, but she didn't smile back.

"Y'all gots t' git y'all's thangs degether," she said solemly. "We be movin' y'all t' de other jailhouse."

I sat up in my bunk. "What jail?" I didn't know of another facility in Leflore County besides the city jail.

"Don't axe me nothin'—dis mess ain't none o' my bidness," she said, refusing to look me in the eye.

Silently and speedily, we got ready to leave. My bunkmate, Frog Vasser, sniffed back tears as she put her things in an old paper bag. "Maybe dey be takin' us outta here to kill us!"

Mary Lane, the next bunk over, said, "I ain't goin' nowhere wit' these white people. Not to git killed. Hey, Cat—why don't we all go limp when they come to git us?"

"They won't kill us," I said, trying to sound confident, "not while everybody outside knows where we be."

We waited in near silence for two hours, until the chartered black bus came to pick us up. It had been tied up hauling more protesters from the courthouse to jail. We marched out in single file and boarded, along with some of the men who'd been arrested along with us. Laurel didn't even show up to say good-bye.

At the highway, the bus turned north, away from Greenwood. Frog showed me the broken bottle she had kept to defend herself with. Mary Lane displayed a nail file she had managed to conceal from Laurel. We "regular customers" were seldom inspected for contraband. I produced a rusty penknife I had discovered under my bunk bed—and kept there, rather than smuggle it in and out, in case I ever needed a weapon at the workhouse. A few of the men had armed themselves with short pipes they had scavenged from the plumbing under their sinks. If it came to violence, we wouldn't have much to put against shotguns and pistols, but at least we'd have something.

We weren't allowed to talk, but we could sing. So to the great irritation of our guards, we sang freedom songs for an hour—to raise our spirits and depress theirs. Several of them were veterans of our demonstrations, and they knew they wouldn't be able to shut us up, so they didn't try.

I must have dozed off, because I awoke at dusk as the bus bumped off the highway onto a dirt road. We approached a high fence and uniformed armed guards waved us through. The sign above the gate read "Mississippi State Penitentiary."

"Parchman!" the name leaped from startled mouths all over the bus.

People I'd known who had been to other prisons told plain, simple stories about daily life there: work, eat, sleep, over and over again until they were released. Their accounts were as monotonous as prison life itself. But when people told stories of Parchman, they spoke in short grunts and long silences, as if they were trying to forget but could not. As long as I could remember, mothers and preachers had used the place as a bogeyman to threaten wayward children. As Mama used to warn Bud and Simon Jr., "Y'all keep fightin' an' stealin' and you gwine wind up in Parchman wit' de axe mu'd'rers an' bank robbers!"

We local people explained to the others that Parchman was the Devil's Island of the Delta. Sprouting up like a boil between Ruleville and Tutwiler, it was one of the last of the old-style "penal plantations." Prisoners wore stripes, just like in the movies, and overseers rode horseback through the cotton fields, wielding bullwhips and cattle prods against anyone who broke a rule or wasn't working hard enough. It was a rock-hard facility for hard-core criminals, the last place on earth any sane person would send detainees whose only crime had been caring too much about injustice. Of course, that was the point. The white authorities had grown tired of our little game and had upped the ante. If a civil rights arrest meant Parchman, even the most dedicated freedom worker would think twice about "going limp" in front of the cameras.

Frog's bottle, Mary's file, my knife, and a half-dozen rusty pipes clanked to the floor of that old bus, startling our drowsy watchmen. Nobody wanted to be caught with a weapon during Parchman's infamous "strip search" and spend the first week in the sweatbox.

In the dingy holding tank, where we'd been segregated by sex, stripped, showered, and sprayed with lice killer, we were assigned a "top sergeant" to tell us the rules and make sure we knew what would happen if we violated even the smallest of them. Earnestine Whitehead was a colored inmate who was rumored to have killed a white man, so she knew Parchman was her home for life. She'd decided long ago that it was better by far to be "one of them" than one of us. As a result, she was meaner than any hired guard and more trustworthy than the cons—she simply had nothing to lose.

She explained the rules while she searched us for drugs and weapons. No hole was too small to escape inspection with her flashlight, and what she couldn't see into she probed with her longest finger. She confiscated the clothes we wore along with our other effects—including chewing gum and smokes—and marched us, buck naked, past the snickering male guards to the cell block. The men were checked in through another section. I never saw them again during our thirty-three-day stay.

"Ain't gonna have no sangin', no prayin', no talkin' 'mongst yo'selves," she said as we padded along the cement floor in our bare feet. "Dem overhalls you wore in gonna be rags by de time y'all gits outta here."

"Don't need no overhalls to be a freedom fighter—weren't born wit' no pances on," I said. I heard some of the women gasp behind me. After the startled look left Earnestine's face, she gave me an evil smile.

"I guess you s'pose to be de big hen 'round here!" she shouted. "Well, li'l gal, I be de rooster in dis here barnyard. You gots a problem wit' dat?"

"Don't say nothin', Cat," Mary Lane whispered behind me. "Don't give 'em no excuse." We all knew SNCC's standing orders for such situations: go with the flow and stay alive; take mental notes until you can speak with an attorney, a Movement staffer, or someone from the Justice Department. I knew the girls behind me were counting on me. I also knew there were lots of ways to be a leader without opening your mouth. We walked the rest of the way to our cells in silence. The others hunched over, trying vainly to hide their nakedness, but I held my head high, chest out, strutting like a majorette.

The "routine" in Parchman was a big change from the work-house. We slept one to a cell, on iron slabs that, although they had no mattress and no covers, did have thirty-three (by my exact

count) airholes that served mostly to pinch your skin when you
turned over. When one girl complained, Earnestine told her to
"cover up wit' de crickets" that flew in by the hundreds through
our barred, screenless windows. A typical meal was molasses and
biscuits with weak coffee: enough to keep us going but leave us not
much good for anything else, including going to the toilet. Those
sticky biscuits, plus lack of exercise, plugged us up like wet concrete. This made the six squares of toilet paper we got issued once
a week more understandable: If you can't crap, you don't have to
wipe. For some reason our gums puffed up, too, swelling outside
of our mouths. We knew it was shower day when the male guards
lined up to observe us. We never got back our personal items,
including prescription drugs and smokes. But the worst part of
Parchman for me was that they left the hot lights burning all the
time, making it impossible to sleep. After two weeks you didn't
know if it was day or night. After three weeks, you didn't care.

I didn't realize how much my mind and body had degenerated
until a group of white women toured the prison. Like a scene in
some crazy dream, they walked by our cells in tea dresses and
flowered hats, pausing here and there to comment about one
flipped-out sister or another, comparing us to monkeys in a cage,
which was just what one of them called us. We didn't have the
energy or the gumption to shout back, so we just sat or lay listlessly
on our bunks. I wanted to shout, "What you lookin' at, white gal?"
until I realized her only answer could have been "a pathetic black
girl with feces running down her legs, a raw mouth, bleeding gums,
and a belly swollen with malnutrition." I felt like an inhabitant of
some other world, like something evolved from the fetid environment around me, not a human being, least of all myself.

Our uncertainty about our fate made our situation worse. We
had already been held a lot longer than any of our other detainees.
We knew from our occasional glimpses of the other inmates (who

were allowed to work and converse and exercise and smoke, as well as have other privileges, like reading and listening to the radio) that we had been singled out for "special treatment," which Earnestine oversaw with relish. Worst of all, we knew nothing of what was happening in the outside world. Was the Movement still alive? Who was missing or had been killed? Did our relatives and leaders know we were here? How long until we got out?

The short time I spent in Parchman seemed like an eternity. It confined the mind and spirit as completely as it confined the body. I found myself chained to the moment, my entire being caught up in getting through it. I thought about Mama, Cedric, and the rest of my family, and about the friends and freedom volunteers who were undoubtedly trying to get us released. I thought about the work others were doing and worried that I wasn't there to help out. Whatever energy I had left I expended on helping my prison mates get through their stay.

One day, I heard the girls weeping; even Earnestine was sad. Then the air was filled with a lone untuned voice singing a song that was meant to be consoling but somehow came out comical. First I heard Frog laughing, then Mary, then the rest of the prisoners. Even the guard and Earnestine joined in. I laughed until I cried, and that's when I knew that the tuneless voice belonged to me. Frog—one of Greenwood's finest gospel singers—picked up the song and sang it so beautifully that all the rest of us joined in.

It was a hard time for everybody, but none of us went soft. Just as things looked bleakest, our fate began to change. Governor Ross Barnett came for a visit—perhaps to satisfy himself that his vicious plan to reward protesters with "a little taste of state hospitality" was actually bearing fruit. He walked along our row of cells, staying as far back as he could, then paused before my door. He had a face like a hatchet—all sharp-eared and foxy—a tidy haircut, and a mouth like a shark.

"Hey, gal," he said. "How you like Mississippi's hospitality?"

"Just fine, boy," I sassed him back, surprised at the weak, froggy croak my once-booming voice had become.

The color drained from his face; he tried to speak and nothing came out. His bodyguards closed rank around him and he stalked off. A short while later, guards came and took all of us out for what they called a "bug test." They must have been expecting the governor, because they were all wearing their dress uniforms. They declared us to be infected with lice and ordered Earnestine to shave off our hair. Mary Lane's once gorgeous locks fell first, then my long-neglected nappy natural, then everyone else's. To keep the nicks and chunks of flesh gouged out by Earnestine's rough handling from getting infected, she rubbed stinging ointment into our scalps.

That night, I went to sleep with the sound of my sisters' sobbing in my ears—knowing that my smart remark to Governor Barnett had probably caused it. As the night deepened and the duty guards got laxer about enforcing the "no talking" rule, I heard whispered comments about "dat Cat" and "who do she think she is?" and "she gonna git us all locked up forever!" Like the apostle denying Christ, I cursed the Delta, the Movement, even Mama for bringing me into the world.

Then a strange thing happened.

Low and mournful, I heard a woman's voice. First she hummed, then she sang:

Nobody knows
The trouble I seen
Nobody knows
My sorrow . . .

It was Earnestine. Her voice washed over me like warm water. Then Frog Vasser's melodious voice joined hers. Before long, our whole cell block was singing softly—sorrowfully—into the burning night. She couldn't say it openly, but Earnestine hated that white governor as much as the rest of us. Her heart was with us—caged though it would be long after the last of us had gone home to friends and family.

I looked around the cell at the names carved on the cement or into the steel bunk, wondering where they came from, what they'd done to get thrown in there, where they were now. Right then, I decided to lift myself up from my own sorry state. I wasn't going to wait for any Miss Candy Quick or Master Sergeant or a choice man like Ike to save me. I wasn't even going to wait to see a lawyer or a chaplain or a doctor. I knew part of my problem was two weeks' constipation, which had built up poisons in my body that were affecting my mind. I put a finger way up my rectum and dug out what I could, including enough blood to make me feel faint.

My cellmates were singing a new tune now:

You can't hurry God,
You just got to wait on him.
He may not come when you call
But he's right on time.

I hummed along to keep from passing out. Then I heard Frog laugh in the next cell. I called out, "Why you laughin'?" and she called back, " 'Cause you can't sang!" so I hollered back what I was doing and she laughed some more, so I laughed, too. Then Mary Lane and others started laughing, then we all went back to singing, and we had ourselves an angels' choir in that old prison and there was *nothin'* they could do about it.

I cleaned myself up as best I could and felt a hundred percent better. I lay back on my bunk and listened as my sisters' voices drifted off and I drifted off with them into a feverish twilight state.

Before I slept I visited Bob Moses and Sam Block and Willie Peacock and Dick Gregory and Miss Hamer and Medgar Evers and even Emmett Till, whom I hadn't thought of for a long time, and they all smiled and said, "Now you know, Ida, why you gotta lead the others to the jailhouse. You one tough nut to crack!"

THIRTY-THREE DAYS after arriving at Parchman, we were released. I was still in pretty bad shape—sore, feverish, and infected inside and out—but I do recall someone saying something about the Justice Department and John Doar being involved. It just felt good to put on my street clothes again and make tracks. It would have been nice to wash up, but it wasn't shower day, and the warden wasn't about to make an exception in our case. To my surprise, Earnestine Whitehead showed up and helped me fasten the back straps to my overalls.

"What y'all be doin'—marchin' and all—it don't matter none to me," she said. "I be a lifer. But for my chilluns an' gran'chilluns, it do. Keep it up, Cat. Don't let 'em stop you."

We left Parchman in a church bus—the center vehicle in a motorcade that was hailed and feted all the way to Greenwood. We made a stop in Ruleville, where Miss Hamer, who would gain fame as a co-founder of and spokeswoman for the Mississippi Freedom Democratic Party, got on board and cheered us. In that powerful staccato voice of hers, she sang "This Little Light of Mine" as she went down the aisle, kissing every last stinking one of us. When she got to me, she hugged me close, whispering with tear-filled eyes, "You got the light of freedom!"

A good-sized crowd lined the streets of Greenwood to welcome us home and to see how we had fared. Friends and relatives shouted out to us as we passed:

"Hey dere, Cat! You be a freedom fighter!"

"Hey dere, Cuttin' Frog! Us'n glad t' see you!"

"Hey dere, Mary Lane! We be rat wit' you de next time!"

The bus pulled up in front of the Turner Chapel AME Church and we filed off, moving through the crowd and shaking everyone's hands, getting hugged and patted on the back like a football team coming back from having won a championship.

"C'mere, ol' nappy-head gal!" Mama said, rubbing my stubbly head and hugging me from her wheelchair after I climbed onto the porch. I hugged her back until it hurt.

"I be real worried 'bout y'all," she said as we finally pulled apart. "Dat dere Freedom Rider brung me a great big sack o' groce'y an' gi'e me twenty dollars to git by. Den dat dere white freedom 'oman you work wit' gi'e me a jar o' snuff an' ever' Saddity she c'mere wit' yo' pay. Dey was real nice, Ida Mae."

"What? You mean they didn't brang you no RC?" I teased her.

Mama laughed. "Dat white 'oman axed me: *Miss* Ida Mae, does you need anythang else? Ain't dat somethang? Dat be de first time dat a white 'oman *ever* puts a title t' my name! Den I sont her t' de sto' fo' de RC's." We laughed and hugged some more.

"You see, Mama?" I said. "The Movement take care of people."

There was one person, though, who didn't welcome me home like a hero. Three-year-old Cedric stood behind Mama's wheelchair and hollered. When I reached for him, he began to cry and ran behind Mama's legs, his little fist catching the folds of her smock and pulling them across his face like a curtain being drawn closed.

"Stop dat runnin', boy—'cause here be yo' mama," Mama chided him. But he didn't budge. It was a moment of great pain for me, being shut out like that, but there was nothing I could do about it.

I looked around our little house, remembering the time not too long ago when I was sure I'd never see it again.

"It be like the Bible say, Mama. We got to wander in the desert before we kin see the promised land. Don't you wanna vote, Mama?"

Mama grunted. "Dat's what Bro Pastor axe me. He come 'long yestiddy and say dat de Lawd tell him we oughta vote. I 'spect he be lyin' on de Lawd. Vote! Now what colored man gwine be fool 'nough t' try t' git 'lected?"

"Maybe Mr. Mitchell kin git elected," I said. Mama was sweet on Mr. Mitchell—a kindly neighbor who looked in on her from time to time. When he came, Mama would hang a sheet around her bed. Grunts and the odor of Juicy Fruit chewing gum would emanate from her makeshift room.

"Hush yo' mouth, Ida Mae!" Mama snapped. "Anyhow, you git in dat tub over yon'er an' wash yo'self real good. I kin smell you clear 'cross dis room!"

I started undressing—slowly, painfully. Every joint was on fire. My insides felt like I'd been hooked up to electricity. "I hurt, Mama," I said.

She stared at me a second. "Git dat Lysol an' dat Epsom salt an' dat camphor, chile, an' put it in de water. I ain't got no mo' use fo' dem white folkses after dey stick y'all in de pen. I knows dey mistreat y'all, Ida Mae."

I eased into the hot tub and sang softly while Mama helped clean me up:

My Mama is a freedom fighter
And I'm her fightin' chile.
We gonna fight right here
Till the battle be won.
Whose side you be on?
Whose side you be on?

"De Freedom Riders say dat preacher—Luther Kang—gwine march wit' y'all be sont t' Parchman," Mama said as she scrubbed my back. "Be sho' you brang him by here—so I kin smoke him over."

"I will, Mama." I closed my eyes and sank deep in the tub, relaxing for what seemed like the first time in my life as Frisgo started barking at something outside, raising a chorus of other dogs.

Sixteen

THE DAY AFTER WE RETURNED FROM PARCH-
MAN, I SAW DR. JACKSON. HE SAID I WAS MALNOUR-
ished, exhausted (we never slept more than a few hours at a stretch
with those damn cell lights on), and filled with "bad bugs"—from
my torn rectum to the stubble at the top of my head. Rest, sweet
water, and good, wholesome food—plus a few antibiotics and
painkillers—were the order of the day. But after my first visit back
to the SNCC office, I saw that rest was a luxury none of us could
afford, at least for the next few months.

The death of President Kennedy had been a body blow to every
civil rights worker, black or white, although it had forced Congress
in July 1964 to pass his long-delayed Civil Rights Act. Still, the act
faced a record seventy-five-day Senate filibuster before it would be
law. In the meantime, COFO had hatched a new plan.

Bob Moses's symbolic "Freedom Vote" in November 1963 had
attracted some 90,000 blacks—mostly because, as a protest against
the Democratic Party's own primary, it did not require our people
to run the white gauntlet in order to cast a ballot. It all took place
"in the family," so to speak, and this gave Bob an even better idea.

What COFO had in mind this year was not just another protest
vote, but the formation of a brand-new party—the Mississippi
Freedom Democratic Party (MFDP), which could then exert a
valid claim to represent the people of Mississippi at the Democratic
National Convention. Integrated teams of white and black workers
would go out into the field with the requisite petitions, since our
previous experience showed that blacks just had a harder time

saying no to a white person than to another black—their impulse to "go along and get along" was just too great. This backfired when it came to recruiting for demonstrations. People would say yes when a white worker asked them to join a scheduled march, then they just wouldn't come. It worked wonders, though, when it came to getting signatures on a page.

It was a bold plan, coming as it did just a few months after the shocking assassination of a U.S. president, but boldness was the tenor of the times. Deathly opposed to us, of course, were the so-called Dixiecrats—the white southern Democrats, mostly seg-regationists, who had controlled state politics for generations.

Back in the SNCC office, Miss Hamer and Lawrence Guyot had us all busy canvassing for the MFDP. We were excited because we'd heard that busloads of students from up north were coming to Greenwood to help with the campaign that would come to be known as "Freedom Summer." Then, too, Dr. Martin Luther King, Jr., was coming to Greenwood.

As the big day approached, the preachers argued over whose church was most suitable to host the distinguished guest. The women in our community acknowledged to be superior cooks outdid themselves with fried chicken, turnip greens, two-egg-and-hot-water cornbread, candied yams, pies, cakes, and all kinds of other good things to eat. Since I was too excited to stay cooped up all day in the Freedom Library, I took some "direct action" of my own. With a couple of other workers, I visited each of the chefs, sampling their wares, making sure they got praised for their efforts. The houses selected for "official visits" got scrubbed to a fare-thee-well—dusted, swept, mopped, and waxed—and everyone took extra pride in fixing up the neighborhood: trimming lawns, pulling weeds, removing trash, washing windows, and covering broken panes. Sunday best was laundered; kids' ears were washed and runny noses wiped.

Most of the community was openly active in the Movement at this point, but even people who had never marched a step in our demonstrations reminisced fondly about past protests. Those of us who had actually been beaten, shot at, or arrested received admiring glances, like war heroes on Armistice Day. For the first time I could remember, the whole community *acted* like a community, taking pride in what it was, and in what it was becoming.

Mama wore her flowered dress, even though it wasn't so comfortable to sit in. "You brang dat man by here to meet Dossie Ree," she said. "I knows you kin do it, 'cause ain't nosomebody been to de jailhouse mo' den you."

"I don't know, Mama," I said. "He might be bringin' the television folks with him—and everysomebody will see you and know that you be a freedom fighter."

"Lawd amercy." Mama waved my fears away. "Ain't gwine stick my head out de do'—nosuh! You knows you can't hardly look out de window no mo' lessen somebody be snappin' yo' picture." She was right. The media already swarmed like locusts over Greenwood —twice as thick as when Dick Gregory was here.

"This is something to see!" Reverend Lowie Red said as he leaned his chair against the plate-glass window of his barber shop on Walthall Street. I loved to hear him speak, with his great, stentorian bass and his actor's diction. "Lights, camera, action! Microphones, notebooks, and pens! Everybody wants to see, hear, and read about the Delta today. Now, you take these reporters— they're running around, trying to catch anyone who'll give them a good story. The later it gets, the better your chance to see your name in the paper 'cause they've got deadlines to meet."

He pointed to the crowd across the street. "You know how come all these news people are here? Because of all those white youngsters come down for the Freedom Vote. It's what they call

good copy. And look at those policemen on the roof of the Chinaman's store. You think they're going to let any grudge-bearing
hothead harm Reverend King in Greenwood? Not likely! They
don't want the world to see their ugliness!"

Just then Larry Still of *Jet* magazine came up with his tape
recorder and notepad and began interviewing Reverend Lowie and
his customers. I faded back, as I often did when the microphones
came out. Some of the civil rights workers had talked me into
going to Mississippi Vocational College in Itta Bena to take the test
for my high school equivalency diploma. I'd passed, but I still
lacked confidence. I was ashamed of my Delta accent and didn't
think I could command the big words needed to communicate the
Movement's big ideas. There was a time for talk and there was a
time for action, and I knew which was which. If my name was
going to be in the papers, I wanted it to be for getting arrested,
not saying something dumb. Although I did give a few interviews,
by and large I had a pat answer for the media: "Y'all be there to
take my picture in the demonstration—that be when I do my best
talkin'!"

Dr. King was to arrive at the local airport, which had never
received anything more glamorous than a crop duster. Most of
Greenwood's black community lined the runway to await the big
event; some older folks even brought chairs. Many of the onlookers
had never seen an airplane up close, nor did they know anyone
who had flown in one. There were sharpshooters on the airport
roof, and plainclothes policemen mingled with the crowd.

With Dr. King were the Reverends Andy Young, Ralph Aberna-
thy, and Bernard Lee, and Miss Dorothy Cotton, who immediately
struck me as the most sophisticated Negro woman I had ever seen.
It was hard for me to take my eyes off her long enough to take in
the great man himself.

When I did, I was surprised to notice that he was not as tall as the men around him, and that he had a kind rather than forceful face. On top of that, he looked a little jumpy, which seemed odd, considering some of the things he'd been through and the big crowd of black well-wishers (and relatively few whites) who turned out to greet him. He made a few brief remarks at the airport, saying he was glad to be in Mississippi and no one could doubt that Mississippians wanted their freedom. Then he was rushed through the crowd, shaking hands and patting people on the back as he went.

In Gee Pee's sea of friendly faces, he seemed to relax. The local leaders had planned a "community walk" for Dr. King, so that even housebound people like Mama could see him up close. A calvacade of cars with horns blowing led the way. People ran out of their houses to shake Dr. King's hand and to have him sign copies of last Sunday's church bulletin. He went up on porches to greet the handicapped. Mothers thrust babies in his face, and the drunks along McLauren Street picked themselves out of the gutter and saluted him.

Since I had been at the front of every other parade and demonstration in Greenwood for the last year and half, I didn't feel shy about elbowing my way to the head of this one. Dr. King began to talk to me as if I belonged at his side. Clipboard in hand, I briefed the leaders on the names of local people who came out to introduce themselves and their families. I wrote down the names of residents who had taken the occasion to enroll themselves to register to vote. Bro Pastor walked beside us, in his frock coat, along with Edward Cochran, Sam Block, and Willie Peacock. Directly behind us walked the pastors from the churches where mass meetings had been held, and a large crowd of people followed along behind them. You could see that behind the oratory and the headlines, Dr. King was a preacher first. He genuinely liked all kinds of people, and they returned his affection.

Up ahead, I saw Mama perched on the porch, fanning herself nervously, waiting for us to pass.

"Can somebody tell me about this woman we're going to visit?" Dr. King asked.

"She be my mama, Ida Mae Holland," I answered. "Mama can't walk, she be in a wheelchair for the dropsy. She used to be a midwife and she house the Movement people. She got two boys and one girl besides me. She like to eat sweets, she drink RC colas, and she dip snuff."

After greeting a couple of neighbors, we eased to the south side of the street and Dr. King climbed the steps. He was in shirtsleeves now, his jacket thrown over his shoulder. He extended his hand to Mama.

"How do you feel today, Miss Ida Mae?" Dr. King asked with a smile.

Mama smiled back politely, eyes big as cabbages, magnified behind her glasses, and shook his hand. "I be feelin' toler'ble well deday, Reverend Kang," she responded.

Dr. King turned to one of his traveling party like there was something important he forgot. "Bernard, why don't you go to the store over there and get Miss Ida Mae some ice cream, some RC's, and a jar of snuff?"

"Lawd amercy!" Mama slapped her cheeks, thrilled as all get out. "Y'all c'mere an' rest yo'self, Pastor Kang!"

Dr. King eased into the rocker while as many of his party as possible squeezed onto our porch and tried to look comfortable. Cameras whirred and flashbulbs popped. Mama tried to look unimpressed.

"I tol' Ida Mae—dat gal over dere be mine"—she pointed me out on the steps—"t' work wit' y'all an' be mannerly."

Dr. King smiled. "We need everybody to register to vote, Miss Ida Mae."

"I be jest tellin' Susie an' Lou Emma dat I be gwine t' de cou'thouse t' reddish," Mama said, pointing out the houses of her neighbors to lend credence to her story. "Yassuh, I tell you—bence y'all c'mere an' tells me t' go reddish, 'spect I will. A lotta folkses need t' gon' an' git reddish!" She looked into the crowd. "Heap sees but few knows." Then she turned to Dr. King. "I say dat 'cause us'n here in de Delta don't know dat de very one dat be scorn be de one dat he'p de most." She took a deep breath. "Now, I wanna tell y'all dis for years—"

Dr. King took Mama's hand (people would come by our house later to see the hand that Dr. King held) and said, "Tell us, Miss Ida Mae, because history is important for our people."

Mama told him and the crowd all about Dossie Ree and her work. In her best play-like voice she concluded, "Unbeknownest to de white folks an' de colored, her be a mem'er o' de NAACP since '52!"

"Women have always been the leaders in our Movement," said Dr. King.

"You hear dat, Dossie Ree?" Mama said. "Uh, Dossie Ree— c'mere an' 'duce yo'self t' Reverend Kang. He be de preacher from 'lanta, Georgie, had all dem folkses walkin' on dey footses over yon'er in Alabamy." She spoke extra loud so the crowd around the house would know she knew exactly who was sitting on her porch.

The bystanders parted ("Like de Red Sea," as Mama would later describe it) and Dossie Ree appeared in her best dress, Easter hat, and high-heeled shoes. Her children watched from behind the screen door with Cedric, round-eyed with wonder. "Howdy do, Reverend King," she said, making a kind of curtsy and taking his hand. "I be *Dollie* Ree Johnson." This was the first time I had ever heard her real name.

Dr. King gave his seat to Dossie Ree, bowed to her and thanked her for her help. He stared at her for a long time, as if he was burning her face into his soul. Then he came back down to the street and the procession moved on, me with it.

That night, our mass meeting made national news. The freedom songs, testimonies, and prayers rang out, but none with greater force or melody than Dr. King's remarkable voice and the simple message it carried. For over a year we had been so concerned with protest marches, demonstrations, passive resistance, and how to avoid being shot, bombed, and lynched that we'd all but forgotten the reason we'd been put on this earth: to love one another, even our enemies. The Reverend Dr. King said that while he wanted the whole town to participate in our marches, he wanted us to remember that primary mission, too. We all had our roles to play in the Movement. Reminding us to keep love in our hearts was his.

When the meeting was over, it was time to take Dr. King and his entourage to the airport. As the local staff with their clipboards tried to sort out who went with which car, I wound up sliding into the passenger seat of a car driven by Reverend Lowie Red, who knew Dr. King from his early college days at Morehouse and had been assigned to transport him on this last leg.

The caravan followed its police escort through town, then sped out onto the highway. Dr. King waved until there was no one left to wave at, then lay his head back against the seat and closed his eyes. I thought he was asleep until his big voice boomed inside the car.

"What grade are you in, young lady?"

Before I could say anything, Reverend Red began to answer for me. "You see, Reverend, Little Cat here—uh, that is, Ida Mae, was on the wrong road in life." He went on to catalogue every crime and misdemeanor I had ever committed—plus a few that I hadn't. I didn't think I could speak with his authority or grace, so I just lowered my head in shame.

"Well," Dr. King said finally, glancing wearily out the window, "she's going to do better, Reverend Red. You keep up with her and let me know what she's doing."

I sensed Dr. King's eyes fall upon me in the darkened car. I looked back over the bench seat.

"I'm goin' to be Somebody, Reverend King," I said in the fullest, firmest, most pear-shaped tones I could manage.

"You do that, Ida Mae," the deep voice replied. "You go to school and be Somebody—but put God first."

Police, sheriff's deputies, and what looked like the whole U.S. Army had surrounded the little airport when we arrived. Mississippi officials wanted no incidents while Dr. King was in their care, and that was fine with us. The private airplane bearing him away was warmed up and ready to go. It was airborne within minutes after his party climbed aboard. We all stood and watched it climb out of sight, then sighed with relief. We looked around at each other—local staff, key volunteers, SNCC field secretaries—and then at the dozens of white officers nervously fingering their weapons, eyeing us back. I'm sure it flashed into every head, no matter what color, at exactly the same time: If they didn't arrest us or blow us away now, they'd just have to do it tomorrow, or next week, or next year. And at this point in our struggle, it wasn't entirely clear just whose side time was on. With all deliberate speed, we went back to our vehicles and slammed the doors tight.

Reverend Red said, "I'm going to be watching you, Cat." He smiled when he said it, but I knew he meant it, too. It became our catch phrase—our private joke and greeting—whenever we saw each other after that.

The next day, Mama held court. Everybody in Gee Pee had to visit her and make 'mirations over her playing hostess to, and receiving gifts from, the famous Dr. King. She told and retold her story so many times that eventually she had to change the details a little just to keep it fresh and exciting. But the one thing that never changed was the ending:

"Dat ol' gal o' mines, she be Somebody wit' de Freedom Riders," Mama beamed proudly. "I tole Luther Kang dat, too!"

B Y T H E summer of 1964, COFO/SNCC and its supporters had staged 10,000 demonstrations, during which some 5,000 black people had been arrested; still we had fallen well short of our goals. Only 28,500 of the 422,000 eligible blacks in Mississippi had been registered to vote. As our protests and marches became more like battle zones, and our jails more like P.O.W. camps, SNCC leaders felt it would be wise to send a few bloodied veterans north to motivate the people who were donating money, material, and loved ones to the cause.

One day, I had been trapped by a documentary filmmaker who asked me to talk into his camera about my experiences in Parchman prison. A short time later, Willie Peacock and Sam Block came to me and asked if I would mind going north on a speaking tour with Rosemary Freeman, Alberta Barnett, and John Handy to raise money for SNCC. I was flattered, but I also thought they were crazy. True, I had lots of stories, and told them with style and energy, but my Delta accent was thick and I'd spent a lot more time out of school than in it. Surely our educated leaders would be more effective than me in getting our message across to people in a position to help.

They didn't think so. Neither did Bob or anyone else whose permission was needed to set the travel machinery in motion. And that is how the Movement came to fulfill my lifelong dream of getting out of the Delta.

Mama was sad and proud when I told her. From her wheelchair on the front porch, she pointed to the sky and asked, "Gal, you don't mean you gwine fly up yon'er in de sky like de birds?"

"Yas'm, Mama," I said.

"Well, I knowed you be a big liar—but I didn't b'lieve you be a fool, too." She shook her head. "I 'spose you gwine turn in all de money you git—I bet you a fat man dat dem dere other Freedom Riders don't brang alla dey money back!"

I hugged her and tried to soothe away her fears. I brought Cedric to the backyard when I heard a plane passing over and pointed to the sky and told him that his mama was going to be flying up in the sky. I must have scared him because he started crying and wrapped his small arms tighter around my neck.

Our tour was to include Chicago, Detroit, New York, Maine, Vermont, and Minneapolis/St. Paul. We were expected to be away for two to three weeks. I made certain that everybody in Green-wood knew that I was going. People pressed scraps of paper into my hands containing the addresses of and messages for their northern relatives. Miss Nollie B. loaned me her matching set of luggage, which I filled with Eva Mae Brown's clothes. May Liza curled my hair, Pearlie made up my face, and Dossie Ree gave me a pair of stockings and advice on being careful in the big cities. We had a small celebration at Edwards Plaza Hotel.

We rode in first class, which, along with my new dress and fake leather briefcase from Mr. Fred's Dollar Store, made me feel less countrified. My first sight of Chicago, with its tall buildings and its lake and its million lights flickering, made my heart beat faster and weakened my knees. I'd had no idea such wonders existed. But I kept my composure so calm that no one would guess I'd never been out of the Delta before.

Our tour took us to private homes, schools, community centers, and churches. It was organized by the Northern Friends of SNCC, who provided a local escort, meals, and a place to stay, usually at the escort's house. In my speeches I described what was happening in the Delta and what had happened to me, especially at Parchman. I never used a prepared speech. I would make a list in my mind of the things I wanted to cover. Then I would simply speak, all my practice play-liking with Mama paying off at last. I'd boom like the white policemen or go strident and sassy like the marchers, my voice creeping into every crevice and crack of the house or church or concert hall. Then my tone would drop low and servile, so that my audience leaned forward to hear, like the old folk in Gee Pee. Sometimes reporters from the local newspapers would be present, along with a photographer.

In Chicago, I spoke at several suburban churches. Many Delta blacks had migrated to the area, and local interest was keen. Those who could afford it were free with their checkbooks. Most of the migrants I met said they were some kin to me or knew some of my relatives. We stayed in Chicago for several days, and I accepted invitations to countless apartments and houses to visit and eat and tell people what was going on in Greenwood and the rest of the South they had left behind. On one visit, I learned that Simon Jr., whom we hadn't heard from for several years, was in prison for murder, although nobody knew more than hearsay about his arrest.

After Chicago, our escort, the civil rights activist Reverend Charles Sherrod, took us through other parts of Illinois, and then we went to Detroit, where the reception was cool. Race relations were worse there than in Chicago, and black people in Detroit had their own view of the Movement. They didn't identify as much with the plight of southern blacks, and they thought we were hogging all the headlines. They wanted to know why we were marching and going to jail, and why we weren't at work. Many people thought we were Communist-inspired and working against the government.

It was the first time I realized that black people had their own minds on just about everything. Civil rights was a political issue, not just a personal one, and reasonable people could differ on what it meant, and how its goals should be achieved.

Naturally, many of the people we met on our tour were white, which put me in a box. Aside from working at the Freedom Office, I had no experience whatsoever meeting white people on an equal footing. Even looking a white person in the eye was considered impudent—and it often took all the energy I had just to resist the long-ingrained habit of looking away. I took advantage of the airplane rides between stops to research good "white folks' manners" with my seatmates, who were almost always white.

Chatting with them, I had the freedom to pretend I was anything I wanted—a lawyer on one plane, a schoolteacher on another. That role prompted my seatmate to ask me about my school's curriculum. Since I had never heard the word before, I didn't have an answer. Instead, I pretended to get airsick. By the time I had stopped "vomiting" and the stewardess had given me water and a cold towel for my forehead, he had forgotten his question.

As usual, though, events in the Delta overshadowed most conversations, even casual ones. The trial of Byron de la Beckwith, the white man from Greenwood accused of murdering Medgar Evers, was a litmus test for sympathy with the Movement. At the time, the outlook for conviction was not good. My old nemesis, Governor Ross Barnett, had appeared at the courthouse in Jackson during

Myrlie Evers's testimony and made a big show of support for the defendant—at one point even shaking his hand in front of the jury.

In the end, despite what appeared to be an airtight case by the prosecution, a mistrial was declared. In fact, despite more legal action in 1964, Beckwith was not convicted of killing Medgar, but only of carrying explosives with the intent of blowing up a Jewish teacher, which got him only five years in jail. (Twenty-five years later, the case was reopened when new evidence came to light, and a year later de la Beckwith was indicted by a grand jury. In February 1994—thirty years and eight months after the murder—he was finally found guilty and sentenced to life in prison.)

The de la Beckwith trial was eclipsed only by an equally high-profile and horrific crime. Each day, when we called the SNCC office to report in and receive instructions, we asked, "Have you heard anything about the workers?"

The three civil rights workers in question—two white students from up north, Michael Schwerner and Andrew Goodman, and James Chaney, a black student from the South—had disappeared, the first casualties of Freedom Summer.

"I'll tell you what I think," the well-dressed white businessman sitting next to me said as he leafed through his newspaper. "I think that Negro boy took those two white students out crawdad hunting and they got lost."

Since I had not been given a first-class ticket to antagonize potential donors, I responded with a joke. "Well, as long as they been gone, they coulda caught enough crawdaddies to feed ever-somebody in Mississippi!"

The white man didn't meet my eyes. He only grunted and turned back to his newspaper.

The eventual discovery of the civil rights workers' gunshot bodies, buried in an earthen dam, cast a pall on workers in both the

South and the North. By degrees, white reaction to the Movement had escalated from lynchings of ordinary black folk to murders of black rights workers to assassinations of black officials and the white workers helping them. The state government in Mississippi was openly calling the arrival of Freedom Summer workers an "invasion" and had declared certain types of civil rights activities illegal, including picketing of public buildings and passing out leaflets in support of boycotts. The Highway Patrol had been expanded and given broad new powers, including authority to infiltrate civilian organizations. Most ominously, Parchman state prison had been designated as the official facility to house civil rights detainees.

These developments put new urgency in my talks up north. My audiences got larger and listened more closely. Each day, it seemed, the newspapers and TV and Mississippi SNCC gave me some new atrocity to announce, explain, and lament.

In Great Neck, New York, my hosts were Dr. and Mrs. Charles Goodrich, whose rambling, beautiful home, with modern appliances and expensive furniture, seemed like a storybook to me. An escort took me into Manhattan, where I saw such wonders as moving stairways and trains that ran underground. But for some reason, I could not force myself down into the bowels of the earth to board that silly train, and she drove me back to Great Neck really amused. She couldn't understand how a little hick who had no fear of police dogs, riot guns, and nightsticks could nearly faint at the white man's technological "hoodoo."

That night with the Goodriches was memorable for two other reasons. It marked the first proper, sit-down meal I'd ever taken with a white family. I had helped serve food to white families in Greenwood and had been around them while they ate. I had even "broken bread" with some of the white workers in Greenwood—one or two poor meals inside a shotgun house or rural shack, almost in secret. But now the Goodriches and their children sat me down at the backyard table beside their barbecue. They put before me a grilled steak about a mile high—the first I had ever eaten.

The rare meat was so tender I could cut it with my fork, and juicy as a watermelon. In the Delta, we cooked everything to a fare-thee-well, mostly for safety because the meat was half-rotten. The filet was therefore a little rich for my system, but I choked it down with a smile, like I'd been eating expensive cuts of beef all my life. At first I couldn't stop thinking how little I deserved to be enjoying these good things while Mama and everyone else was still suffering in Mississippi. But by the second half of the meal the good food had worked its magic, and I found myself reflecting on how good and smart the civil rights workers said I was, how courageous I had been at Parchman, and how a good meal now and then was just my due. I could hear Mama saying, "I owe dis some-teet t' my owndearself."

But later that night, as we were getting ready for bed, several cars roared up outside. A voice cried, "Nigger lovers get outta town!" and a brick shattered the plate-glass picture window in the Goodriches' living room. Mrs. Goodrich and I grabbed the children and jumped behind the sofa as a couple of shots rang out. Then the cars peeled away.

After our ears quit ringing, Mrs. Goodrich peered out from what used to be her picture window, shaking like a leaf. The kids thought it was exciting. I had to admit, between the family's hospitality and the presence of the northern Klan, I felt right at home. We put the kids to bed and cleaned up the mess while Dr. Goodrich phoned the police, but I was determined that no rednecks were going to spoil my trip. I stripped back the covers on my bed so that I could see all its finery—the double mattress and matching sheets and soft pillow, better than Black Mary's bridal suite!—and settled into it.

I fell asleep at once, but soon armies of roaches and marching rats invaded my dreams. The bugs carried matches, which the rats struck with their teeth. A giant fire blazed in my subconscious and I woke up screaming.

Mrs. Goodrich was sitting beside me on the bed. "It was just a bad dream. You're safe, Ida Mae," she said.

"I know you're afraid," Dr. Goodrich said, mussing my hair, as I supposed fathers did on such occasions. He turned to his wife. "She's just a young girl—"

"I know," Mrs. Goodrich replied, "it's so hard on the children." She gave me a hug and held me until I got drowsy. At least, I reflected as I fell back to sleep, I hadn't peed the bed.

The next morning I awoke feeling refreshed, alert, and alive. I couldn't remember much about my nightmare except that it had been another "fire dream," as I now called them. I had almost succeeded in forgetting about the attack on the Goodriches' house as well, until I went into the living room and saw the big sheet covering the window.

I spent the next few days getting medical examinations and treatment at the New York hospital where Dr. Goodrich worked. My teeth had never been cleaned or checked by a dentist until that visit, and my bowels had never been quite right since Parchman. I spent my evenings giving lectures before large audiences—mostly Jewish white people. Occasionally, as I spoke of this atrocity or that, someone in the audience would call out, "We remember! We remember!" I couldn't make sense of this until someone explained to me that they were referring to their own near-extinction at the hands of another kind of klan.

Before leaving New York, I had another milestone experience, though I would not recognize its full significance for many years.

For the first time in my life, I met an interracial couple living openly together. You can imagine my surprise when Mrs. Childs, a black woman living in Manhattan, introduced me to her white husband. I stayed with them for a few days, and again saw strange and beautiful things. I knew that Mama wouldn't believe me when I told her about the doorman who stood in front of their apartment building wearing a uniform. I must have gone in and out over a hundred times—just to have him open the door for me!

Along with the usual fund-raiser, the Childses had arranged for us to go to the theater later in the week. We were going to see *The Dutchman*, by a black playwright named LeRoi Jones (later known as Amiri Baraka). I was full of anticipation. Although I had seen lots of play-like in the Delta and a few minstrel shows, I had never seen a full-fledged professional theatrical production, and everyone I spoke with was raving about this one. And I still harbored dreams of performing myself.

How can I explain, then, why the experience was so disappointing to me? First of all, having been unable to summon the nerve to go down into the subway system, I could not imagine a "subway car"—the play's setting. Second, I could not for the life of me suspend my disbelief about a Negro man talking in such a way to a white woman. It all seemed so unreal to me, it might as well have been depicting life on another planet. But watching the play, somewhere deep inside it began to occur to me that if I could ever get it on stage in a real theater, a play about *my* life and experiences could really move people.

I had a chance to share these ideas backstage with the playwright. Despite my puzzled reaction to his work, he was full of encouragement for me.

"You read as many plays as you can," he told me, "and write down everything that happens."

On the eve of our departure, we were invited to the home of

another playwright, Lorraine Hansberry, whose *A Raisin in the Sun* is another icon of American drama. Unfortunately, between the injuries I'd received at Parchman and the treatments I'd had to cure them, I felt too bad to go out with the other workers. Had I fully appreciated Miss Hansberry's stature, perhaps I would have forced myself out the door.

The next day, we went on to Boston, then Maine. In Maine we stayed with Reverend and Mrs. Dick, who treated us kindly and insisted that we sign their guest book; when I wrote my name on the page, I felt like a queen. By now I'd grown so confident as a speaker that my play-like sometimes brought tears to my eyes as well as to my listeners'.

Our last stop was in the Twin Cities of Minnesota, where we were hosted by several families who rolled out the red carpet for us. We were hailed and feted everywhere we went: Luncheons and dinners were held in our honor, and reporters and children followed us everywhere. Not surprisingly, I took an instant liking to Minneapolis. The town was clean and its tall buildings well kept. Every dog I saw was on a leash. The sprawling university appealed to me particularly. And I liked the idea that the river it straddled was the same one that, a thousand miles south, watered the Delta where I was born.

Prompted by nobody, I said aloud, "I'm gonna come back here an' go to this college!"

"That's nice, Ida Mae," my host, Shirley Ricketts, said, giving me a polite little wink. "We think highly of our university. It's one of the top ten!"

"I'll help you get in," said Judy Barnes, a girl my age, who was sitting in the backseat. "I go to school there."

I leaned back and tried to picture myself walking my walk down the mall, a stack of books under my arm.

A question from Shirley Ricketts brought me back to the present. For the moment, I reminded myself, my job was to tell tearful stories to the local folks, get them to write their checks, then get my tail back home, where I had a mother and a son. Not that Cedric regarded me as a mother anymore. I was the stranger lady who popped in now and then to tend Mama's sores and to play-like I was his mother. But it wasn't me putting him to bed or waking him up day after day. It wasn't me wiping away his tears, or feeding him, or listening to his baby talk and talking back to him through the long afternoons and into the night. I hadn't been there.

With my thoughts still in turmoil, I surpassed myself that night, like a performer hitting her peak at the end of a long-running play, and we set a SNCC fund-raising record. As we mingled with the crowd afterward, a man came up to me and introduced himself as Zev Aelony. It turned out he was the inmate at Parchman whose name, carved in thin but defiant letters in my cell, helped give me the courage to keep going. We hugged and cried like kinfolk.

At the airport the next morning, Shirley Ricketts and Judy Barnes shook my hand and thanked me again for helping to make the evening a success. Then, as I was about to board the plane, they added, "You come back, Ida Mae. We'll help you go to the university."

For once I was tongue-tied. I had half-convinced myself that, as eloquent as I might be at talking about the past, I was a big failure when it came to planning the future.

I settled into my seat for what I knew would be my last first-class ride for a while, and thanked God the seat next to mine was empty. I didn't feel like talking about the Delta for a while—about the Movement and the terrible things people were capable of doing to each other. All I wanted to do was hug my mama and hold my son.

The flight was smooth and gentle. But when we began our descent and I thought about what lay ahead of me, I was tempted to crawl into the overhead compartment or under the seat to hide.

Chauffeured cars were a lot more comfortable than police vans. A cheering audience was a lot better than jeering rednecks or a snarling line of police dogs. I knew the trip had changed me; I just didn't know how much. Nor did I know just how much the situation in the Delta, too, had altered while I was gone.

Seventeen

When I got home, Greenwood was like a city under siege. Strange-looking white "invaders" from the North and East and West, most of them young, wandered the streets like an occupying army. Not to be outdone, the police and the Highway Patrol paraded around in their heavy armor, with a new militant attitude. The COFO/SNCC office had been wired with a WATS line and was staffed twenty-four hours a day, so we could instantly contact other SNCC offices—even Julian Bond in Atlanta—and COFO outposts all over the country—not to mention the U.S. Justice Department.

"I tell you, Aint Baby chile," I heard Dossie Ree tell Mama one morning, "de bottom rail be on de top!"

She was referring to the way life in the colored sections of town had been turned upside down by the Movement. People who hadn't set foot in school for decades now crammed the Freedom Schools. Men who had literally never looked a white woman in the face now stood toe-to-toe with the registrar and argued for their rights. All over town, blacks and white civil rights workers broke bread together, watching and learning and laughing with each other as old habits, misconceptions, and stereotypes began to melt away. Colored folks trod the sidewalks in the white district like they owned the town, and white girls from New England used our outhouses like they were born to it. We even saw black men walking hand-in-hand with white girls. We got used to hearing ourselves introduced as "Mr." and "Miss" by the white workers from up north, who had to remind us time and again to drop those titles when we addressed them.

"I 'spect you right," Mama replied. "Even li'l Ida Mae be up yon'er in de Nawth—ridin' in dem big planes through de air—" She tossed her hands like it was all too much for her, but I knew she was secretly pleased—not only with the changes in our community, but with me.

We had, however, argued a lot about my duty to Cedric. By temperament I had never been much of a homebody, and the Movement had given me a good reason not to turn into one. I asked myself whether it was better for Cedric to have a full-time mama who was bad at the job or a new society, but the truth was, for me there was never really a choice. I had pushed Cedric into Mama's arms, partly because she had been a good mother to me and I knew she would do a better job than I could at my age, but also because I was still hungry. "Yo' eyes be bigger den yo' belly," Mama used to say to me, but she understood that I was committed to a cause greater than myself and greater than her and greater than my child.

"I glory in yo' spunk, gal!" Mama told me in an unguarded moment. She said it like a fact and I believed her. I still didn't think I would ever be her equal, but at least, I believed, I would not be her nemesis.

Still, most white people—especially those born and raised in Mississippi—were puzzled and angered by the new status quo. By the end of August, the mystery surrounding the disappearance of Goodman, Schwerner, and Chaney had been cleared up, but their killers were no closer to justice. Over the summer there had been thirty-seven church burnings and more than eighty beatings of civil rights workers and would-be voters. Testing the teeth of the new Civil Rights Act, a handful of blacks in Greenwood had attempted to integrate an all-white theater. The show ended early for them when they got chased out by a mob of angry whites.

As "the establishment" proved more and more intractable—in the courts, in the new federal administration, and in local politics, as well as in the streets—the ideology at SNCC's core began to change. Bob Moses's original strategy in Mississippi had been to enroll more black voters, and let social justice largely take care of itself. But the second "Freedom Vote" had drawn no greater response than the first had, even though six thousand more ballots had been distributed. After two years of hard canvassing, it was apparent that voting didn't mean much to impoverished, illiterate black citizens who lacked a rudimentary understanding of their place in the world.

There had always been those hanging around the Movement who espoused radical socialism, but their voices had usually been suppressed by our more moderate leaders. Now they began to be heard. This process was inadvertently boosted by the moderates themselves, who now felt morally bound to take responsibility for the well-being of anyone who joined or supported the Movement. Although I wouldn't realize it until years later, these two forces working together—the gradual rise of the "super snicks," or radicals in the Movement, and the sense of dependency we created among the people we were trying to help—laid the groundwork for many of the problems we would later encounter. Some even went so far as to accuse our Moses of "leading us back into the wilderness," but that was going too far. Like any war, ours had taken on a life of its own.

Lots of Mississippians went to the 1964 Democratic Convention by bus. Alberta Barnett and I flew to Atlantic City, where we had a great time walking the boardwalk, seeing the sights, hearing the sounds, and attending receptions—like the one hosted by Jacqueline Kennedy, whose hand we were privileged to shake. We took the bus back to Greenwood, giggling and play-liking all the way home.

But Lyndon Johnson and Hubert Humphrey conspired with the Dixiecrats to block the Mississippi Freedom Democratic Party's full participation at the Convention, and we left Atlantic City without getting our rightful place there. After that, the Movement—and black people generally—saw no other road to take but increased militancy. Whereas we began 1964 with integration and equality as our goal, led by such big-spirited souls and unifiers as Bob Moses and Martin Luther King, Jr., we ended it with the Movement slipping more and more into the hands of charismatic radicals like Stokely Carmichael and H. Rap Brown. The Nobel Peace Prize Dr. King received in December was hailed as a victory laurel for our cause, but to me it seemed more like a funeral wreath for the Movement as we'd originally conceived of it.

By then, Greenwood was no longer a hotbed of activity. Bob Moses and most of the SNCC field secretaries had moved on, and almost all of the white summer volunteers had gone back home. With them went the news reporters and TV cameras. Miss Hamer, Annie Devine, and Victoria Gray were still protesting the seating of five white congressmen, but on the whole, nobody wanted to stir up white people's anger and nobody was there to help or to tell the world. So a quiet pall hung over Greenwood, like the day after a big party when everyone wants to get some rest. Even the Klan had been strangely quiet.

"IDA MAE! Ida Mae!" Mama whispered in the near-dark, shaking me as I slept. "Wake up, gal, an' lissen!"

I sat up on my mattress, heart pounding. "What is it, Mama? What's wrong?"

"Dem dogs," she said. "Lissen how dey be barkin'."

"Aww, Mama," I slumped back down. "They just treed some cat—"

"Gal, I knows how dogs sound when dey tree de cat, an' dey ain't runnin' no cat up no tree! Sound t' me like dey gots a crook in de th'oat! C'mon now—git up an' go see what de matter be—"

"Aww, Mama—" I said. But I swung my legs to the floor.

"An' don't turn dat light on, neither!" she added, wheeling back to give me room to stand, "or de whole town be out dere lookin' and talkin'."

I stood with the back door open, shivering in the February dawn. I doubted whether anyone would want to break into our house; we didn't have anything worth stealing. Still, all the neighborhood dogs were barking, in a rhythmic, unearthly chant. Nothing seemed wrong, exactly, but then again, things didn't seem quite right.

"It be just Frisgo and a whole buncha dogs, Mama," I said, crossing my arms for warmth. My wet nightgown clung to the back of my legs.

"Den hook dat ol' hound up t' de wood house," Mama yelled. "Dat'll fix him!" Her nose wrinkled and she fingered my mattress. "I 'spect you pee de bed mo' den dat boy o' yo'n!"

I chained Frisgo to the wood house and came back in. The sun was almost up, so I filled the tin tub with lukewarm water. All the sweet-smelling soap the Goodriches had sent home with me was long gone, so I had to bathe with the harsh Octagon soap Mama used for laundry.

I had a big day ahead. A squad of us local workers, determined to make ourselves feel useful again, had assigned ourselves the task of integrating the lunch counter at the white hotel. I had rehearsed many times how I would take my seat in the plush "white only" hotel (I had never been inside, so I could only imagine how it looked) and politely ask for my cup of coffee. Of course, there were limits to my daintiness. My trusty overalls were starched and ironed. They were still my "jailhouse" uniform—clothes I could afford to get beat-up and arrested in.

I dried off and dressed, then patted my natural into place. Then I went out on the porch to wait for the others to come by and pick me up.

"Gal," Mama called, "I hope you put some Yodora underneath yo' arms, since you gwine down yon'er t' set next t' white folkses." She wheeled over to the screen door and peered out nervously. "Don't know why y'all gots t' git some-teet an' drank coffee wit' de white folkses who don't want y'all 'round. Steada runnin' down yon'er t' cause trouble, you oughter be takin' care o' yo' boy."

"All right, Mama," I said, "I'll git Cedric up and gi'e him his bath and git his clothes on."

"Never mind, old pee-de-bed gal!" Mama said, rolling back. "Don'cha tetch dis here chile—you be liable t' drown him!" Then her voice turned as she cooed to Cedric, "C'mere, Mama li'l ol' stankpot—yo' granny gwine take care o' you!"

I shrugged and sat back on the steps.

Later, I would spend many sleepless nights trying to recall exactly what happened next.

"I 'members de very day," May Liza would say confidently. "De dogs be barkin' all funny like. I sont one o' my bad-tail chilluns t' de sto' t' git me some snuff. I look outta my do', an' dat Frisgo be makin' some kinda racket—jumpin' 'round in a circle, dis way and dat. I could jest 'cern him twix de houses, hitched t' de wood house wit' a railroad chain 'round his neck. His tail be pointin' t'ward Dossie Ree's house—I mean Do*llie* Ree's—and his footses be beatin' de air. I say t' myself: It be a good thang y'all gots him tied up. Den I go on back in de kitchen. Den I seed you jump off'n de porch and run down Dixie Lane alley—an' after dat, yo' lil' boy run out t'ward the sto' by Aintee's house."

Miss Susie piped in then, because she seldom let May Liza have the last word on anything.

"I 'spect you be runnin' after some man or 'nother," she said, dipping some snuff. "I went on in my middle room an' den I heard a big racket—sound like a bomb went off! So I run t' de do' an' look up an' down de street." She spat neatly into her homemade cuspidor. "Dat be when I seed y'all house afire."

I had heard May Liza's and Miss Susie's versions at least a dozen times, but both ended up at the same place. Mama's words—her surprise, her terror—consumed my imagination:

Who dat? Who? Nossuh. Nossuhree. I don't know what you be talkin' 'bout. I knows nothin' 'bout dis here freedom mess! Looka here—what you doin'? Oh, Lawd—he'p me, sweet Jesus! Oh my Lawd! Oh Lawd! I be afire! He'p! He'p me! Fire! Fire! Ida Mae! Ida Mae! Lawd amercy—Lawd —Lawd—Lawd—

I imagined her big face slack with terror, uncomprehending yet knowing exactly what was happening, that her time had come. I imagined her screaming, struggling, tumbling forward out of her wheelchair—steel now hot as a fireplace poker—flames racing up her smock to light her hair.

"Dat be when I seed pore Ida Mae," Miss Susie said. She always shook her head and sniffed back tears when she got to this part. "She *be* crawlin' on her knees out de do'. De house 'hind her don't be nothin'—jest burnt t' de groun', jest dat fast!" She tried to snap her chubby fingers. "I broke out in a run. I be hollerin' an' callin' for anysomebody t' come hep dat poor soul an' put out de fire."

That was May Liza's cue to take over the story. "Dat be when I

heared Miss Susie hollerin'! I run t' de do' an' dat be when I seed
yo' house afire. I didn't put on no shoes or nothin'—jest broke
outta my house hollerin' for Pearlie! Den I seed Miss Ida—" May
Liza usually looked away now, or covered her face. "She be a big
ball o' fire by de time me an' Miss Susie gits t' her."

That always led to a big argument between Miss Susie and May
Liza over just who pulled Mama the rest of the way from the
burning house.

"I tell y'all, dat fire be so hot," Miss Susie swore, "I be reachin'
for Ida Mae an' de fire be reachin' for me! I still got de marks on
my arm where I jest retch in dat fire an' took her hane!" If Miss
Susie was wearing long sleeves, she'd roll them up to show her
burns.

"I guess Miss Susie did git burnt," May Liza rejoined, "but it be
me who grab ahold of Miss Ida's hand an' pull her off'n de porch!"

That was where I came in. I remembered running after the
crowd from the low end of Dixie Lane alley, in front of Mr. Walter
Foreman's Blacksmith Shop. I heard the explosion and saw the blast
of hot, black smoke turn February into summer, day into night. I
heard a scream, too, and I turned to face that way, back the way
I'd come, but I couldn't move. Instinctively, I knew that trouble
had come for me, but there was nothing I could do. My feet
stayed glued to the ground, like in a nightmare. More screams—a
younger voice, probably Miss Susie's son Paul, who helped me pull
my legs from the molten lead that held them and run in unreal
slow motion back to my blazing house.

*Smoke rising in a big, black mushroom cloud—a strange and terri-
ble stench, like rotten meat. "We remember," the Jews of New York had
said . . .*

I skidded out the mouth of the alley to East Gibb Street and saw
a ball of fire floating across our yard toward the rose bush by the
concrete steps. The ball rolled over and turned into Mama. I

jumped forward, calling—commanding—the outstretched hands of those around her to roll her on the ground and put out the fire.

The faster I ran, the slower time moved.

More people—startled, screaming, uncomprehending—gathered in our yard. As I got closer, I saw that all Mama's skin and hair had burned off, leaving charred flesh and pink muscle. I was just about to grab her when the strong arms of Paul and a neighbor man hooked my waist and yanked me back.

"You cain't do nothin', Cat!" they said.

A woman shouted, "I got yo' boy, Cat—Cedric he be safe!"

But my eyes were fixed on Mama. Other men turned over her smoldering body, leaving flesh on the dirt and grass. Somebody brought a sheet and covered her. Neighbors dashed around, yammering and wailing, holding their noses with one hand and patting out flames with the other. Someone pointed to Frisgo's barbecued body dangling by a blackened iron chain from the charred post of the wood house. Our old house was a gutted ruin, its frame burning greedily like a stove full of crackling wood.

My eyes rolled up and my lungs shut down, stopped taking in the stinking air. I slumped over the arms that held me.

WHEN MY head cleared, I was sitting on the ground. The pungent fumes, strong as smelling salts, made me jerk upright just as Mr. Simon pulled up in the hearse that served as his makeshift ambulance.

Mama was still alive, but barely.

I rushed to her side but somebody said, "Don't touch her!" because her skin came off in your hand. Dogs were already sniffing the charred flesh left where she'd rolled.

The men loaded Mama into the hearse and I piled in after her.

Mr. Simon lit out for the hospital, horn blowing and lights flashing. White and black folk alike jumped back as we screeched down Main Street, just missing Mr. Scarecrow McGee.

I found the only unburned place on Mama's body—the palm of her hand—and held it gently, even as we rolled her down the corridor of the Leflore County Hospital, through the same doors she'd passed countless times to tend mothers and babies. The colored emergency waiting room was already filled with sad, docile patients but we rushed to the head of the line. I explained to the white nurse on duty who Mama was and what had happened and asked that the nurse call Dr. Aaron G. Jackson. She made an unpleasant, prissy face and buzzed for the colored orderly. Afterward, she slowly buzzed for Dr. Jackson, like she was doing me a favor.

Fortunately, Dr. Jackson was at the hospital. Mama was wheeled into the operating room, her body jumping under the coarse cover. I went to wait in the colored waiting room. There was nothing else I could do.

The next time I saw Mama, she was being delivered to her bed in the colored wing, bandaged from head to toe. She moaned pitifully as the orderlies lifted her from the gurney onto her bed. I found the unburned pink palm again and held it until Jean arrived. Our cousin T.C., who'd been on his way to join our sit-in, had tracked her down after he'd stopped in to see Mama and had found instead our smoldering house and distraught neighbors.

Jean glared at me with bloodshot eyes. "I knowed you was gonna git somebody kilt—messin' wit' dese white folkses!" she hissed. "Now you see how come I won't have nothin' t' do wit' dem Freedom Riders!"

"Ain't my fault, Jean," I said, though I didn't believe it myself.

"Is too! Dossie Ree seed de white folkses dat done it. Dey oughta burnt you up 'steada Mama. Pearlie say Ceg woulda got burnt up, too, 'f'n Mama hadn't sont him t' de sto' t' git some snuff!"

I knew that I had broken an important rule of the Movement: never take on the power structure without knowing that reinforcements were available. But much as I deserved it, I didn't need my sister's reproof. My stomach churned and vomit rose in my throat, but I choked it back. I put Mama's hand gently back on the sheet and took a chair on one side of the bed while Jean sat on the other —a different kind of sit-in. We kept our vigil until the nurse told us for the third time to leave.

For more than a week, Mama just lay there, wheezing through her scorched throat. Then the bandages came off, and her wounded flesh lay naked to the air under a tent-like sheet. A steady stream of friends and relatives came by to pay their respects, but we couldn't tell if she knew anyone was there. It wasn't clear whether the visitors knew I was there, either—one by one, they refused to look into my eyes.

While I was out in the hall, taking a break during one of these visits, I overheard one white LPN tell another, "I can't stand the smell of that colored girl!"

"Shhhh!" the other one answered. "She can't help it. Besides, she won't last much longer."

When I went back in, Mama's eyes were open for the first time since the fire and she was pulling at the tubes in her nose and mouth that hung like swamp runners from the bottles and bags around her bed. The nurse came in and reconnected the tubes and said condescendingly, "Now, we gon' be a good girl and not pull the tubes again—ain't that right, Aintee?"

When she was gone, Mama's glazed eyes pulled me to the bed. Her lips trembled like she wanted to speak. I put my ear down close.

"You want water, Mama? You gotsta use the bedpan?"

She said hoarsely, "Tote me t' vote, gal."

I burst into tears. I couldn't hug her, so I just clutched the edge of the bed and squeezed till my knuckles turned white.

A few days later, with Jean at her bedside, she died.

NOW I'M going to tell you something that you may not believe. I have run it back and forth in my mind so many times, for so many years, that I don't know what to believe myself, so I'll just give it to you straight.

Shortly after Mama died, I stood by her bed and looked down at the sheet that covered her face. Jean was out of the room, Dr. Jackson was off attending to another patient, and the nurse was on the phone making arrangements to have Mama's body transferred to the funeral home. It was just me and Mama alone, as it had been for so much of my life. Cried-out and calm, I folded the sheet down from her face. Her eyes were still half open, and the skin was clammy and turning gray, but that wide old face was placid— not the way they make you look in a mortuary, but like it was all finished, satisfied with what it had done in life and glad to be free of it. I traced the outline of Mama's lips with my dog finger, the way a little girl idly plays while she's sitting on a parent's lap, and told her:

"I'm gonna be Somebody. You rest now. I swear 'fore God, Mama—I'm gonna be Somebody."

Now here's the part that drives me crazy. After I made my promise, I swear I saw Mama's lips pull apart. Whitish-yellow spittle formed at the edge of her mouth, and she said, clear as day:

"Gwine see—thank de Lawd."

I was startled, as you might guess. I reached down and took her by the shoulders and cried, "Mama?" But she had nothing more to say. I thought about calling out, but to what purpose? The doctor had pronounced her dead, and who was I to resurrect her? I heard the nurse's footsteps in the corridor and looked over my shoulder. I suppose I should've been scared or spooked or felt guilty or something, but all I was was happy. Giddy, in fact. Joyful—as in the rapture of the Lord.

Funny thing is, I continued to hear her voice every now and again after that, and at the funniest times: fussing at Cedric, when I was about to do something stupid, waiting to go to sleep, waiting to get up. Sometimes it made me cry, but it never made me sad or angry. I have heard it, off and on, for the past thirty-odd years.

Eighteen

The attendants at McDonald's Funeral Home were taking Mama's casket out of the hearse to give to the pallbearers when Mr. Gravedigger Gransberry ran over to Miss McDonald and said, "De grave ain't ready yet!"

Miss McDonald walked a short distance from the crowd of mourners to peer under a sheltering palm, where the workmen were still excavating the grave. With apologies, she invited us to return to the line of long, black cars and wait in comfort.

The delay didn't make burying Mama any easier. Jean still blamed me for Mama's death, and we sat as far apart in the backseat of the lead Cadillac as her wide hips would allow. Mama's brothers, Cal and R.L., and her sisters, Annie, Mattie, and Thelma, just looked at each other helplessly and talked among themselves.

The only person who knew just what to do was Mabel, Mama's niece—who'd brought her northern smarts back home with her from Newark, New Jersey. She had promptly taken control of the funeral, plunking down several hundred dollars to upgrade Mama's functional "Sharpshooter" casket to something closer to the top of the line and to purchase Mama a burying gown that was twice as nice as anything she'd ever worn in life. As we climbed back into the cars, I heard Mabel tell off Miss McDonald in her citified accent, "My aunt paid a quarter a week to you for twenty years, Miss McDonald! It doesn't seem dignified to me that we, the relatives, should have to wait and watch the diggers finish her grave. Seems to me you would have taken care to do things right, since her burial was *paid up!*"

Miss McDonald rose on the balls of her feet so she could better look down her nose at Mabel, but even then she was at a disadvantage. Mabel was half white, with a skin tone even lighter than Miss McDonald's—not to mention that she held the purse strings.

"The weather was bad yesterday—they couldn't dig," Miss McDonald mumbled.

Mabel wasn't deterred. "They could've put a tarpaulin up over the gravesite."

While Mabel and Miss McDonald sorted out blame for the delay, Bro Pastor squirmed in the front seat of our car. Although he was normally a patient man, he seldom had opportunities to preach— not being ordained—so funerals were his specialty; and even then, an ordained preacher had to be present for the burial. He said he would give the owner of the funeral home a good talking to about keeping the dead waiting!

After a while, Miss McDonald stuck her head in his window and told Bro Pastor we could begin. We reassembled behind the hearse and Bro Pastor led us around the briers, over the mud, and through the tall stalks to a patch of damp earth covered with outdoor carpeting and some folding chairs. After giving us women a moment to straighten our snagged stockings and the men a chance to button their suits, he turned his eyes skyward and began.

"Lawd, Lawd, Lawd—here I is one mo' time, beggin' you to throw yo' strong arms of protection 'round sister Ida Mae. Lawd, I knows dat you knows dat I be talkin' 'bout our own dear Aint Baby. Take her to de place dat you promised you would, many years ago, 'f'n she would carry de cross and follow 'hind you. Well, Lawd, dis here poor ol' critter done what you tol' her to. She retched down, Lawd—way down—an' took dat heavy cross—"

We *amen*ed him, with much shaking of heads and fluttering of hankies.

"Den she be strugglin' wit' it on her back, Lawd—on her back!"

We echoed him, agreeing that Mama's life had been hard. The Mothers of the Church, all in attendance, looked radiant. Miss Magnolia Johnson bawled into a clean diaper, as did Miss Sweetney Matthews.

"An' den, Lawd," Bro Pastor went on, two-stepping slowly in place, "Sister Aint Baby took a step—den she took one mo' step —den she took 'nother! I tell you, Lawd, dis here poor ol' chile, de one dat be layin' here in dis box, underneath our veil of tears, dis poor ol' servant o' yo'n—yo' *faithful* servant"—we murmured our agreement—"toted Calvary's cross!"

Bro Pastor now stood at attention, arms upraised as if he himself was nailed to that cross, then drew them down violently over his chest. He shut his eyes and the words flew out of him. This was God, now, talking back. As a mortal man, and unordained minister, Bro Pastor hardly got a word in edgewise:

"Yassir. Yassir. Oh—yassir, Lawd! I did, Sir. I sho' be de one dat prayed her mama, Sophie, on in. Well now—I do declare! You don't say? Thankee, Lawd, thankee. Yassir, I sho'ly will tell dem!" Bro Pastor bowed low as his short conference with Higher Authority neared its end. I always used to think Bro Pastor's meetings with the Lord were a joke, but now I wasn't so sure.

"What dat you say, Lawd?" Bro Pastor cupped his hand to his ear. We did, too. "I knows dat be de truth, Sweet Jesus. I knows dat her ol' mama gwine be mighty, mighty proud when Saint Peter answer de knock at de Pearly Gate, and dere be standin' Sister Ida Mae!"

The crowd muttered in relief and palpably relaxed. Mama had made it into heaven, thanks in part to Bro Pastor.

"An' Lawd—I gots one last thang to ask you—" Bro Pastor crouched, eyes closed, arm extended like a man about to hang up the phone. "Bence I gots yo' 'tention, Lawd, I hears Aint Baby's freedom-fightin' chile, Cat, be gwine way up Nawth, to Minny-sody—"

The crowd murmured again and half the heads turned my way. I had only mentioned to a select few about my plan to take my Minneapolis hosts up on their spur-of-the-moment offer. But then, news about me always traveled fast in Greenwood.

"Walk wit' her, Lawd!" Bro Pastor pleaded. "See dat she don't fall in wit' no sinners. Let her make somebody outta herownself. Yassir, Lawd—dat be fine! Den we kin all be, uh, *elufindated!*"

T.C., Jean, and I were blubbering into our hankies, along with everyone else. Next to us were two empty folding chairs. They were for Bud, who was in Chicago—distraught at the news of Mama's death, he'd walked head-first into a telegraph pole and knocked himself out—and for Simon Jr., still doing time in an Illinois prison. Bro Pastor called their names, anyway. Then he scattered the first handful of dirt on the casket and the rest of us followed suit—family, then Mama's many friends, her white folks, and a number of civil rights workers.

We walked back to the cars two abreast, like majorettes in a parade, or protesters in a demonstration. Old Lady Woodard, a Mother of the Church, slipped and fell, splattering herself and everyone around her with mud. When she tried to get up, she fell again—drunk as a skunk. Some of the civil rights workers helped her up, and when we saw that she wasn't hurt, we began to smile. Then we began to laugh. Jean and I laughed so hard, we hugged each other and forgot about blame. Before we crossed the bramble knoll, I looked back one last time and saw that Gravedigger Gransberry and the other diggers were laughing, too.

• • •

THE FACT was, Mama's death made me put aside my plans to leave the Delta. It did not, however, make me a better mama to Cedric. It was not uncommon in the black community for grandmothers to raise their grandchildren as their own, and fortunately we had a spare—Ike's mother, Muh Dear.

Soon after Mama's burial, Ike and I started dating again. We pledged ourselves anew to each other and even discussed marriage. We rented a fairly new three-room shotgun house on Taft Street and furnished it with a bed, couch, end tables, and kitchen table from Malouf's. I was the envy of May Liza and Pearlie, who still lived in the run-down part of Gee Pee.

We actually did get married, one Saturday evening at Ike's friend's house on Avenue I. I don't remember what we wore or who performed the ceremony. But I do remember T.C. being there and Ike's cousin Sammy, and how I wished that Mama was there to see me, and how happy I was—at least for a moment. Then, looking out for Jean, who was late arriving, I saw that Ba-Ba, Ike's other woman, had come to our wedding. She wanted "t' see my ol' man git hitched up!" she told several people later.

From that day on, Ike and Ba-Ba made no secret of their relationship. I walked around in a daze, making excuses for Ike's behavior even while I was making plans to get out of the Delta or to get a job at the Baldwin piano factory, so that I could be on my own.

Meanwhile, the Movement was passing me by. We activists still gathered every other week to talk about the "good old days," but with few of the civil rights workers left, we weren't very active. And after Mama's death, I had a hard time rationalizing the gains we had made as having been worth all they'd cost us. True, there was talk about black children going to the local white schools, but I had heard that kind of talk a decade ago. Dr. King led the march from Selma to Montgomery—the last great battle in the voter registration wars, which ended with the passage of the Voting

Rights Act. But even that was overshadowed by the six-day riot in Watts, the black ghetto in Los Angeles, a sign of black people's social and economic frustration. And earlier in the year, Malcolm X, an early voice for black power rather than integration, had been assassinated in New York.

I began to see that I had to get out of the Delta. A child does not need to dwell in her mother's house forever to be a loyal daughter, I realized, or stay in her birthplace to remember where she's from. One night, after I'd seen Ike and Ba-Ba together, I wrote to the people I had met in Minneapolis. They sent my train fare.

Five months after Mama died, I left Greenwood for good. The night before my departure, Ike didn't come home at all. I packed Cedric's clothes in his old diaper bag, glad that I had someplace safe to leave him. In the morning, he seemed to sense that I was leaving. He didn't want me to leave his sight, and he cried and held on to me when I left him at Muh Dear's house. But I left him there without a glance backward because I didn't want him to see my tears.

I went quickly to Eva Mae Brown's house and borrowed two outfits and a cloth suitcase. Then I went back to my house and finished packing, pinning my GED scores to my bra. I took a long look around, then went to the corner store to call Buddy Boy's cab to take me to Winona so that I could catch the *City of New Orleans* passenger train north. It was not the triumphal exit I always imagined—my picture emblazoned on a canvas tent or Big Show playbill —but a personal "black migration" all my own. Like so many others before me, I headed north to find a life that, simply by being "normal," would be better than the extraordinary one I had left behind.

• • •

IN AUGUST 1965, I celebrated my twenty-first birthday in the Twin Cities. With the help of my friends, I enrolled in the General College at the University of Minnesota.

That first year, I moved from family to family, envying my home-girl and fellow freedom worker Rosemary Freeman, who had a permanent family to live with. The onset of winter caught me off guard. One kindly woman had given me a used fur coat, which I promply put in the trash can—only to scour the dump heap look-ing for it when a balmy autumn gave way to sleet and snow. I didn't know it could get so cold.

Shirley Ricketts felt sorry for me and my unsuitable coat. During the week I stayed with her family, she made a lot of soups and stews to warm my stomach. I stayed for a few months with Toni Lang and her children in St. Paul. I was so cold there that I practically welcomed the heat from the burning cross the Klan lit on their lawn one night to scare them and me. Soon after, I went back to Minneapolis to live with yet another host family, the Winikaitis. They were the first hippie family I ever met. After that, I shared a condemned apartment on 22nd Avenue South with Judy Barnes and some other young hippies.

The president of the National Council of Negro Women, Dr. Dorothy Height, had sent me my first scholarship money. I carried an armload of books around campus, because I thought the more books you had, the higher you were in college. Unfortunately, I spent more time walking the mall than actually working, and before long I had walked myself into D's and F's in most of my courses.

In the North, I was not immune to the black rage that was sweeping the country. In the summer of 1966, black ghettos in Chicago, Cleveland, and sixteen other cities burned. The great American system of checks and balances, of government by the consent of the governed, had had its chance to take black Ameri-cans into the fold, and it had decided not to. So the genie got out of the bottle; Pandora's box flew open. Black society, in large measure, continued to be separate, occasionally equal, rarely better off, and in the main saw less and less reason to pound futilely on the white man's door. The Civil Rights Movement of the sixties ended with neither a whimper nor a bang, but an unraveling of the social contract that was supposed to stitch all of us together.

In fact, the more tolerant atmosphere of the North encouraged shows of temper that were still unthinkable in the South, a freedom I found appealing. The angrier I acted, the more sympathy I got, so I looked harder for things to be angry about. I became a professional "white hater," a reputation that made me popular in both the white liberal and black communities.

I found myself planting new roots in Minnesota, though not all of them grew straight. I wrote to Muh Dear every day, enclosing a few lines for Cedric. I still helped SNCC any way I could. I spoke at fund-raisers and coached civil rights workers going south. But my real interest went back to the streets. I was a neighborhood worker for Pillsbury House Settlement Services (and later a community coordinator for The Way) and hung around the colored bars such as Cassius' Lounge and the Afterhours Joint, where I made friends with the junkies and hookers. I didn't turn tricks—I didn't have to, thanks to a day job at Dayton's department store—but I sure understood the feelings of those who did. Sometimes I posed as a reporter for *Ebony* magazine, which really opened people up. In America, I discovered, people would say things in the newspaper or on TV that they wouldn't tell their preacher or best friend. In those dingy bars and alleys, I became a little of both.

This affinity for Minneapolis street life made me a rogue on the mostly white campus. Those who were sympathetic to the Movement saw me as a colorful hero. Those who weren't felt my outrageous behavior only confirmed what they silently thought.

I got married a couple of times—once to a black man, once to a white—and each marriage worked for a while, then withered and died. During most of my married life, I dropped out of school to be the wife I thought I could be. After a while, I realized I could use a few more lessons—the academic kind.

It took me thirteen years to complete my work for a bachelor of arts degree in black studies, which was awarded in 1979. I stayed on for another five—working, studying, consorting, helping, and mothering (I got Cedric from Muh Dear in 1971)—to get my master's in American studies. I could've stopped there, but when I looked back down the ladder at how far I'd climbed, it seemed foolish to not go the distance, to become if I could the "third doctor lady"—not just to follow in Mama's footsteps, but to make a new path all my own. Dr. Horace Laster, my mentor, and his family insisted I go all the way to the top. Hearing his and Mama's encouragement, I thought I would give it a try.

On May 25, 1985—twenty years after I'd left the Delta—I marched down the University of Minnesota mall, the only black face among all the black-robed doctoral candidates. I hadn't made much fuss over my bachelor's and master's commencements, but this time I had invited everyone I knew, from both sides of the river, from the Movement, and from home, to come and share my triumph.

Shortly before I got my Ph.D., I had added "Endesha" to my name. It was a gift from a very wise man, Dr. Maulana Karenga, the creator of Kwanza and a scholar of African history and culture who helped me to fill the gaps in mine. The name comes from Swahili, and it means "driver—she who drives herself and others forward." I was still Ida Mae Holland, but now I was also something more.

When my name was called, I bounded up the last few steps into the arms of two proctors dressed like clowns. Flouting convention, I hugged them, then puffed out my chest as they hung the doctoral hood over my shoulders. Only a dozen yards of stage separated me from the university president, who held out my degree. Dr. Elaine Tyler May, my American studies adviser, was waiting for me on the low end of the stage, fairly buck-dancing with joy.

I eased into my streetwalker's walk and crossed the stage to uproarious cheers, whistles, and applause.

"Go on, Cat gal! Walk dat walk!"

"Li'l Ida Mae, ain't you somethin'! Lawd, Lawd, Lawd!"

Somewhere in the midst of all that hollering, I heard my Mama's voice. "Step high, up yon'er, wit' de birds!"

Now, you might think my story is over—and I admit, this would sure be a good place to end it. If I had dropped dead right then, Bro Pastor would've laid me to rest, too, with a smile —but in a way, that fine afternoon was only the beginning.

Back in 1979, as I cast about for an easy course to complete the academic units required for graduation, I had spied in the catalogue what I thought was a class in acting. Now, as you know, I had always been fond of play-like—it was in my blood from Mama—and I could think of no better way to reward myself for all the semesters I'd spent in classrooms and libraries than to spend the last one on a stage.

As it turned out, my class in acting was really an advanced seminar for playwrights taught by Dr. Charles Nolte. Instead of admitting my mistake, though, I decided to bluff my way through.

I wrote two plays that semester, both based on my life in Mississippi—*Second Doctor Lady,* about Mama, and *The Reconstruction of Dossie Ree Hemphill,* which was also about Mama but from the perspective of her friends. I read patches of both in class, and everybody—including me and Dr. Nolte—wept. It seemed I had found the right class after all.

After the second play was performed, my past once again caught up with me. The late Lorraine Hansberry, whom I had missed meeting in New York during my tour for SNCC, rewarded my puny effort with a prize: a $1,000 National Lorraine Hansberry Award for the second-best play of 1981.

As I finished my studies, I kept writing plays. So scarce was black theater in Minnesota in those days that people lined up for two and three blocks to see my plays directed by Dr. Elton Wolfe. I began to be hailed as "Second Doctor Lady" as I puttered around the campus.

Now I'll tell you another secret.

Although people claimed they loved it and were moved to tears, I could never sit through a whole performance of *Second Doctor Lady*. I never minded seeing and hearing my work performed—I'm not one of those playwrights who wants to change every line as soon as it leaves an actor's mouth—but I always left before the scene containing Mama's death. Those responsible for her killing had never been found, and although I had been absolved by Jean and my own conscience over time, it was still an unhealed wound on my soul.

After the Hansberry award, I found myself forced by special circumstances to sit through a whole performance. I got increasingly tense as the firebomb scene approached. As the moment of Mama's death drew near, I covered my face. But the world I had created in my play went on without me, reaching out to the stunned and silent audience.

At the end of the play, the ovation was astounding. I glanced down one aisle and saw a little black woman—obviously blind—gripping her escort's arm and pounding the seat in front of her with her white-tipped cane. At that moment, all the bitterness and rage and fear and remorse I had kept bottled up since that terrible morning evaporated into the air, borne up by the cheers and applause the audience gave my Mama. It was not that her death didn't matter anymore, only that it now mattered to the world, not just to me. By freeing her of my grasp, I had finally freed myself.

I HAD come a long way from the Mississippi Delta. I had seen and done many things that I'd never expected I would do, even in the wildest dreams of my Delta girlhood. Some of my country ways had fallen away, as if they'd frozen up North and dropped off me like icicles fall off a tree. But somewhere deep down inside, under my sophisticated manners and chic woolen clothes, there was still a girl who wanted just one more chance to go barefoot and feel Mississippi mud ooze between her toes. I got my chance on October 18, 1991, which—thanks to Miss Frances Robertson and a committee of former schoolmates and dear friends —the mayor of Greenwood had officially declared Dr. Endesha Ida Mae "Cat" Holland Day. I was goin' home!

I flew into Memphis from New York, where I was teaching at the State University of New York at Buffalo. From Memphis, Greenwood councilman David Jordan and his wife chauffeured me and my theatrical business manager, Habibi Minnie Wilson, through the Delta to Greenwood. Newswoman Jane Pauley's crew from NBC's "Dateline" had arrived before me in order to document my homecoming.

The first thing that struck me was how much the landscape had changed. Not the tabletop land or levees or trees or the rippling heat—those would go on forever—but the people. In 1990, Mississippi had over 825 elected black officials—more than any other state in the union. Machines had replaced the endless lines of sharecroppers and day laborers picking cotton or hoeing weeds; backbreaking labor for subsistence pay had become a thing of the past. Nearing Greenwood, I saw a Wal-Mart store and roadside video rentals along the highway where, a generation ago, I had turned tricks among the farmers.

"It's a fine new day," I said to Councilman Jordan.

Wrapped in a colorful *gele* and *kente,* I presented my doctoral diploma to the people of Greenwood. I rode as grand marshall in the high school's homecoming parade to the steps of city hall. There, before its scrolled and fluted brick façade, where I had been arrested, dragged, and kicked on my way to jail, I received a commendation signed by the governor of Mississippi, Ray Mabus, and a key to the city from Greenwood's mayor, Louis E. Fancher. As testimonials in honor of "Dr. Cat" poured forth from old friends and new, I looked out at the crowd of black and white faces who had come to make my day. My brother Bud, his hard, chiseled features softened with emotion, sat next to Jean, the image of our Mama; next to her, I imagined our brother Simon Jr., who was a victim of ataxia—the same hereditary, debilitating nerve disease that put Mama in her wheelchair and has recently set me to hobbling with a cane. Later, we would all go to the cemetery and dedicate a fine new headstone for Mama's grave.

That evening, after the hoopla and merriment and memorializing were over, I sat alone and took a look at the certificate signed by Governor Mabus. It said, "Her history has served as a model for all people and shows how, with determination, we can overcome obstacles for a better life."

Amen to that, I thought.

I'VE BEEN asked on occasion if I have any regrets about my life—anything I'd do differently if I had it to do over again. My answer is, "Take your pick!" Let this book fall open to any page and you can find something on it I would correct, undo, or redo if I had the power. Mostly, I wish I could erase the feeling of Mr. Lawrence breaking and entering the treasure house of my youth. I would also have taken little Cedric with me to Minneapolis when I left Greenwood in 1965, since I have come to realize the importance each mother has in shaping the future—not just the future of her child, but that of everyone her child will touch, and everyone *those* people will touch, around the world to the end of time. Since I've let Mama take her ease among the stars, these are the thoughts that crowd into my mind most often when I'm alone.

But everyone has a past, and these things are a part of mine. They've shaped my view that our time on this sad and happy earth is a gift. I can't change them, but I can share the wisdom they've given me:

If you're so far down and out you feel you can't get back, I assure you from the bottom of my soul, the journey home is shorter than you think.

If your mama is still living, give her a great big hug and kiss from me, and always remember where you came from.

If you happen to be a white man or white woman living in the South, or anywhere else the Movement touched, I want you to see I made it. Those black boys and girls you see around you, whether in a grand or sorry state, can make it, too. You may give them something hard to push against or you may give them a helping hand—that's up to you. But I can tell you from experience that the helping hand feels a lot better.

Finally, if you're young, make a promise right now that you will never, *ever* give up your dreams. If you've been a ho', be a doctor, too. If you've hurt a man, be a healer. The world began when you were born. It will be whatever you make it.

Acknowledgments

I DIDN'T DO IT BY MYSELF! THE WRITING OF
THIS BOOK WAS HARD. I SHOULD HAVE KNOWN THAT
this event would be no different from many of the forward
movements that have characterized my life. Therefore, I should
have known that a lot of people would help me.

I am forever grateful to: the Creator, whose arms encircled me
as I wrote; my dear late mother for her example, triumphs, and
legacies; my son, Cedric, the dreamer and the love of my life; my
sister, Dr. Jean Beasley, who's more beautiful and stronger than she
knows; Habibi Minnie Wilson, a source of inspiration and sister
love and a rising star; and my son's grandmother Mary "Muh Dear"
Davis, for nurturing and caring for him as I prepared for our
future.

Many thanks to my literary agent, Kimberly Witherspoon, for
her remarkable expertise and competence in the publishing world,
who first encouraged me to write this book; to Judith Regan, who
saw its possibilities; to my editor at Simon & Schuster, Becky
Saletan, for her perseverance and editorial skills; and to Denise
Roy, for her expedient work. Special thanks to writer Jay Wurts,
for his many helpful suggestions, and to Victor Kervia Smith, my
assistant, for his help in fueling this book's progress.

I am especially indebted to my friend and researcher Dr. Carol
Fairbanks for the historical gems she unearthed; to Kay Mills and
Dr. Nicole Boand, whose advice helped me to avoid the pitfalls that
await the nonfiction writer; and to Marie Carter, make-up artist
and keeper of my outer beauty.

I wish to thank the following attorneys for their timely advice and legal help: Carl Bucki, Mary A. Donovan, Nancy Rose, and Bob L. Johnson.

Also, to the University of Minnesota and my advisers for preparing me to write about my life: in the Afro-American and African Studies Department, the late Dr. Anita Bracey-Brooks; in the Theatre Arts and Dance Department, Dr. Charles Nolte and Dr. Elton C. Wolfe; and in the American Studies Program, Dr. Joseph J. Kwiat and Dr. Elaine Tyler May.

It would be remiss of me not to extend my sincere thanks to the American Studies Department and the Women's Studies Program at the State University of New York at Buffalo for their encouragement and support.

My heartfelt thanks to my present school, the University of Southern California, for affording me the opportunity, in the Trojan spirit, to teach and write. My sincere appreciation to the president of the university, Dr. Steven B. Sample; the vice-provost, Dr. Barbara Solomon; the dean of the School of Theatre, Dr. Robert Scales; the chair of the Gender Studies Program, Dr. Judith Grant; my strongest advocate, Professor James D. Wilson; and my other colleagues.

I appreciate the efforts of the following angels who helped me as I worked on this book. Some read, others typed, while others fetched fried chicken. Some put their hands to healing my body, and still others gave themselves to praying for my strength: Wanda Beale; my kinfolk, the Caples; Barbara S. Cyrus; Michael Dinwiddle; Shirley Ferrell; Dr. Larnell Flannagan; Burleigh Foreman; Mattie E. Grace; Lorene Graves; Nzinga Ratibisha Heru; the late Dr. Eric "Aula" Hill; Dr. Edna Hood; Uriel and Yvette Jordan; Pete and Virginia Kelly; Martha Maimone; Essie B. McSwine; Community Mother Lillian Mobley; my two promoters, Shelia P. Moses and MaryAnn Walker; Mozhgan Mujab, P.T.; Y. Denise Nelms; Dan

Pothier; my late brother, Simon Redmond, Jr.; Dennus Richards, P.T.; Dr. La Francis Rodgers-Rose; Lawrence Schut, M.D.; Dr. Halisi Edwards Staten; Dr. Melvin Terrell; Marvin Thomas, my personal trainer; Karen Thompson; Dr. Barrie Thorne; Karen Trusty; Douglas Tyler, M.D.; C. Thomas Vangsness, M.D.; Elder Fred Washington; Barbara "Akua Zawadi" Williams; Pastor Betty Williams; Michael Zola, D.M.D.; and the students of my Playwriting, Racial and Ethnic Women in America, and Biography/Autobiography classes. And special thanks to my brother in the spirit, Coach Tommie Smith.

To Bob Moses, Willie "Wazir" Peacock, Sam Block, the SNCC people, and other civil rights workers who touched my life and whom I have cried with, been beaten with, been jailed with, marched with, and eaten with, my humble gratitude. The seeds that you sowed in the sixties have come to fruition in the nineties. And a special thank you to Dr. Maulana Karenga for my name, "Endesha."

I want to thank Val Ward, the first person to read aloud and critique my entire unedited manuscript; Shirley Jo Finney, who read aloud and critiqued the entire edited manuscript; and Rick Eyler for his help with the galley proof.

My sincere appreciation to the people I have leaned on over the years: my Maryland family, Horace Laster, M.D., Janice Laster, and Frances "Rafiki" Travis, Queen of the Chicken-Pushers Club (of which I am a member); my theater intern, Connie Bullock; and my personal assistant, Joy Shannon.

I thank my Mississippi friends and informants who are mentioned in this book (including those whose names were changed, for reasons of poetry or privacy) for helping me to remember, taste, smell, and hear our region of the South. I also thank Greenwood City Council president Arance Brooks Williamson; the late Alberta Barnett; Willye White, the Olympian; and others from the

Greenwood community: attorney Alix and the Honorable Betty W. Sanders, Senator David Jordan, the late Harry and Frances Robertson, Lillie Shotwell Russell, Margaret Bush Cochran, Sharon McCormick, William Speed, Lee Purnell, my uncle R. L. Connor, my cousin Dr. T. C. Gavin, June Johnson, Maeola Anderson Cox, my brother Charlie "Bud" Nellum, Jr., and my Minnesota and nationwide host families, friends, supporters, and street people.

For the unselfish sharing of their photographs with me, I thank Matt Herron, Baba Simba Mlee, my cousin Margaret Hodges Daniels, my aunts Thelma "Doll" Powell and Josephine Garner Grissom, and all my other kinfolk.

To Anthony Chase and Javier Bustillos for their promotion, friendship, and encouragement from the beginning, and to my friends and supporters in Mississippi, Minnesota, New York, California, and places in between—a hearty thank you.